A HISTORY OF

MOUNTAINSIDE

1945–2007

IT WAS ONLY YESTERDAY

CONNIE MCNAMARA

On Behalf of the Mountainside Historic Preservation Committee

THE History PRESS

Published by The History Press
Charleston, SC 29403
www.historypress.net

Front cover: (Top) View of Hoppe's Hotel 29 from original painting by E. Hoppe. Extachrome by Helen S. O'Brien. *Courtesy of Allan Attanasio.* (Bottom) Mrs. Singer's third-grade class at Deerfield School, 1957. *Courtesy of Richard Benninger.*

Back cover: (Top left) Children's Country Home. *Courtesy of Allan Attanasio.* (Top right) Moving the Hetfield House in 1985. *Courtesy of Mountainside Historic Preservation Committee.* (Center) Welcome to Mountainside. *Photo by Chris Petraccoro.*

First published 2010

Manufactured in the United States

ISBN 978.1.59629.801.9

Library of Congress Cataloging-in-Publication Data

McNamara, Connie.
A history of Mountainside, 1945-2007 : it was only yesterday / Connie McNamara and Mountainside Historic Preservation Committee.
p. cm.
Includes bibliographical references.
ISBN 978-1-59629-801-9
1. Mountainside (N.J.)--History. 2. Mountainside (N.J.)--Social conditions. 3. Community life--New Jersey--Mountainside--History. I. Mountainside Historic Preservation Committee (Mountainside, N.J.) II. Title.
F144.M98M35 2010
974.9'36--dc22
2009051625

Dedicated to the residents of Mountainside:
past, present and future.

CONTENTS

ACKNOWLEDGEMENTS

My thanks to all who have assisted in the publication of this history: borough officials, community leaders, residents and out-of-towners who provided information, photographs and encouragement. I owe particular gratitude to the Mountainside Historic Preservation Committee for its initiation of this project and for its continued support throughout the years this book was in progress. Recognition is due Worrall Community Newspapers and both the Mountainside Public Library and the Westfield Memorial Library for permitting access to local newspapers covering this period of time. The Union County Parks and Community Renewal, in the person of landscape architect Sean Ryan, graciously assisted in material on the parks surrounding our borough. Special thanks to three others: Dr. Alexander E. Gates, professor of earth and environmental studies at Rutgers-Newark, who explained thoroughly yet simply to me the whys and wherefores of Mountainside's geologic evolution; Peter F. Goggi Jr., who assisted with manuscript formatting; and Ruth Cruz, editor and graphics guru extraordinaire, whose expertise and advice cannot be measured. To my husband, Bill, and son, Doug, *muchas gracias* for your patience, confidence and inspiration. Without these individuals, Jean Hershey's *History of Mountainside: 1895–1945* might have been a stand-alone work. I trust that this history provides insight into the borough's growth and development. May you learn, laugh and wax nostalgic but, above all, be proud to call Mountainside home.

INTRODUCTION

Geological Beginnings

In the midst of the most densely populated state in the country—the only state in which all twenty-one counties were officially classified as "metropolitan" by the 2000 census—sits a 4.1-square-mile municipality that seemingly has been left unscathed by the blight of urbanization and industrialization. This pristine jewel of single-family residences is surrounded by parkland, mountains and one of the world's most prestigious golf courses. Yet just a few miles away are many of the nation's top retail stores, Fortune 500 companies and transportation and communication links to national and international destinations, as well as to the financial and cultural giant New York City. One might conclude that the evolution of the borough of Mountainside was a perfect combination of serendipity and strategic planning.

Natural surroundings play a significant role in Mountainside's serenity and beauty. About 220 million years ago, the supercontinent Pangaea, which had been in existence for nearly 100 million years, began to break apart. One of the rift systems that developed and continued to widen became the Atlantic Ocean—hence, the division of North America and Africa. One of the schisms that failed to widen and instead filled in with sediment was the Newark Basin. Twenty million years later, volcanic activity began deep beneath the southern portion of this basin. Lava rose

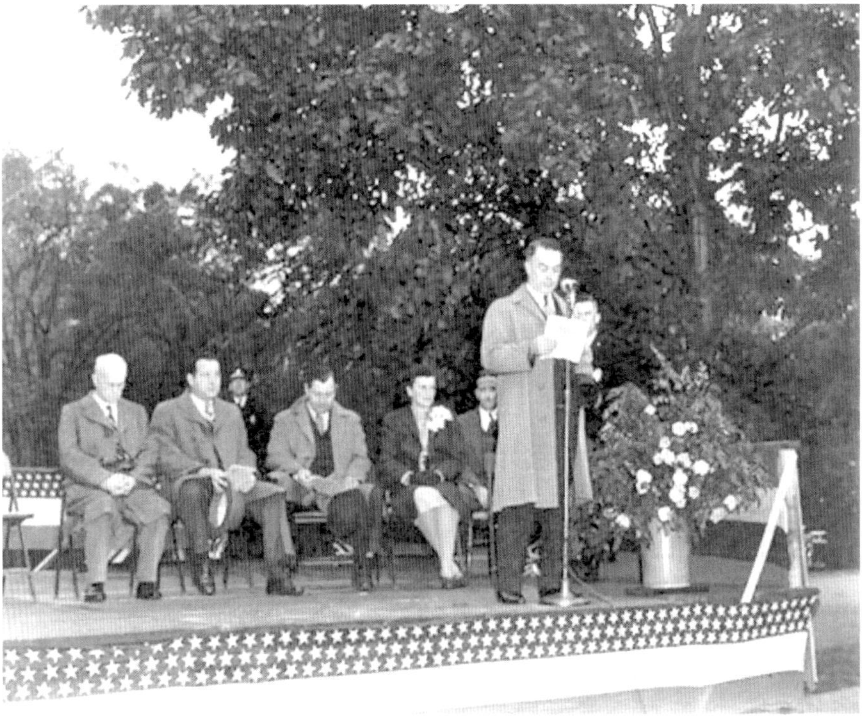

Mayor Meril C. Hoy addresses residents on the occasion of Mountainside's fiftieth anniversary. *Courtesy of the Borough of Mountainside.*

to the surface. Since the volcanic rocks were tougher than the sediment being replaced, they remained and composed the three basic floes that we know today as the Watchungs. (The word *watchung* comes from the Lenape Indians and means "high hills.")

The Watchung ridges are lava floes that haven't completely eroded away. Mountainside rests on the easternmost lava floe. According to structural geologist Alexander E. Gates, professor and chair of the Department of Earth and Environmental Sciences at Rutgers University in Newark, the composition of rock in the Mountainside area and that in Africa are exactly the same because the two landmasses were once joined.

Nearly half of Watchung Reservation's 1,945 acres, and most of the 147-acre Echo Lake Park, lie within the borough's borders, making almost one-third of its area parkland. The unspoiled woodlands offer recreational resources—from walking and hiking to boating, fishing and horseback riding—while the nearby community pool provides yet another venue for contact with nature.

A trip downtown to Mountainside's two-block shopping area along Mountain Avenue reveals some of the only sidewalks in town, yet the pace is as unhurried here as it might have been at the beginning of the twentieth century.

Careful planning and strict regulations are responsible for the winding roads that meander down the side of the mountain and curve through the sloping landscape below. Foresight rather than fortune has seen fit to enhance the natural beauty of the surroundings while at the same time curtailing the speeding that often is more prevalent on straight and parallel byways.

Even along the 2.7-mile stretch of Route 22 and in the two major industrial areas where some four hundred light industrial and commercial businesses operate, the tenor is low-keyed. Strict zoning prevails and safeguards the borough from fast-food chains, car dealerships and unsightly buildings in general. Mountainsiders work hard to maintain their bucolic surroundings and take pride in this pacific gem in the midst of exurban activity.

THE FIRST FIFTY YEARS

The American Revolution had been over for more than a century, but a minor skirmish occurred in the middle of Union County during the last years of the nineteenth century. Residents of the northern section of the township of Westfield felt strongly that they were not reaping the benefits of tax dollars spent.

On July 16, 1895, resolutions proposing independence were presented to the community. A committee of three—William Miller, Charles Badgley and Joseph W. Cory—was responsible for seeing that those resolutions were carried into effect. A vote on September 24, 1895, verified the will of the people, and the borough of Mountainside was incorporated on October 22, 1895, with Cory as its first mayor.

The borough's four square miles of farmland had a landscape that remained basically unchanged throughout the first decades of the twentieth century. Running water came to town in 1913, and gas mains were laid in 1925. In that same year, the Somerset Bus Company was the first industry to come into Mountainside; it linked the borough with Plainfield and Somerville to the west and Springfield, Newark and New York to the east. Hall & Fuhs opened for business in 1929 as one of the first distributors

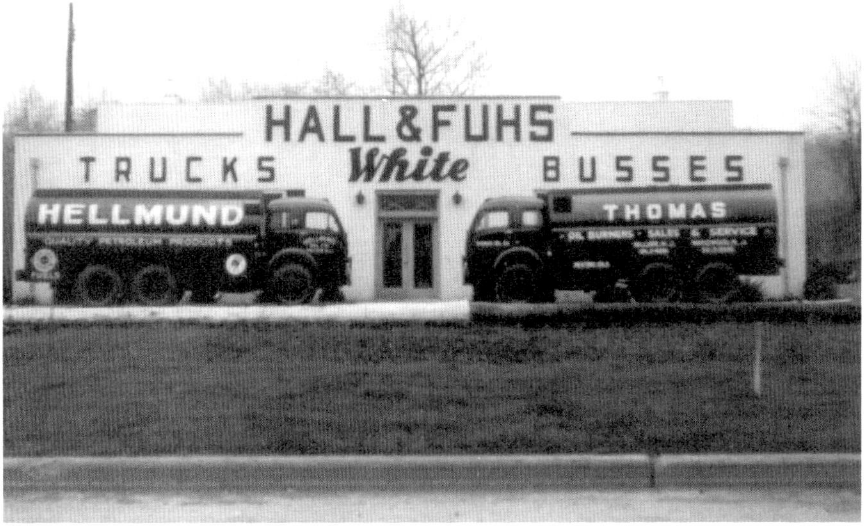

Hall & Fuhs in its 1950 location on Route 22 East. *Courtesy of Tom Costigan, Hall & Fuhs.*

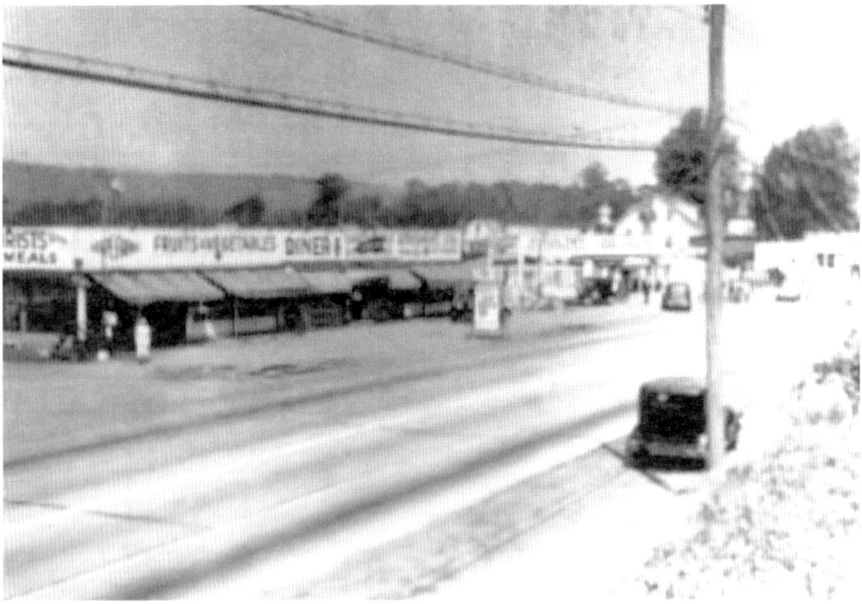

Hoppe Farms, circa 1950s, was located on Route 22 West adjacent to Hotel 29 and was operated by two generations of the Hoppe family. It was purchased by the Pfeifer family in 1969. In 1986, Manor Care bought the property and constructed its facility. *Courtesy of the Borough of Mountainside.*

of White Motor Trucks in New Jersey. Schoonover's store, located at the present-day entrance to Echo Lake Park, was purchased by Harry Bliwise in 1914 and moved across the street to its present location when work began on the park in 1924. Maxwell's Furniture Restoration was established in downtown Mountainside in the late 1800s. Its current owner is the fourth generation of master craftsmen to provide services, and the business bills itself as New Jersey's oldest restoration shop. Maxwell's, along with a dozen or so family businesses from the early part of the twentieth century, continues to make up what we know as "downtown" to this day. Mountainside's strict zoning laws have prevented further expansion, thereby maintaining a small-town environment.

A short distance away, however, is the 2.7-mile stretch of U.S. Route 22 that runs through the borough. Originating as dirt-surfaced Springfield Road in the 1800s, it was paved with concrete around 1918 and then became part of Route 29, one of the original national highways, in 1926. Late in the 1930s, this major thoroughfare became a dual highway. Renamed Route 22 in 1954, it has helped Mountainside to both grow and "grow up" in terms of population and sophistication, respectively. Nearly 650 miles of roadway from Cincinnati, Ohio, to Newark Liberty International Airport have encouraged an influx of industry in small pockets of an otherwise residential community. Accessibility via this major artery has connected Mountainside to the world. Conversely, it has brought with it noise, pollution, heavily trafficked roads, accidents and congestion. While literally dividing the borough, Route 22 paradoxically has led to greater unity among its residents in their attempts to resolve the complex issues that come with progress.

Advancements during the early twentieth century included the creation of a regular police department in 1934; prior to that date, constables, chief marshals, justices of the peace and recorders presided over the law. When the volunteer fire department started in 1910, it was no more than a bucket brigade until 1915, when Henry Weber's horse and buggy pulled a used chemical engine to fires in town. Motorized equipment came on the scene in 1917, when Charles Heckel purchased a Reo truck. A viable fire engine appeared in the form of a Flying Thomas in 1921, when Heckel's son Lew drove to Buffalo and, according to Heckel family records, purchased a "motor drawn fire apparatus & hose." Vehicles continued to be upgraded primarily through fundraising activities. A rescue squad did not get going until 1938, with police and firemen taking courses in first aid until official volunteers came on board.

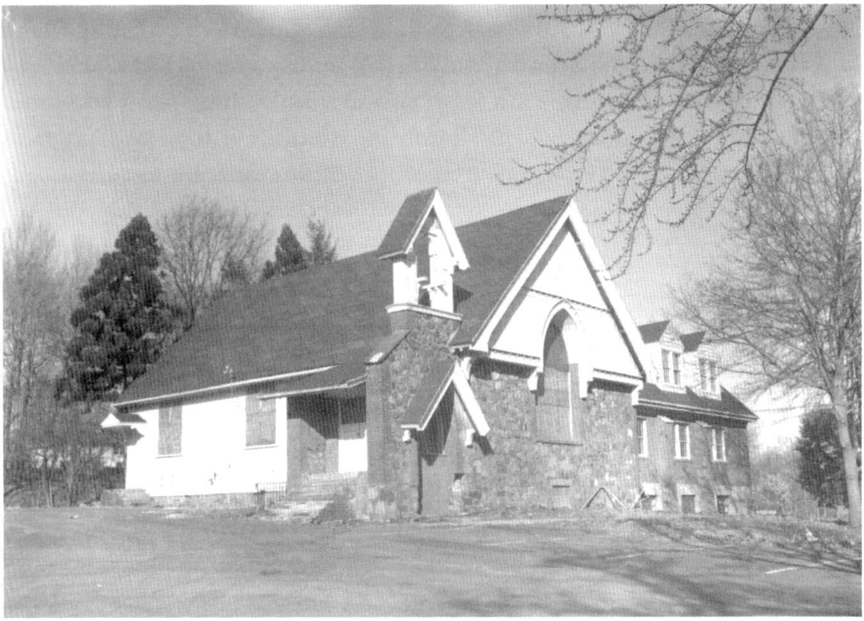

Mountainside Chapel on Route 22, February 1975. *Courtesy of John Sharkey.*

During its first half century, Mountainside's only tangible religious edifice was the Locust Grove Union Chapel, which became the Mountainside Union Chapel in 1911. Other specific denominations worshipped in nearby towns. Only in the 1950s did population and interest spur on the establishment and building of additional religious centers.

When the first brick schoolhouse was constructed in 1900, Mountainside was still part of the Westfield school system. Four years later, the two boards of education became separate entities. Remodeling and an addition in 1924 provided space for the steadily growing school population. Both the purchase of additional land and the construction of a new brick building adjacent to the Mountainside School faced numerous placements on the ballot before becoming reality in 1935 as the Echobrook School. It remained the only school in town until the burgeoning population of the late 1940s necessitated the construction of a second building—Deerfield School, completed in 1952.

While we do know that in 1895 sixty freeholders (landowners) petitioned for the formation of a new town, the exact number of residents of the proposed borough is not known. However, between 1900 and 1930 the population tripled to 965 and grew to just a little over 1,000 by 1940. In

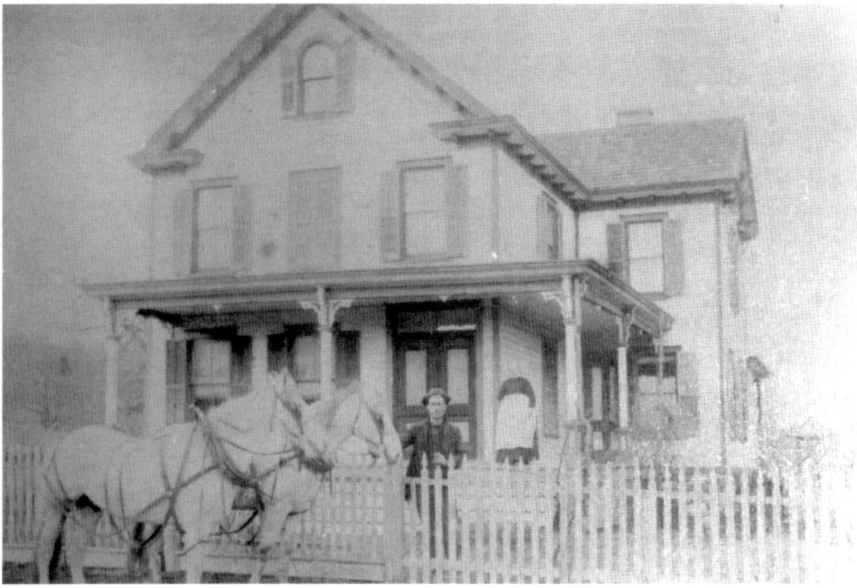

The Darby house on Summit Road, circa 1890. *Courtesy of the Westfield Historical Society.*

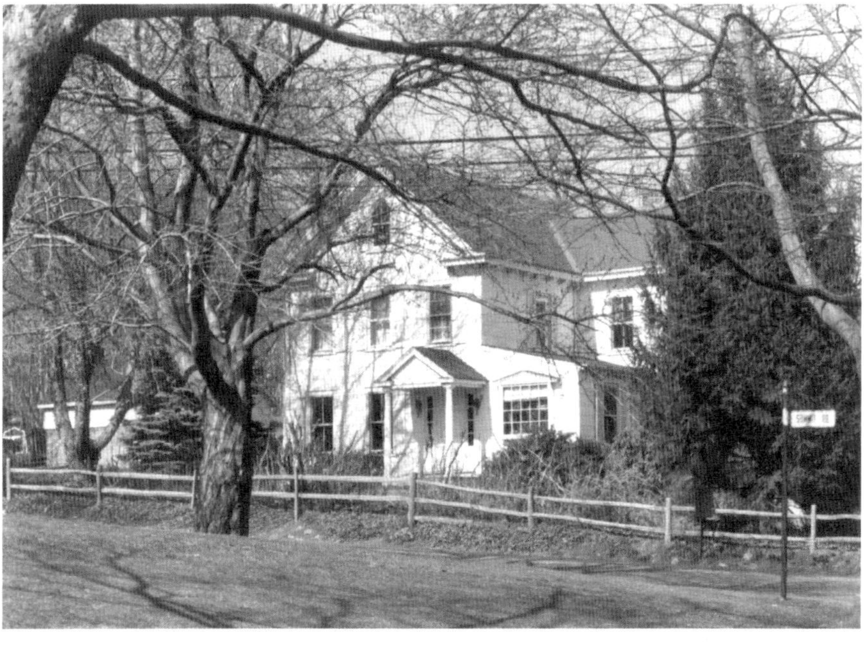

The Darby house was later owned by the Dietz family, circa 1981. *Courtesy of the Mountainside Historic Preservation Committee.*

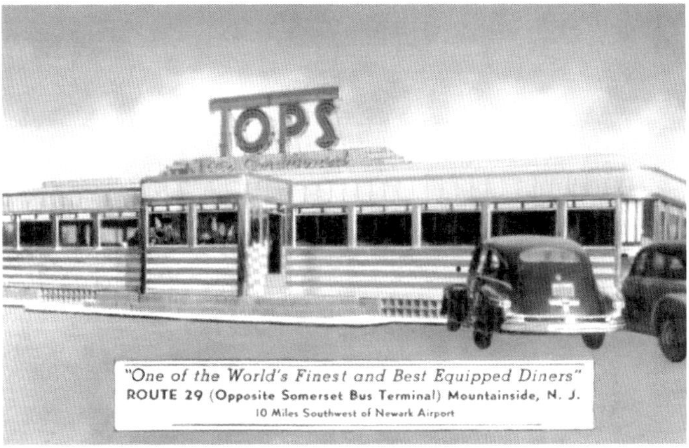
TOPS
"One of the World's Finest and Best Equipped Diners"
ROUTE 29 (Opposite Somerset Bus Terminal) Mountainside, N. J.
10 Miles Southwest of Newark Airport

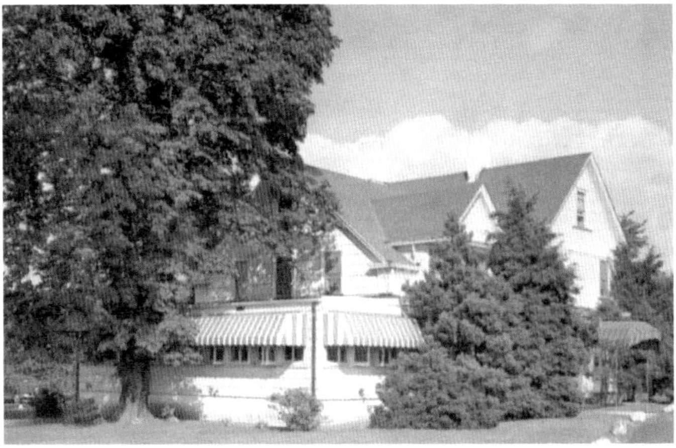

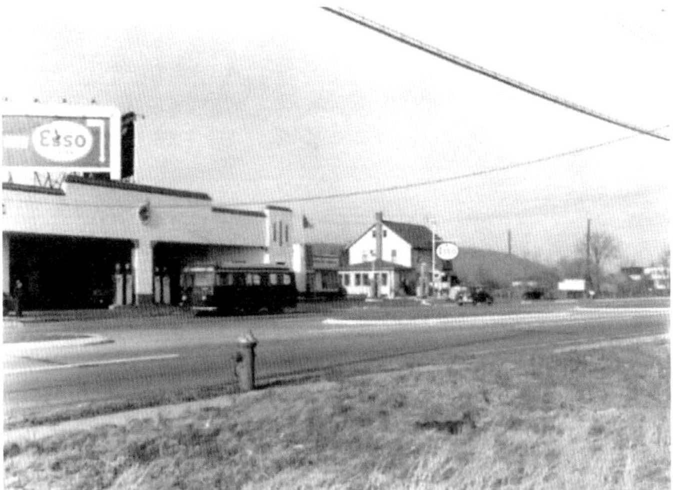
Esso

the next ten years, the town's population reached the 2,000 mark. The post–World War II years witnessed growth throughout the New York metropolitan area, and Mountainside was no exception. Restoration of peace, return of the military, development of an interstate highway system and increased automobile production were several of the catalysts behind suburban magnetism.

TABLE 1. POPULATION

YEAR	POPULATION
1940	1,148
1950	2,046
1960	6,325
1963	6,679
1970	7,520
1971	7,530
1972	7,525
1973	7,530
1974	7,530
1980	7,118
1990	6,657
2000	6,602
2002	6,687
2004	6,690
2005 (est.)	6,635
2006 (est.)	6,644

Opposite, top: "*TOPS* is the spot to stop." It was a ninety-seven-seat diner on Route 22 East on the site of the current Echo Queen diner. *Courtesy of Bob Hain.*

Opposite, middle: La Martinique offered fine food in a romantic atmosphere. It was located on Route 22 East, the present site of L'Affaire. *Courtesy of Bob Hain.*

Opposite, bottom: Somerset Bus Terminal. *Courtesy of the Borough of Mountainside.*

Chapter 1

REMINDERS OF OUR ROOTS

Historic Sites

While Mountainside is relatively new in comparison to early colonial settlements on the East Coast, many of its homes have been standing since pre-Revolutionary times, or shortly thereafter. The following landmarks reflect the early settlement of western Union County and provide Mountainsiders with a continued prideful look back on their early roots.

Woodland Avenue–New Providence Road Historic Sites

These buildings still surround the downtown area of the borough as the twenty-first century unfolds.

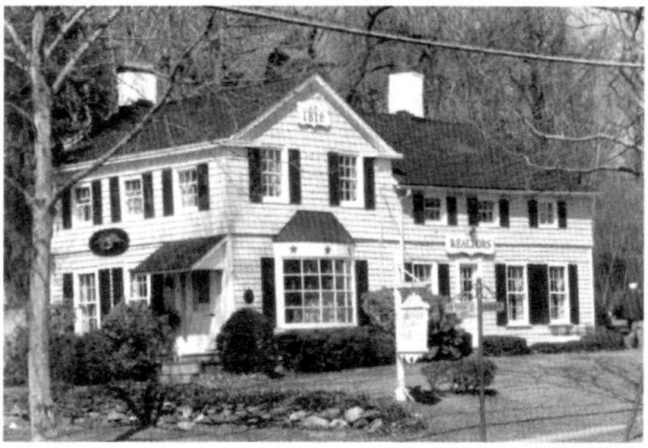

Barrett and Crain House, 1981. *Courtesy of the Mountainside Historic Preservation Committee.*

Barrett and Crain House

Located at the corner of New Providence Road and Mountain Avenue, this two-story wooden structure was erected in 1818. According to Jean Hesketh Hershey's *History of Mountainside: 1895–1945*, it was the first site of the Children's

Country Home (later Children's Specialized Hospital) in the 1890s. For a number of years, and minus its two original porches, it was the home of realtors Barrett and Crain. In 1996, Patterson Interiors purchased the stately home.

Crane Hill House
27 New Providence Road

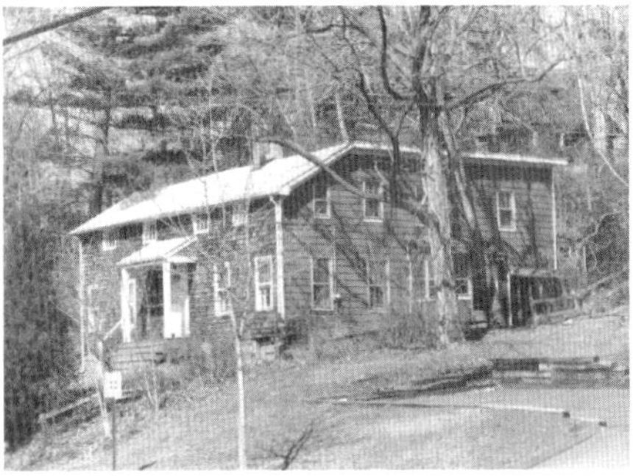

Crane Hill House, 1974. *Courtesy of the Mountainside Historic Preservation Committee.*

Resting on a fieldstone foundation, this two-story structure may have been erected as early as 1740. It sits on an elevated bank overlooking New Providence Road, hence the "hill" part of its name. Residents have traced its ownership to descendants of the Crane family, who settled in Elizabeth in the late 1600s. Jonathan Crane, one of the founders of the Presbyterian Church of Westfield, is believed to have lived here around 1740.

Hamilton House
590 Woodland Avenue

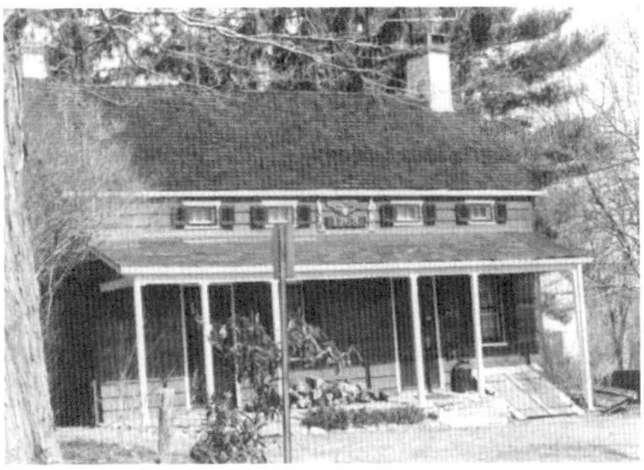

Hamilton House, 1974. *Courtesy of the Mountainside Historic Preservation Committee.*

Built in 1763, this one-and-a-half-story pre-Revolutionary dwelling rests on a fieldstone foundation. It was built by Aaron Miller for his son Abraham, both early settlers in the Westfield-Mountainside area. Ownership later passed to Jacob Hamilton, who died there in 1908. His son Henry then lived in the house all his life. The property was later sold to the Mathes family.

Other Historic Sites

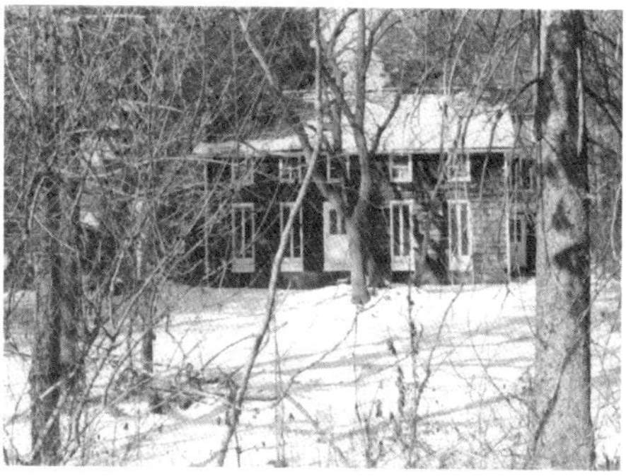

The J.P. Boyd residence. *Courtesy of the Mountainside Historic Preservation Committee.*

J.P. Boyd Residence
1618 U.S. Route 22 West

Owners of this dwelling believe that it may have been constructed as early as 1722, making it among the oldest homes in the borough. It may also have been part of the extensive Baltusrol estate.

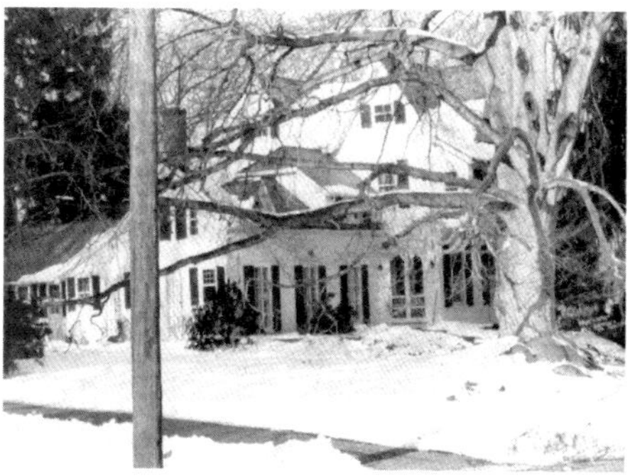

Buck House. *Courtesy of the Mountainside Historic Preservation Committee.*

Buck House
737 Hillside Avenue

The smaller section of this house was constructed around 1760; it reveals "stomach" windows on the upper level. (These are attic windows built into the top molding of the house; often one must lie down on the floor to see out the windows.) The larger section, built in 1816, has a number of varied window sizes and numerous roof gables. This home exhibits a combination of different building periods from pre-Revolutionary to the early nineteenth century.

The Smith Williams House
1248 Route 22 West

One of the oldest homes in the area, it stands next door to the original site of the Hetfield House. Built around 1790 by Deacon Andrew Hetfield,

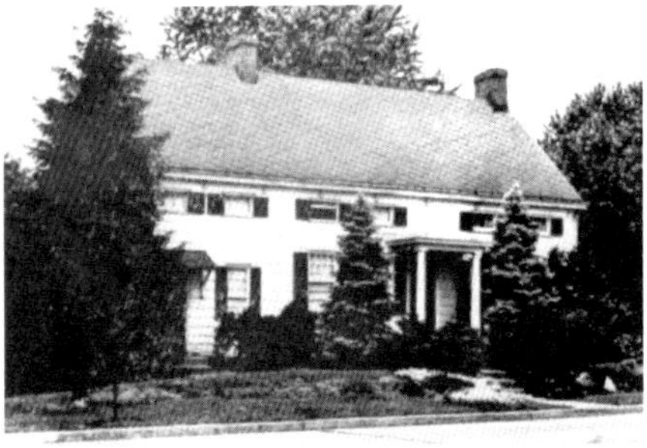

The Smith Williams house, circa 1980. *Courtesy of the Mountainside Historic Preservation Committee.*

it was a wedding present to his daughter Abigail, who married Smith Williams, a shoemaker and tanner. Their daughters, Phoebe and Ann, were born in the house, and Ann lived there all ninety-five years of her life. The property was purchased in 1918 by Mr. and Mrs. Fred Rumpf; he served two terms as mayor. After his death, his widow sold to Egan, Fickett & Co., a Florida citrus fruit distributor, which preserved the original façade of the building so that it would continue as a landmark.

Badgley House

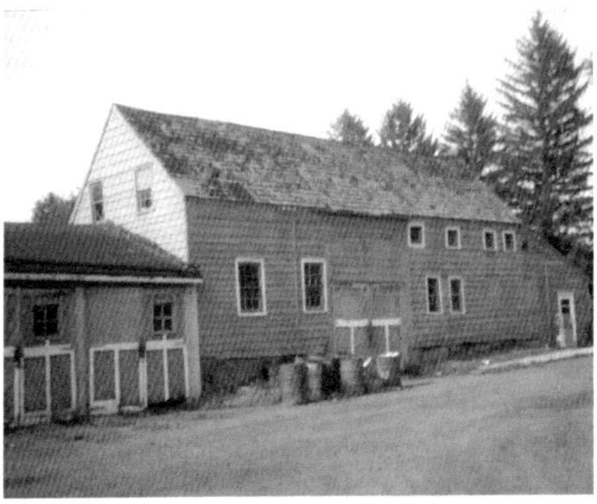

Badgley House, 1976. *Courtesy of the Westfield Historical Society.*

Located off New Providence Road in Watchung Reservation about one hundred yards north of Trailside Museum, Badgley House is said to have been one of the oldest homes in Union County and the oldest building in Mountainside. The structure was destroyed by arson on May 2, 1984. According to the Union County Planning Board's Survey of Historic Sites, Badgley House was "a visible link to the first permanent settlement of the Mountainside area in the late 1600s." This report states that John and James Badgley built the house sometime between 1735 and 1738 as "one of the first outpost settlements in the western portion of present-day Union County." According to a study in the 1970s by two Scotch Plains architects, A. Detwiller Jr. and his son, Frederic C. Detwiller, the easterly section of the building was similar to the seventeenth-century "saltbox" design found in homes on Long Island, from which the Badgley family migrated, and may have dated from sometime around 1675. (A saltbox is a frame house with two stories in front and one in back.) The house is thought to have served as a refuge for area settlers during Indian raids and also as a haven for colonists during Revolutionary War conflicts in the area. Additionally, historical accounts report that settlers of the Westfield area hid their treasures and valuable clothing and jewelry in the secluded Badgley House to secure them from British raiders. For a time before the fire, the Union County Department of Parks and Recreation used the structure to store tractors and other maintenance equipment. In 1976, the home was placed on the National Register of Historic Places.

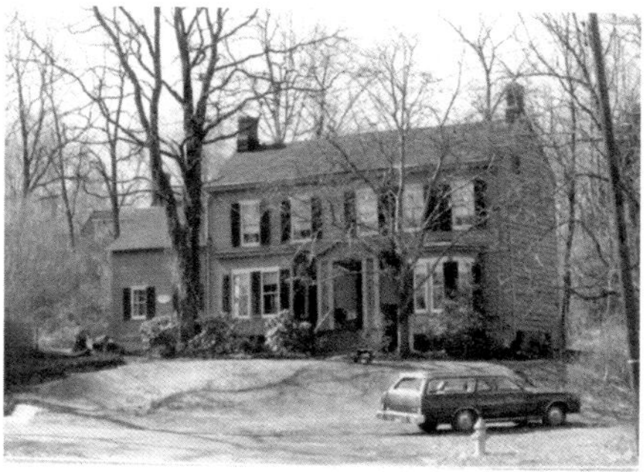

The Hetfield House in 1981 on Route 22. *Courtesy of the Mountainside Historic Preservation Committee.*

Deacon Andrew Hetfield House

Perhaps the single most recognized and celebrated structure in Mountainside is one that literally lost its footings twice in its 250-year history. When Deacon Andrew Hetfield of the Presbyterian Church of Westfield built this home in 1760, it was located across from what would become Echo Lake Park on Route 29 (now Route 22), which was then a dirt road. In 1929, it was moved back from the highway about fifty yards when the road was widened. In 1985, it was moved again to its present location adjacent to the library on Constitution Plaza.

The Georgian colonial-style house was constructed in three stages. The oldest section on the far left of the house, built around 1760 by Deacon Hetfield, consisted of a kitchen with a large hearth on the first floor and a sleeping loft on the second. As the family's needs changed, they altered and expanded the house. In about 1820, the Hetfields added a one-story, two-room portion that more than doubled the size of the house. A final two-story portion on the right side, as well as a second floor over the middle of the house, completed the house by 1830. Bay windows to the right of the entrance were added ten to twenty years later; those on the left were added in the 1870s.

Hetfield, born in Elizabethtown in 1740 and a participant in the Revolutionary War, later served as a deacon and elder of the Presbyterian Church. The house remained in the Hetfield family until approximately twenty years after World War I, when it was used as a tearoom. During the Depression, the family rented out rooms, and during the 1930s, MacKinlay Kantor, American author of *Andersonville*, was one of the tenants. In 1935, the Rosencrantz family rented the house and turned it into an antique business known as the Dutch Oven. In 1946, daughter Walda Rosencrantz purchased the home and continued the antique business until developers Walter and Robert Kuczynski bought the property in 1984. The Kuczynskis planned to demolish the old house to make room for a commercial building. At that point, the Mountainside Historic Preservation Committee, led by Fern Carter Hyde, stepped in and convinced the owners to delay their plans while the committee members raised funds to move the building to another location.

The Kuczynskis donated the house to the Borough of Mountainside, and on June 29, 1985, the Deacon Andrew Hetfield House was moved a half mile to land between the library and the firehouse on Constitution Plaza. The structure was added to the New Jersey Register of Historic Places and the National Register of Historic Places in 1989. (See chapter 5 for additional information on moving day for the house.)

Chapter 2

THE POSTWAR YEARS

1945–1959

In 1940, 23 percent of Americans lived on farms. A decade later, that number had declined to 15 percent. By 1960, the percentage of farmers had been halved. Industrial growth was changing the country, and Mountainside was following the trend. Local landholders were selling to developers, and the town's population was booming.

1945

In 1945, Councilman Meirl Hoy, acting mayor during the absence of Mayor John Moxon, sought the mayoralty nomination on the GOP ticket. According to petitions filed with Borough Clerk Robert Laing, there would be no contests in either party for the primaries on June 12. Hoy was elected mayor with a total of 199 of 220 votes. Total registered voters in the borough numbered 766.

Mrs. Jessica Dunn, widow of Charles A. Dunn, former Mountainside police recorder and justice of the peace, was planning to operate the service station formerly leased by her husband. She had been asked by Standard Oil Company of New Jersey to continue operating Dunn's Esso Station, located at Route 29 and New Providence Road. Charles, first of the borough's official family to enter the armed forces, was killed in action on June 9 while serving with the marines of the Sixth Division.

The Bronze Star Medal was awarded posthumously to Staff Sergeant Robert E. Johnson, son of Mr. and Mrs. Forrest B. Johnson of Poplar Avenue. It was presented to his mother at a ceremony on Governor's Island

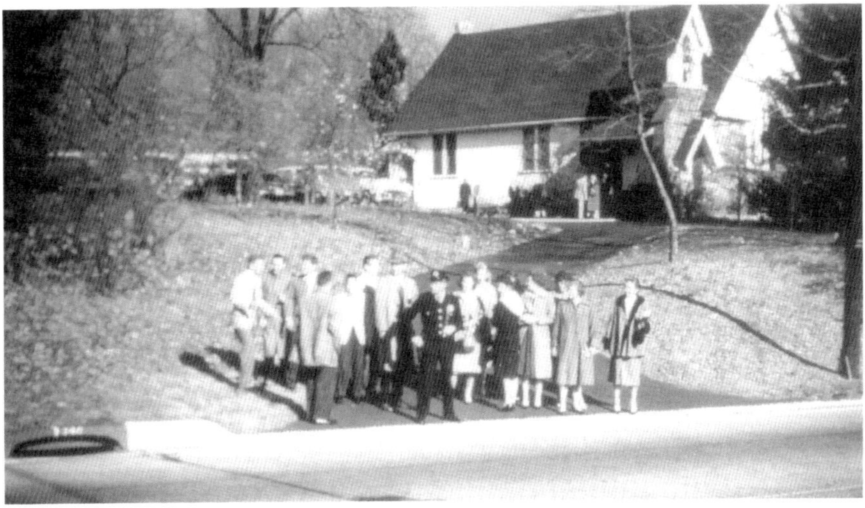

Students escorted from Mountainside Gospel Chapel by police officers cross the highway to attend Sunday school at Borough Hall due to overcrowding in the chapel. *Courtesy of Mountainside Gospel Chapel.*

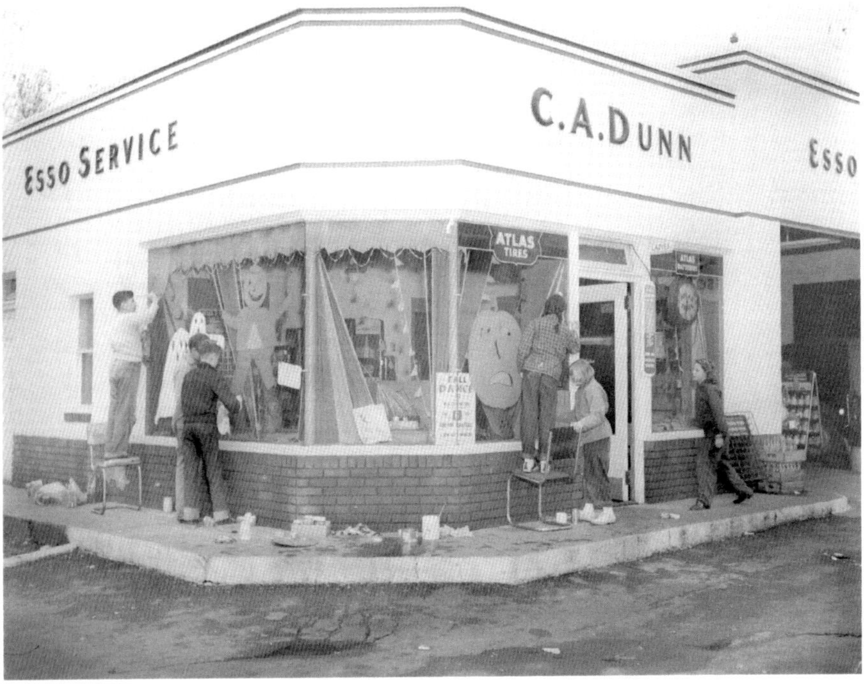

Dunn's garage on Route 22 and New Providence Road, circa 1950. *Courtesy of the Mountainside Historic Preservation Committee.*

on September 14, "for heroic achievement in connection with military operations against the enemy July 26, 1943." Twenty-four-year-old Johnson had also been awarded the Purple Heart posthumously in February. He was killed in France on D-Day, June 6, 1944.

Mountainside celebrated its fiftieth anniversary on Sunday, October 14, with a Golden Jubilee in Echo Lake Park. Festivities took place at the flagpole facing the lake. Descendants and early settlers participated. Among them was Joseph H.W. Edwards, overseer of the poor of the borough for many years and the only surviving member of the original borough government. The following is an excerpt from an editorial that appeared in the *Westfield Leader* of October 18, 1945:

> *We feel a little like the British Empire felicitating the United States on the anniversary of the Declaration of Independence. When Mountainside "seceded" from the town of Westfield we lost a very fine section of our town, but gained a stimulating and friendly neighbor. In the past few years Mountainside has grown phenomenally. It is a fine residential community,*

Pauline Tims on Moving into Mountainside

Pauline was from Brooklyn, a city girl who met her future husband, Richard, through family. They married and lived in Plainfield for a short time. In 1945, they built a house, the first on Stony Brook Lane. Pauline and Richard were married for over fifty-four years when he passed away in 2000.

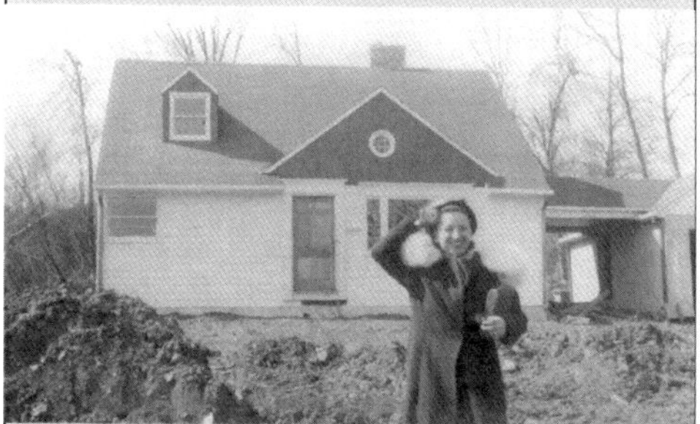

Pauline Tims in front of 1332 Stony Brook Lane, the first house on the street in 1945. *Courtesy of Pauline Tims.*

> *There were woods all over and lots of wild birches in the area. A stream ran in back of our house, the reason for the name of the street. At the beginning I didn't think I could adjust to life in the "country."*

> *with beautiful homes, an excellent school, a community chapel, several fine clubs, good community services, such as the Civil Council, Fire Department and the Rescue Squad, Girl Scouts and Boy Scouts and Cubs, and good stores.*

Farmer and longtime resident Leo Benninger died on December 6, after a short illness. In addition to his wife, Mary, he left four sons (George J. of Mountainside; Charles and August, both members of the Westfield Police Department; and Al, a captain in the U.S. Army Signal Corps stationed in Germany) and two daughters, Beatrice Schneller and Caroline Pfeiffer.

1946

In 1946, diplomas were presented to twenty graduating eighth graders.

Residents received a letter signed by fourteen (five Westfield residents and nine Mountainside residents) charging that stores on Mountain Avenue were being constructed too closely to the sidewalks. The letter further contended that there would be a loss of "beautiful balance" with the setback of the adjoining buildings.

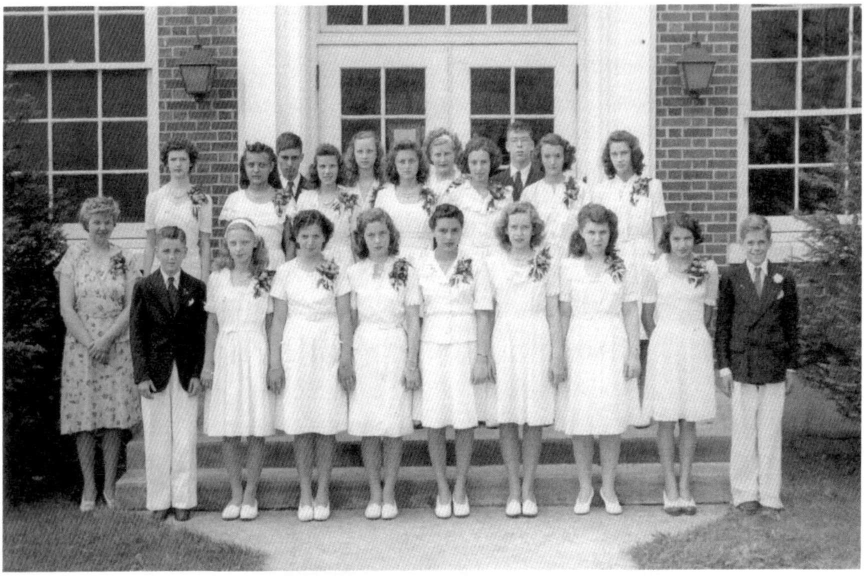

The graduating class at Echobrook School, 1945. *Courtesy of the Mountainside Historic Preservation Committee.*

1947

In 1947, the *Westfield Leader* reported that a fire "poured down" Route 29 early on Tuesday morning, September 9. A westbound tank truck went off the pavement near the entrance to the Chatterbox about one hundred feet east of Central Avenue at 5:45 a.m. Flames spread down the highway for about one-fifth of a mile, causing extensive damage to nearby property and power lines. Fire departments from surrounding towns were on the scene to help extinguish the flames. More than $20,000 worth of damage was done to the affected area.

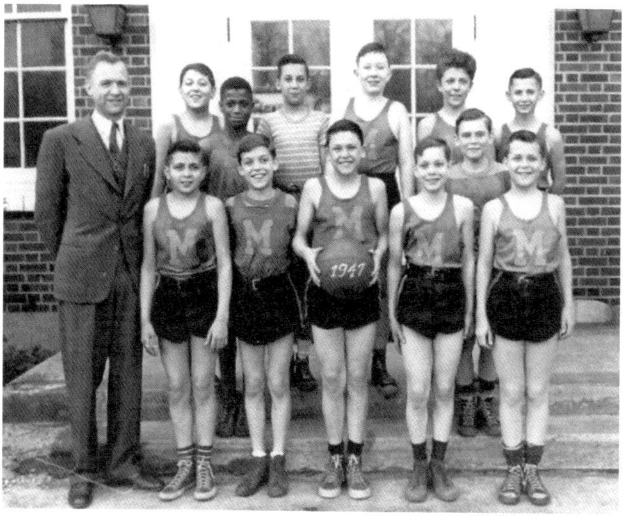

The 1947 boys' baseball team. *Courtesy of the Borough of Mountainside.*

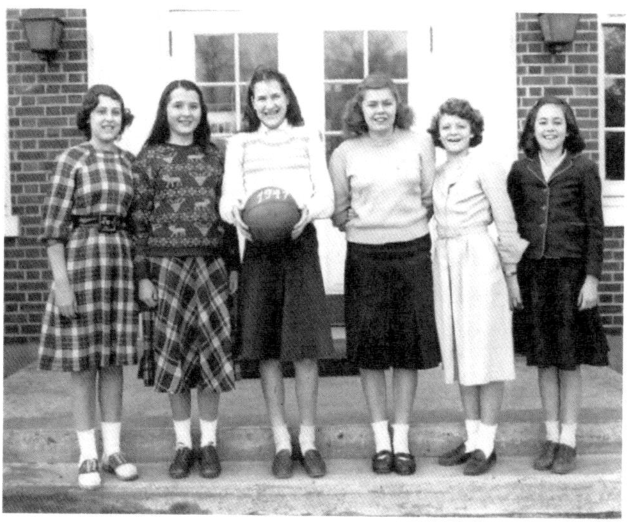

The 1947 girls' softball team. *Courtesy of the Borough of Mountainside.*

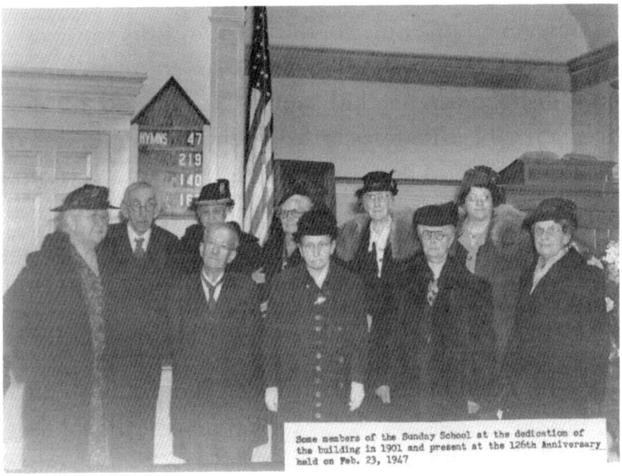

The Sunday school members present at the 126th anniversary of Mountainside Gospel Chapel on February 23, 1947. These same people were in attendance at the dedication of the building in 1901. *Courtesy of Mountainside Gospel Chapel.*

A twenty-five-foot tree, donated by Henry Vaughn-Eames of Woodland Avenue, secretary of the planning board, was erected in front of Borough Hall. It is believed to have been the first community Christmas tree in the borough's history. Members of the fire department decorated the tree with lights.

Albert J. Benninger entered the Union County freeholder race and won.

December saw the delivery of a new Cadillac ambulance for the rescue squad. The purchase was made possible through the generosity of Mountainside residents in contributions to the Community Association over the previous nine years and from a savings plan by squad members. The ambulance was equipped with a resuscitator and oxygenator, along with other first-aid devices.

1948

In 1948, a battle erupted over numbering property. The planning board proposed that all streets running parallel to Route 29 be numbered as follows: beginning at the Springfield line, houses would start at 1000 and increase from that number to the Scotch Plains border; those houses running in from the highway would start at 200. Groups of residents protested that high numbers "citified" instead of fitting the small-town atmosphere. Others didn't want to change the then current house numbers because it would require a great deal of effort. G.L. Keppler, representing the Westfield Post Office, informed the group of the difficulty of effecting proper mail service when house numbers are erratic. He didn't care what numbers were used, as long as they were consecutive.

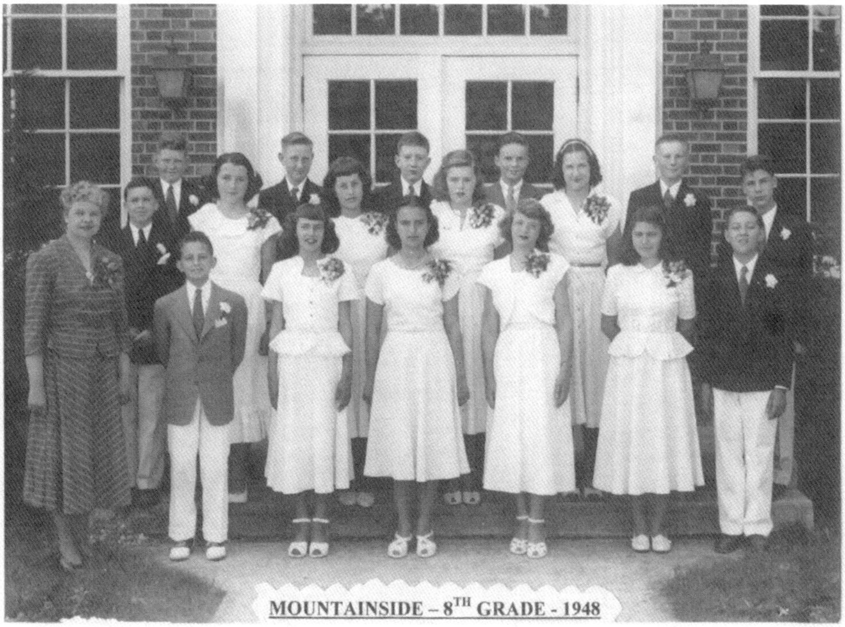

The 1948 Echobrook School graduation. *Courtesy of Carol Clark.*

1949

In 1949, a forty-lane bowling center was proposed. Echo Lanes on Route 22 East would be the largest bowling alley in New Jersey.

On August 11, the *Westfield Leader* reported the first polio fatality in the Westfield area. A nine-year-old Mountainside boy had died on August 9.

Two residents objected to the request for a club liquor license with the move of the Elks from Westfield to Mountainside. Dr. Minor C.K. Jones, Democratic candidate for council, was concerned that "with the number of liquor licenses in the borough at the present time, the average is one bar to every 100 voters." (Nine licenses were issued at the time. The Alcoholic Beverage Control [ABC] allowed one for every one thousand residents. In 2007, the State of New Jersey allowed one consumption license for every three thousand people in the population.) Reverend Milton P. Achey voiced his sentiments against the addition of any liquor licenses, stating that "as the drinking takes place in Mountainside, so does the aftermath of the drinking."

Residents from the Birch Hill and Wood Valley Road sections protested the proposed erection of ten two-family dwellings on Wood Valley Road. The homes were proposed as a "buffer" between the present one-family

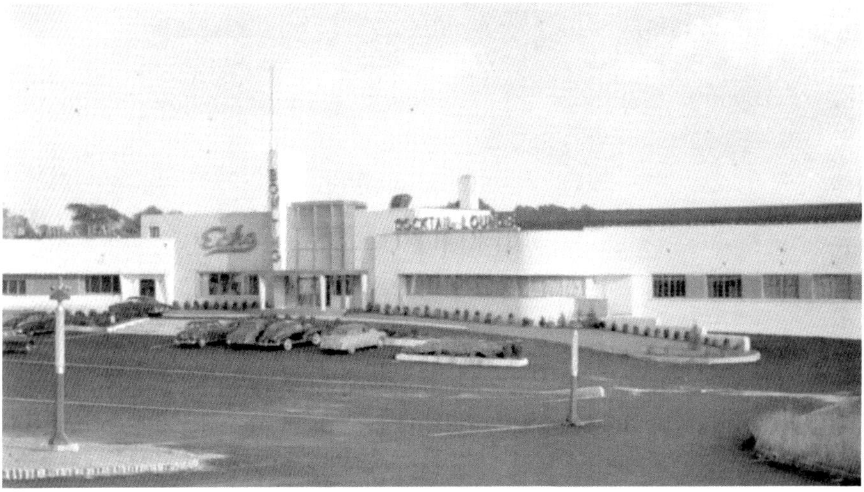

Echo Lanes, once billed as the world's largest bowling alley, is now the site of a Loew's Theater. *Courtesy of Bob Hain.*

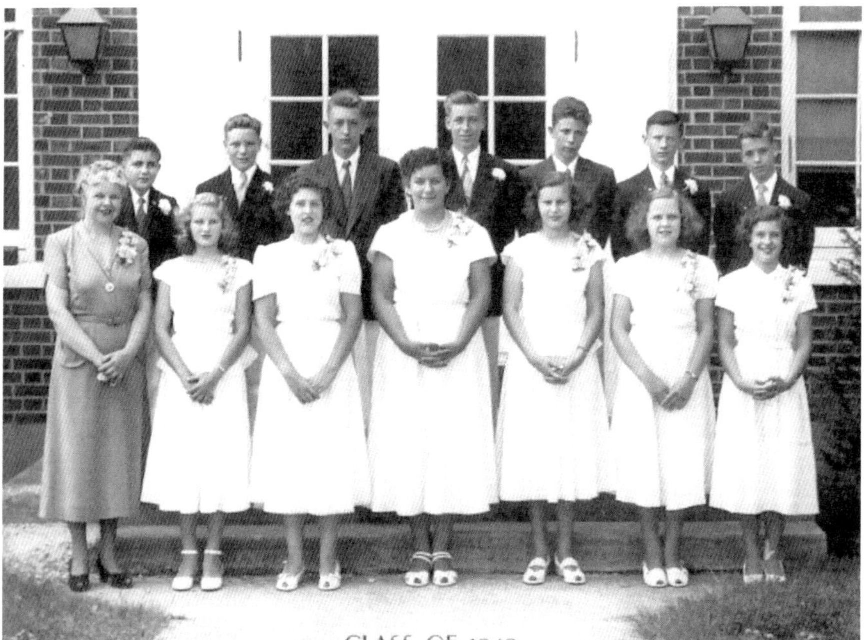

The 1949 graduation class at Echobrook School. *Courtesy of the Borough of Mountainside.*

dwellings and a proposed group of stores to be erected at some future date at the intersection of Wood Valley Road and Central Avenue. Resident William Rader said that such a "buffer" was needed because no one would construct a $20,000 house next to a store. Residents questioned the need for stores in the area. Rader agreed to withdraw the duplex-home application (cosponsored with Herman Honecker), but instead of a park area desired by the residents, he would look into the building of more reasonable one-family dwellings that would run about $12,000 each.

1950

In 1950, need arose for a new school building at a cost of $350,000. That year, school enrollment (ages five through fourteen) was 250. By the end of 1950, the projected enrollment was 330. The proposal was for a building of ten classrooms and "other necessary rooms."

On August 8, voters went to the polls to approve the purchase of twenty-one acres of land on Central Avenue. Twenty were from the eighty-eight-acre Weber farm at the cost of $1,100 per acre. In October, only one-third of the registered voters turned out and approved the planned Deerfield School.

From the opening of school in 1950 until the spring of 1952, during the construction of Deerfield School on Central Avenue, kindergarten pupils attended class in the Sunday school rooms of the chapel.

On the November ballot, a referendum appeared authorizing the borough to purchase a half million gallons daily of sewage disposal from Cranford. This had been a hot question since it was listed as one of the reasons Mountainside separated from Westfield fifty-five years earlier. According to experts, local ground conditions were not conducive to proper working of septic tanks. Mayor Joseph A.C. Komich expressed that the purchase of space was only a step toward sewers and that voters should not expect immediate installation of trunk lines if the referendum were passed. Cost for this first step was $130,000 and a fifty-point increase in the tax rate.

1951

In 1951, gasoline prices nationwide were as low as 16.9 cents per gallon. Most dealers in Union County held prices at 23.9 cents. On Route 22, the average price per gallon was 20.9.

The borough Christmas tree was relocated—Mountainside would now use a forty-foot fir in front of the Mountainside Union Chapel. It was a strategic spot visible from both sides of the highway. The civil council had to purchase additional strings of lights, as well as replacement strings for

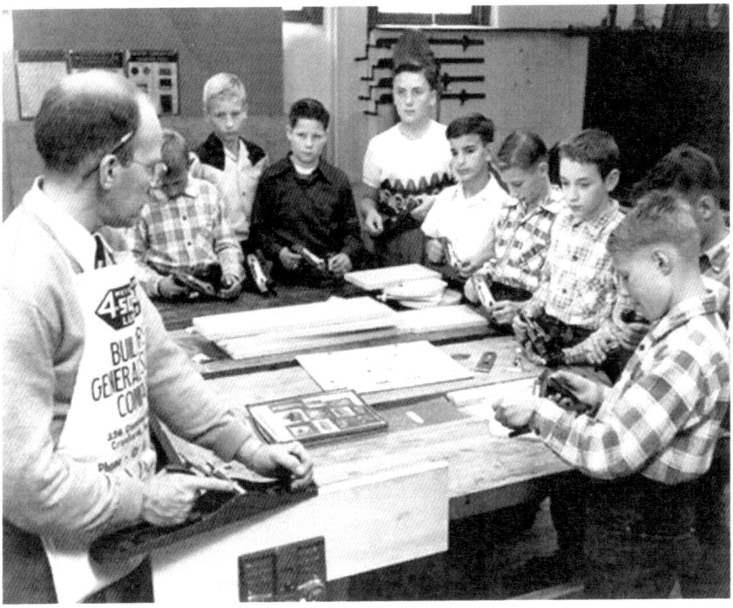

Teacher Al Collins and his class at Echobrook, 1951. *Courtesy of the Borough of Mountainside.*

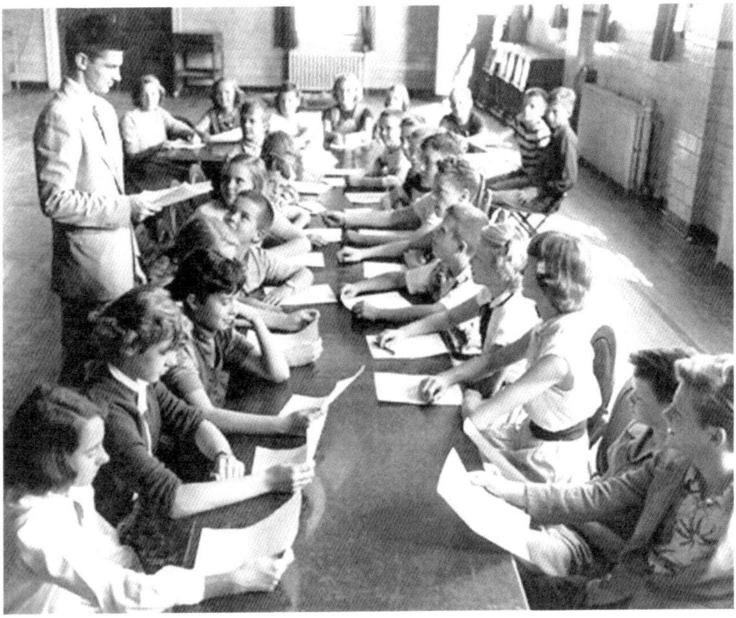

Teacher Bill Tetley and his class at Echobrook, 1951. *Courtesy of the Borough of Mountainside.*

those broken when the previous year's tree blew down in a windstorm during Christmas week. Another change was the time clock installed in the chapel so that the lights would automatically turn on at 5:00 p.m. and off at midnight.

1952

In his annual message to residents in 1952, Mayor Joseph A.C. Komich urged the people "to do their utmost to keep septic tanks in the best possible working order so that we can get by until our public sewage system, now under construction, is completed throughout the Borough, wherever feasible and practical." He explained that initial efforts to buy sewer space for a half-million-gallon flow and to secure an option for an additional half million failed because of legal complications. The borough was forced to purchase the full million-gallon capacity outright.

1953

By 1953, Deerfield School, which had opened in September 1952, needed expansion. A $350,000, nine-room addition was proposed for occupancy in September 1954. The town foresaw an increase of 70 percent in the school population between 1952 and 1957. Voters approved the referendum on April 9.

1954

In 1954, Route 29 became Route 22.

The telephone company began to convert Westfield-area phones to dial, starting with new installations and those who had service moved. Total installation was estimated to be three years away.

Reverend Delwyn R. Rayson was recommended as minister to Community Presbyterian Church congregation. Church and Sunday school had been in operation since May, renting space in Deerfield School. Architects had been chosen, and construction on the $125,000 building on Deer Path was set to begin the following spring. Rayson was installed as minister on October 31.

1955

In June 1955, the school system graduated 51 students from eighth grade. Total enrollment in September was projected at 710.

Groundbreaking for the Community Presbyterian Church took place on Sunday, December 11. It would be a red-brick, colonial-style edifice. When completed, the sanctuary and balcony would seat 350.

1956

In 1956, a referendum was planned for a third school in town. The Community Presbyterian Church was dedicated on December 9.

1957

In 1957, a Nike Missile Base was built in Mountainside's portion of Watchung Reservation. The Nike missile is a surface-to-air type weighing approximately one ton, controlled by a surface guidance system. Eighty officers and enlisted men occupied the base at its height in the late 1950s and early 1960s. Three underground storage areas were located in the launching area, ready at a moment's notice to launch missiles in defense of New York City.

A referendum for a new ten-classroom school was defeated in January: 640 to 410. In November, voters approved a new school in a vote of 805 to 726.

Fire damaged forty-eight-year-old Borough Hall on April 1. Repairs were to be made. Insurance funds would pay for the renovations to the damaged portions of the second floor of the wooden structure.

1958

In 1958, the Trailside Museum Association and Amateur Astronomers, Inc., set a goal of $100,000 for a proposed Trailside Science Center in Watchung Reservation. Approximately $70,000 was to be set aside for building and $30,000 for equipment. It would be located adjacent to Trailside Museum.

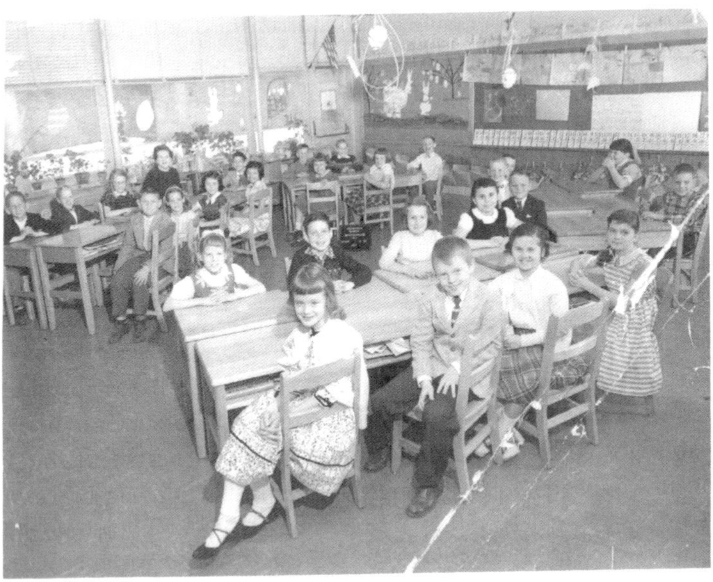

Mrs. Singer's third-grade class, 1957. *Courtesy of Richard Benninger.*

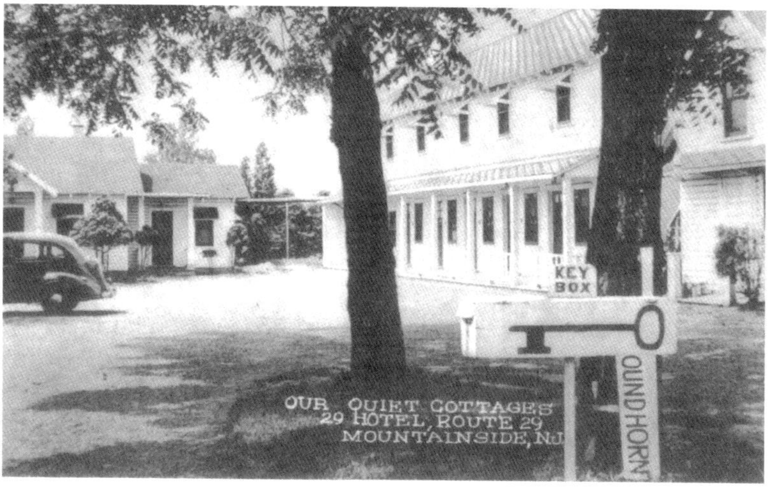

Hoppe's Hotel 29, 1950s, on what is now Route 22 and the site of Manor Care. *Courtesy of the Mountainside Police Department.*

Seventy-three eighth graders graduated from the school system.

Plans for a new Catholic church were announced by Most Reverend Thomas A. Boland, archbishop of Newark. At the time, two Sunday Masses were being said in Deerfield School for Catholics in town. In December, Father Gerard McGarry was appointed pastor of the new church. Cynthia Dorio West was the first baby baptized in the newly formed parish on December 21, 1958.

The board of education announced that it would hire a business manager for the school system. According to Board President Frederick Wilhelms Jr., this would result in a savings greater than the amount of his salary.

Private sponsors began a summer recreation program for grades kindergarten through twelve. It would be directed by John Kyreakakis, a twenty-seven-year-old physical education teacher in the borough. Seven civic groups would provide financial support.

Plans for a municipal building were discussed. The two options were to utilize the Echobrook School building or to construct a new building on the northeast corner of Route 22 and New Providence Road.

A Mountainside branch of the Westfield Post Office was opened on November 1 in temporary quarters at 1170 Route 22.

On December 11, the *Mountainside Echo* made its debut as the community's weekly newspaper.

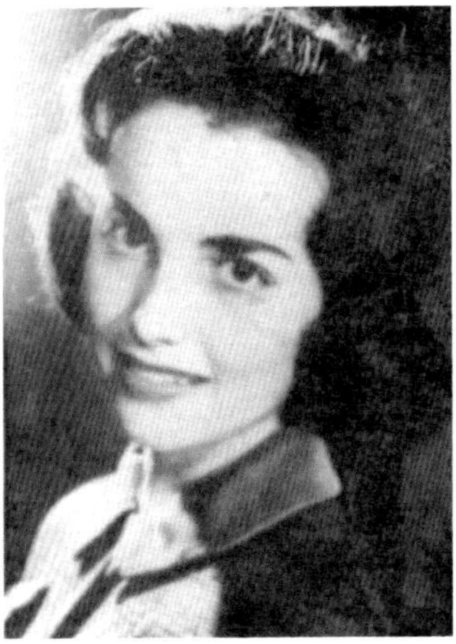

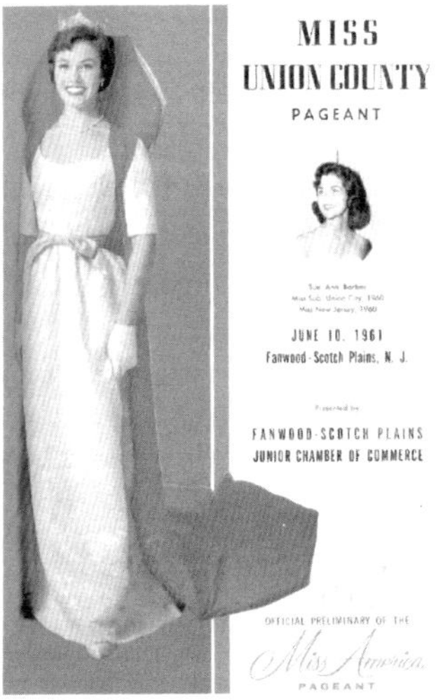

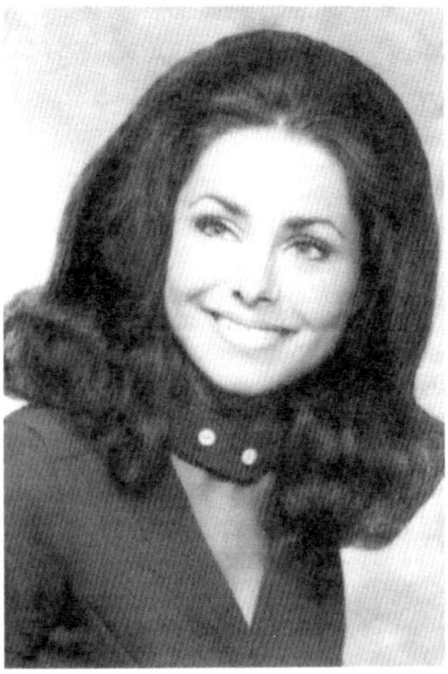

1959

In 1959, the Mountainside Union Chapel was the only church on Route 22 between Newark and Whitehouse, New Jersey. According to *Ripley's Believe It or Not*, it is the only church in the United States that is located in a traffic circle.

On April 2, the *Mountainside Echo* went from tabloid to full-size newspaper and established itself at 2 New Providence Road in the Barrett & Crain Realtor's building.

Echobrook graduated seventy-seven students in June.

All-night parking was outlawed (2:30–5:30 a.m.) to facilitate snow removal and eliminate potential hazards for children walking to school.

Don Maxwell retired as secretary of the board of education after thirty-two years in the post. He was also on the borough council from 1925 to 1927, and he organized the zoning and planning boards with two other men in 1935. Born in New York City, Maxwell came to Mountainside in 1907. He lived on a farm, now part of Watchung Reservation. He worked his way through Phillips Exeter Academy in New Hampshire and New Jersey College of Agriculture (Rutgers) and then joined the family business, Westfield Storage Warehouse. He became interested in antiques and added an antiques department to the business. Maxwell said, "I am not particularly interested in making money. People should be more interested in living a life than in making a living."

Within a decade Mountainside boasted three winners of the Miss New Jersey Pageant: *Top*: Beverly Ann Domareki, 1959; *Middle*: Sue Ann Barber (Torborg), 1960; and *Bottom*: Hela Yungst, 1970. *All photos courtesy of the New Jersey Education Foundation.*

Beechwood School opened its ten classrooms to house kindergarten through third grade.

Beverly Ann Domareki, a resident of Fox Trail, was crowned Miss Union County. She went on to become Miss New Jersey, representing the state and the borough in the Miss America pageant.

The Mountainside Rescue Squad began building a new brick-faced structure with colonial architecture. Herman Honecker, a local builder and one of the organizers of the group in 1939, supervised the construction.

The school population increased. Six new classrooms would be needed by 1961. Projected school enrollment for the following year was 1,300. By 1970, however, there was expected to be a decrease.

Construction began on Our Lady of Lourdes Church and School. The church would seat seven hundred in a building designed by Alphonso Alvarez of Upper Montclair. Planned also were a four-classroom school and an all-purpose room.

The new regional high school being built in Berkeley Heights was named Governor Livingston in honor of the state's first governor, William Livingston (1723–1790).

At the age of fifty, Al Benninger quit a twenty-nine-year political career. He was Mountainside's youngest councilman, elected in 1930 at the age of twenty-one, and went on to become a freeholder in 1948. In 1956, Benninger hit the national picture when he presented a doghouse to Vice President Nixon's family for Checkers, their cocker spaniel. Mrs. Nixon called on Christmas Eve and wanted to know when to expect the doghouse. Benninger said that quitting politics would give him more time with his wife, Elizabeth, their eleven-year-old son, Peter, and their sixteen-year-old daughter, Mary, as well as for his pigeons and fishing. People recall his oft-quoted phrase: "I ain't mad at nobody."

Beyond Mountainside's Borders

The events in this section do not attempt to cover all of the important dates in the history of the period. They are but a handful of primarily national, and some international, occurrences that may have had an impact on the development of the borough of Mountainside. Further, they may provide assistance in placing Mountainside's growth in perspective with that of the outside world.

1945

In 1945, the Serviceman's Readjustment Act (GI Bill of Rights) of 1944 provided $13 billion in aid ranging from education to housing. The United States dropped atomic bombs on Hiroshima and Nagasaki, and Japan surrendered. Soviet troops occupied North Korea, and U.S. troops occupied South Korea. The United Nations was established with fifty-one founding member nations. Harry Truman became president upon the death of Franklin D. Roosevelt.

1946

In 1946, Winston Churchill coined the term "iron curtain." The U.S. Atomic Energy Commission was established.

1947

In 1947, the United States announced the Marshall Plan to help stabilize Western European governments and accelerate postwar economic recovery. The total number of armed forces was cut to 1.5 million. The army fell to 600,000 from a World War II peak of 8 million.

Jackie Robinson joined the Brooklyn Dodgers, and Captain Chuck Yeager, USAF, broke the sound barrier.

1948

Harry Truman was elected president in 1948. The United States reinstated the military draft and recognized the state of Israel. Truman ended racial segregation in the U.S. military.

1949

Twelve nations signed the North Atlantic Treaty in 1949, establishing NATO. The USSR detonated an atomic bomb, beginning an arms race with the United States.

1950

The Korean War began in 1950. Senator Joseph McCarthy claimed he had evidence of Communist infiltration into the State Department.

1951

The postwar baby boom increased the national population by 30 percent in 1951. Peace negotiations began in Korea, and forty-nine nations signed the Japanese peace treaty.

1952

Dwight D. Eisenhower was elected president in 1952, and the United States detonated the first hydrogen bomb.

1953

A peace treaty ended the Korean War in 1953, restoring the partition of North Korea and South Korea.

1954

Brown v. Board of Education found the "separate but equal" doctrine unconstitutional in 1954. Eisenhower invoked the "domino theory," insisting that Indochina must not fall to Communist control. The Geneva Peace Accords partitioned Vietnam.

1955

Jonas Salk created the polio vaccine in 1955. Martin Luther King Jr. introduced civil disobedience into the struggle for integration. The Supreme Court ordered the states to desegregate schools "with all deliberate speed." Rosa Parks refused to sit at the back of the bus, breaking the Montgomery, Alabama segregation seating law.

1956

Eisenhower was reelected president in 1956.

1957

The launching of *Sputnik* by the Soviets in 1957 caused fear that America was falling behind technologically.

1958

In 1958, Congress established NASA to coordinate research and development and the National Defense Education Act to provide funds for education.

1959

Homeownership grew by 50 percent between 1945 and 1960. New homes required appliances, and by far the most popular was television, which increased from 7,000 sets in 1946 to 50 million in 1960.

The suburbs grew faster than the cities in the 1950s. Due in part to the development of the interstate highway system during the Eisenhower administration, auto production increased from 2 million cars in 1946 to 8 million in 1955, which further increased the development of suburbs.

Alaska and Hawaii became the forty-ninth and fiftieth states in 1959.

Chapter 3
EXPANSION
1960–1969

The 1960s began with a new mayor, a court appeal from a developer, a community-wide fight against a jetport in neighboring Morris County and the opening of the Union County Regional High School district's third school. The decade concluded with Mountainside's victory in its attempts to preserve its community, specifically in relation to construction of a cloverleaf at Route 22 and New Providence Road. Still, strides continued to be made, including the building of a new public library and a municipal pool.

1960

In 1960, Albert T. Hartung became mayor, succeeding Joseph Komic, and the completion of the 5.5-mile missing portion of Route 78 was discussed. Donald Robert Maxwell (614 Sherwood Parkway) took over his father's firm. Don Maxwell retired after forty-five years.

Mountainside's growth was the greatest in Union County; its population tripled between 1950 and 1960.

The 139th anniversary of Mountainside Union Chapel's Sunday school was marked by the dedication of a new Christian Education building on February 26.

A Citizens' Advisory Committee spoke against the Port Authority of New York and New Jersey's plan to build the world's largest jetport on the Great Swamp in Morris County. The airport would be located just seven miles from the borough, with runways only five miles away. In July, the Sunny Slope Civic Council urged the borough's governing body to oppose the jetport. One month later, the council came out against the Port Authority's plan and appointed Councilman Chester Fabian to the Jetport Site Association. Raymond Herrgott and Thomas Harding led the citizen group. In October, Harding campaigned to demonstrate to residents the problems that a nearby airport could inflict on Mountainside. The Great Swamp was ultimately saved from destruction in 1964, when the United States Department of the Interior designated the area a National Wildlife Refuge for migrating waterfowl.

The Mountainside Rescue Squad opened its new building on Route 22 near New Providence Road. The squad had been in operation for twenty-one years.

A Route 22 pedestrian overpass was completed for the safety of schoolchildren walking to Echobrook School, located on the south side of the highway.

Groundbreaking for Our Lady of Lourdes took place on May 15; actual construction began on July 7.

The speed limit on the 2.7-mile strip of Route 22 through Mountainside was reduced to forty-five miles per hour for trucks due to a major accident involving a coal truck striking two buses parked on the highway. The reduction restricted trucks to the right-hand lane because the speed limit for other vehicles was fifty miles per hour.

Governor Livingston High School opened on September 8 with a student capacity of 930. Its initial enrollment was 775. The building was equipped with one of the finest electronic labs in the nation. The lab was designed with the help of engineers from New Jersey Bell Telephone Labs at a cost of $2,525,000 for the school. Already only two years away from capacity, an addition was being planned, as was a parking lot, a track and work on athletic fields. These projects were expected to be ready by 1962.

A post office was built on Sherwood Parkway near the business district. Action to secure a post office started in 1957 by the borough council. It had been located in rented quarters in a factory building at 1137 Route 22 since October 1959 and before that in other temporary quarters for about a year. In the 1920s, the Westfield Post Office left the borough's mail at Schoonover's, located on the site that Bliwise now occupies. Schoonover's was part living quarters, part taxi building, part hardware store and part post office substation. Mr. Schoonover had his taxi parked on the Mountain Avenue side of the building. At train time in Westfield, he would be at the station, ready to serve those who needed a ride since there were so few automobiles around.

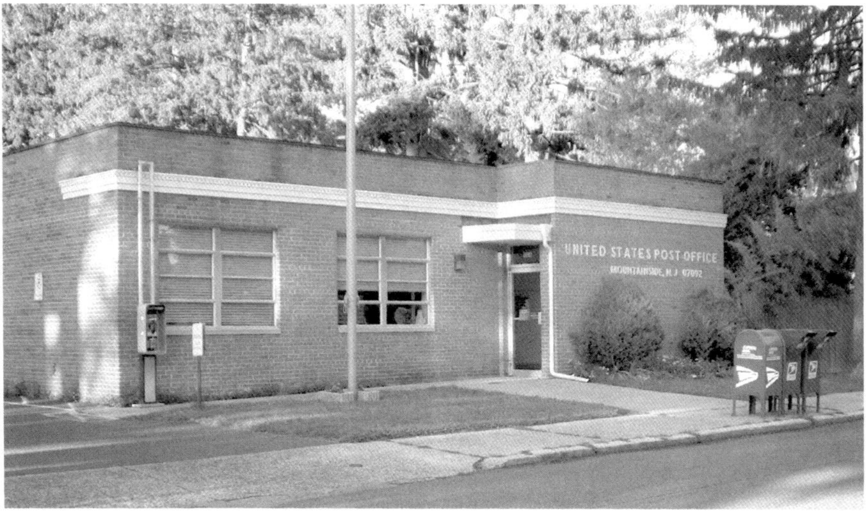

Mountainside Post Office in the early 1960s. *Courtesy of the Borough of Mountainside.*

Reverend Elmer A. Talcott accepted the position of minister of the Community Presbyterian Church to replace Reverend Delwyn Rayson, who was leaving to be a minister in Honolulu, Hawaii. Reverend Talcott would begin on January 1, 1961.

Deerfield School graduated 102 students.

1961

Groundbreaking for the post office was held on Saturday, April 8, 1961; it opened on Monday, August 21. Because many residents were on vacation at that time, the dedication took place on September 9.

Voters approved plans to establish a municipal library.

The first Mass at the newly constructed Our Lady of Lourdes was held on July 23. Approximately 125 first through fourth graders attended opening day at Our Lady of Lourdes School on September 6.

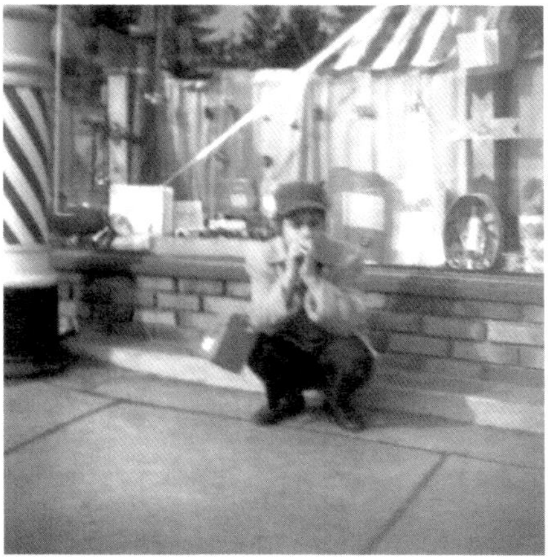

John Decristoforo in front of the Mountainside barbershop, 1961. *Courtesy of Frank DeRosa.*

1962

In 1962, 106 students graduated from Deerfield School.

The board of managers of the Children's Country Home changed its name to Children's Specialized Hospital. Although different techniques of treatment might be used, the *Westfield Leader* reported on September 27 that "the aim is the same: to rehabilitate each child to the greatest possible extent."

1963

An ordinance was passed and adopted on April 19, 1963, appropriating $300,000 for the cost of construction of a building for use as a free public library.

On June 1, a board of recreation commissioners was established.

Forty-two volunteer firemen served the borough in 1963.

Deerfield planned a third addition. At a cost of $207,000, it would include a new library and library office, a workroom and a book storage room, as well as a locker and shower room.

Enrollment in the schools stood at 1,254 at the beginning of the 1963–64 academic year, 41 fewer than in June and 22 fewer than in September 1962.

1964

Question arose at a council meeting on April 22, 1964, about a vehicle overpass at New Providence Road and Route 22. A jughandle was also a possibility.

Approximately 155 students received diplomas from Deerfield, the largest graduating class in the school's history; 325 graduated from high school.

On September 8, Frederick Wilhelms Jr.'s name was placed on the ballot as the Republican candidate for mayor to fill the unexpired term of Orlin E. Johnson, who was moving out of town.

The board of education announced plans to vacate its offices and the office of Superintendent Levin B. Hanigan in Echobrook School. Offices were rented in the Benninger Building on Route 22.

A municipal pool was proposed.

A petition was started urging the borough council to hold a referendum on November 8 on whether the town should permit multiple-dwelling buildings. The planning board officially disagreed because the sewer lines were not adequate to maintain such dwellings.

In December, the board of education released long-range plans for abandoning the use of Echobrook for educational purposes, instead citing the building of additions to Deerfield and Beechwood and the acquisition of a site for possible erection of a school in the next twenty to thirty years.

1965

At the January 1965 reorganization meeting, Mayor Wilhelms announced that a master plan was to be adopted that would hold the key to the future of the borough. Wilhelms also called for a storm-drainage plan and improvements in the business operation of Borough Hall.

Gloria Johnson created the official borough seal.

Plans were announced for a new rectory for the priests of Our Lady of Lourdes Church. It would be designed by Alfonso Alvarez, who was the architect for the church.

Ground was broken for a "7-11" general store at 921 Mountain Avenue. The one-story colonial building would be constructed with used bricks. The Mountainside store was one of seventy-five that the Southland Corp. of Dallas, Texas, planned to build in New Jersey.

1966

The pool opened in 1966, and plans were underway for a new library. An appropriation of an additional $70,000 was made on October 28.

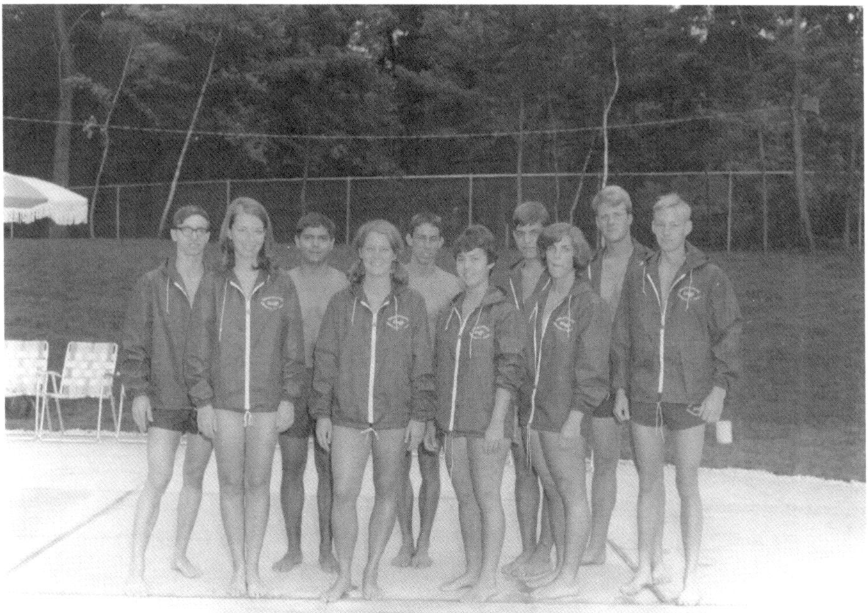

Recreation Department staff, 1966. *From left to right*: Bob Speyth, Pattie Dwyer, Barry Bistis, Carol Dawson, Richie Brown, Rene Dorfman, Lenny Myers, Susan Hartnett, Frank Chambers and Rene DeMonchy. *Courtesy of the Mountainside Recreation Department.*

1967

In 1967, Mayor Wilhelms introduced a program for improvements to Borough Hall and police headquarters, which occupy what is currently the Lord Building on Route 22 near Mountain Avenue. Updating municipal buildings would be a recurring theme for many years to come.

Bids went out for the building of a bathhouse at the pool, and the fall of 1968 was set as the target date for opening a new wing at Deerfield. The planning board gave approval for a water tower in Watchung Reservation, and the library building was scheduled to be finished in November.

1968

In 1968, the Mountainside Music Association donated $800 to the library and a cello to the music department of Mountainside's public schools.

The library opened with Emily Hoffarth as the first library director. She retired in 1970. Her picture remains on the library wall in honor of her years of dedication to the library and to education in the borough.

On March 29, a borough landmark, the former Chi-Am Chateau, burned to ground in a fire estimated to have caused $300,000 in damage. At the time of its demise, the restaurant was known as Three Coins.

1969

Reverend Gerard McGarry marked his tenth anniversary at Our Lady of Lourdes in 1969; it was also the tenth anniversary of the parish.

Police Chief Christian F. Fritz retired after thirty-two years, and Captain Edward J. Mullin was named acting chief.

The rescue squad celebrated its thirtieth anniversary.

Schools opened with 1,235 students. Enrollment would climb to 1,280 by the end of year. The school population was on a plateau that was expected to last until 1975.

Mayor Wilhelms outlined a plan to use the Echobrook School building as Borough Hall and police headquarters.

Thomas Ricciardi won election as mayor.

Mountainside's first ecumenical Thanksgiving Eve service was held at Community Presbyterian Church.

Opposite, top: A Cub Scout pack meeting, 1967. *Courtesy of Ruthie Goense.*
Opposite, middle: Chi-Am Chateau was at the first traffic light on U.S. 22 West from New York City, where Famous Dave's is now located. *Courtesy of Bob Hain.*
Opposite, bottom: Emily Hoffarth and her class at the first school library. *Courtesy of the Mountainside Public Library.*

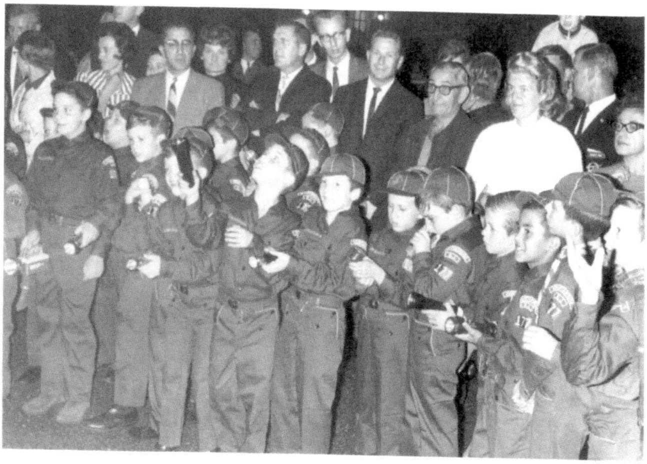

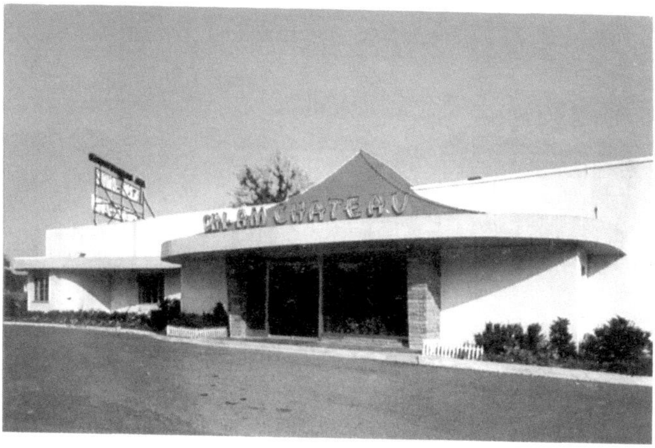
CHATEAU

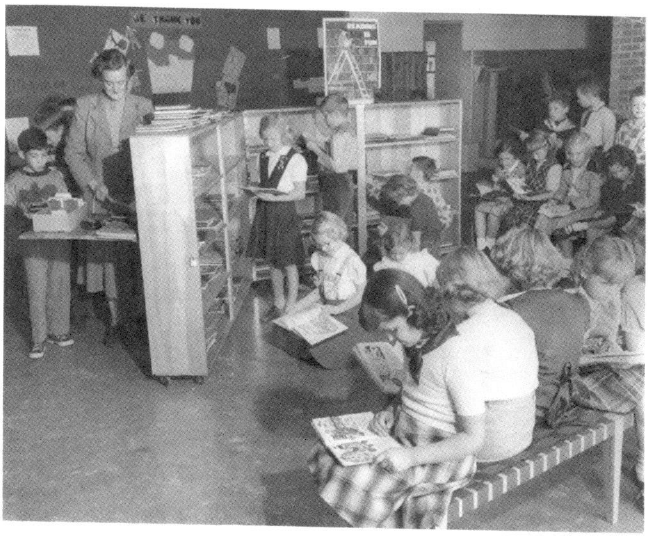
THANK YOU

Beyond Mountainside's Borders

1960

Minimum wage was raised from $1.00 to $1.25 an hour in 1960. John F. Kennedy was elected president, and 90 percent of U.S. homes had television sets.

1961

The Peace Corps was established in 1961. The Berlin Wall was built, and the United States broke diplomatic relations with Cuba.

1962

In 1962, the Cuban Missile Crisis nearly resulted in war.

1963

In *The Feminine Mystique*, published in 1963, Betty Friedan argued that middle-class society stifled women and didn't allow them to use their creativity.

More than 200,000 people participated in the March on Washington for civil rights. Martin Luther King Jr. delivered his "I Have a Dream" speech.

Lee Harvey Oswald assassinated President John F. Kennedy in Dallas, and Lyndon B. Johnson became president.

1964

In 1964, the Civil Rights Act outlawed racial discrimination by employers and unions, creating the Equal Employment Commission to enforce the law.

The United States escalated conflict in Vietnam by bombing North Vietnam.

University students organized to protest limitations on freedom, equality, individualism and democracy.

The War on Poverty began with the Economic Opportunity Act, which established a job corps. Lyndon B. Johnson was elected president.

1965

The Medicare Act of 1965 combined hospital insurance for retired people with a voluntary plan to cover physician's bills. Medicaid provided grants to states to help the poor below retirement age.

Racial riots erupted in Watts (Los Angeles): 34 people were killed, 850 wounded and 3,100 arrested. The Great Society program included a wide range of legislation to improve many aspects of American life.

1966

New York and Chicago experienced race riots in 1966. Betty Friedan and others founded the National Organization for Women (NOW). Medicare took effect.

1967

Race riots occurred in Newark and Detroit in 1967. Thurgood Marshall was sworn in as the first black U.S. Supreme Court justice.

Dr. Christiaan N. Barnard and a team of South African surgeons performed the world's first successful human heart transplant. The patient died eighteen days later.

1968

James Earl Ray assassinated Martin Luther King Jr. in 1968. Sirhan Sirhan assassinated Robert F. Kennedy. Richard M. Nixon was elected president, and the Tet Offensive began. The Vietcong attacked cities, towns and American bases and won a psychological victory. American opinion turned against the war.

1969

Neil Armstrong and Edwin "Buzz" Aldrin became the first humans to walk on the moon.

Richard M. Nixon was inaugurated as the thirty-seventh president of the United States.

Nixon announced "Vietnamization," encouraging the South Vietnamese to take more responsibility for the war, thus enabling the United States to withdraw its solders.

Chapter 4

ENERGY AND GROWTH

1970–1979

The decade of the 1970s began with a celebration to commemorate Mountainside's seventy-fifth year of incorporation, followed by an energy crisis that was a harbinger of conservation measures and a new mindset for the future.

1970

Thomas Ricciardi replaced Wilhelms as mayor in 1970. Emily Hoffarth retired as borough librarian after twenty-four years of service; Johanna Chen of Murray Hill was named the new library director. Jim Green was appointed the first paid recreation supervisor.

Borough residents signed a book that would be placed in a time capsule. This was the first activity conducted by the Committee to Commemorate the Diamond Jubilee. The capsule was buried on the library grounds and would be opened at the borough's centennial in 1995.

Diamond Jubilee was officially underway: Borough Hall was decorated with bunting and an official emblem. A parade began at 11:00 a.m., followed by a picnic/fair at noon on the combined grounds of Our Lady of Lourdes and Deerfield School. Tents housed exhibits by local religious, civil, service and social organizations. Local industries displayed their products. Contests, games and rides entertained children of all ages. Local artwork was also shown.

Six hundred attended the Diamond Jubilee dinner/dance on October 23 at Wieland's Steak House on Route 22.

The borough council held its monthly meeting at the Elks Club, one of the oldest buildings in the borough and the place where gatherings were held by those responsible for the borough's incorporation in 1895.

1971

In 1971, Mayor Ricciardi presented the State Arts Council Certificate of Award to the Mountainside Music Association (MMA) on behalf of the New Jersey State Council on the Arts. MMA was formed in 1960 to help support music departments of Mountainside schools and to encourage the participation and enjoyment of the arts. In the past, $30,000 worth of equipment, instruments and pianos had been donated to schools. The Mountainside Public Library was built to include a music room because of the commitment of the association to supply it with records and books and to equip it with phonographs. In addition, MMA awarded two scholarships to high school seniors who showed particular promise in the fields of drama and music.

School enrollment was expected to stay at the then current level into the 1980s. The borough neared its saturation point of 2,600 homes. The birth rate was falling. Mountainside's birth rate was 6 percent per one thousand as compared with 18 percent per one thousand nationwide.

Due to the planned widening of Route 22, Mountainside Union Chapel voted to begin preparation for construction on property off Central Avenue. It had been at its then current location for seventy years.

Nancy Pollock was appointed recreation director.

Ninth graders had to decide whether to go to Jonathan Dayton High School or to Governor Livingston High School in September 1972.

1972

In 1972, Elmer A. Hoffarth, borough clerk since 1949, announced that he would retire in December. The U.S. Department of Commerce census figures showed a population of 7,520 in Mountainside. The average resident of Mountainside was a native-born New Jerseyan who had lived in the same house for seven years, attended college for a year, was a professional man or an administrator and earned at least $15,000.

The site for a new firehouse was chosen, and an ordinance appropriating $400,000 to pay for the firehouse was introduced on August 15. It passed and was adopted on September 19. The borough council planned to sell $850,000 in municipal bonds to cover the costs of the firehouse, Barnes Tract and the next stage of drainage and sewer projects.

1973

In 1973, the Highlanders, the Governor Livingston marching band, represented New Jersey in President Richard M. Nixon's inaugural parade.

Far View Drive resident and Marine Captain James Egan, MIA since 1966, was named an "adopted son" of neighboring Springfield. The Foothill Club dedicated a "Freedom Tree" at Deerfield School to Marine Captain Egan. The ceremony was held on June 14, Flag Day, with James's parents, Mr. and Mrs. James Egan, participating.

A killer storm hit northern New Jersey on August 2. It started at 7:30 a.m., and by 8:10 a.m. rowboats could be seen paddling about on Mountain Avenue. Two bridges in Echo Lake Park were washed away, and a water main broke, draining a portion of the lake. The storm delayed the opening of Mountainside Gospel Chapel on Spruce Drive. This structure replaced the old chapel on the center island of Route 22, which was purchased by the state for road widening.

Approximately 1,054 pupils were registered in school in September, down from 1,127 who attended in June. The board of education announced difficulty in securing a school fuel-oil contract due to the national fuel shortage. In November, an emergency delivery of fuel oil arrived.

1974

In 1974, the board of education announced that students in the three grades remaining at Echobrook School would be transferred to other schools in September.

Sue Winans assumed the duties of borough recreation director, replacing Nancy Pollock.

Formal dedication services were held for the new Mountainside Gospel Chapel.

A groundbreaking ceremony was held for the new firehouse on April 6.

1975

In 1975, the Trailside Nature and Science Center in Watchung Reservation held a formal dedication ceremony for its new $500,000 building.

On June 7, the Volunteer Fire Department dedicated its new building on New Providence Road.

Traffic once again rolled through Echo Lake Park two years after its roads were closed following the August 1972 storm that washed out bridges and dams. The cost to the Union County Park Commission was $973,000.

The board of education and the borough council announced their agreement on a ten-year lease of the Echobrook School building, which was closed in June 1974 because of declining enrollment.

1976

In February 1976, the board of education approved a reorganization plan for September: Beechwood would accommodate grades kindergarten through three (with 300 pupils), while Deerfield would hold grades four through eight, plus one kindergarten class (550 pupils). In previous years, Beechwood had held grades kindergarten through five and Deerfield, kindergarten through eight.

Marilyn Hart won a three-way race to become Mountainside's representative to the regional board of education. The board of education voted to sell the newer portion of the Echobrook School building to the borough council for conversion into a municipal building. The borough council approved an agreement with the board of education to transfer the title to the 1936 portion of Echobrook School for conversion into a municipal complex.

The Mountainside Rotary Club announced that it had received permission for a third printing of Jean Hesketh Hershey's book *The History of Mountainside*, originally prepared for the borough's fiftieth anniversary in 1945. The borough celebrated the bicentennial year with an all-day festival.

1977

In 1977, the State Department of Transportation's recommendation for the construction of Route 78 through Watchung Reservation was stalled by conservationists. Regional high school students ate lunch on paper plates with plastic utensils as Governor Brendan Byrne's energy crisis orders made water temperatures too cold to sanitize.

Following a wave of vandalism at Deerfield School, Superintendent Dr. Levin B. Hanigan concluded that students caught cabin fever when they were ordered to stay in the building to avoid ice accidents. The borough council adopted an ordinance allowing nonresidents to join the pool in order to remedy budget problems caused by declining membership.

The Regional High School District Board of Education charged athletic directors with male chauvinism, claiming that girls weren't getting equal attention in school sports or athletic contests.

More than four hundred children marched through town, celebrating the borough's twenty-fourth year of organized baseball.

The Jonathan Dayton Regional High School Chorus took the second highest prize in the International Music Festival in Canada, and women could now become members of the police department.

1978

In 1978, the school population continued to decline. Reverend Gerard J. McGarry, pastor since he established the parish in December 1958, retired from Our Lady of Lourdes. Reverend Monsignor Raymond J. Pollard was appointed second pastor at Our Lady of Lourdes.

1979

In 1979, Marilyn Hart, a former member of the Union County Regional Board of Education, became the first woman elected to borough council. On the occasion of her swearing in, Mayor Thomas Ricciardi noted the following:

> *As long as I am talking about people, let me first congratulate Marilyn Hart as the first woman member to be elected to council, and I assure you that I will have no problem working with her, as I have had more than 30 years experience working with another fine woman, my wife.*

Union County began evaluating the feasibility of using underground facilities at the abandoned Nike base in Watchung Reservation to store county government documents. County Manager George Albanese reported that the base included "substantial" underground buildings that could be used mainly for documents the county was required by law to keep but that were not needed for reference.

The three missile silos, which were flooded when the base was closed down in 1963, were drained by county workers. Workers at that time uncovered various military explosives, including grenades and an aerial bomb, which had been left behind when the base was vacated.

Beyond Mountainside's Borders

1970

In 1970, the First Earth Day drew attention to environmental issues. U.S. troops invaded Cambodia, and four students at Kent State University were slain by national guardsmen at a demonstration protesting the U.S. incursion into Cambodia.

1971

Pentagon papers were published in 1971 revealing that the government had misled Congress and the American people about its intentions in Vietnam.

1972

In 1972, Nixon won reelection and authorized a break-in at and wiretapping of the Democratic National Committee headquarters at Watergate complex in Washington, D.C. *Washington Post* reporters Bob Woodward and Carl Bernstein exposed the Watergate break-in and coverup.

Congress passed the Equal Rights Amendment.

1973

In 1973, the Senate initiated the Watergate committee hearings, and the *Roe v. Wade* ruling legalized abortion. A cease-fire was signed, and U.S. forces withdrew from Vietnam. Nixon accepted responsibility, but not blame, for Watergate.

1974

Congress initiated impeachment proceedings against Nixon in 1974. Nixon resigned before the proceedings could take place. Gerald R. Ford became the thirty-eighth president. Ford granted "full, free and absolute pardon" to ex-president Nixon.

1975

In 1975, Saigon was captured by Communists, ending the Vietnam War.

1976

Jimmy Carter was elected president in 1976, and the nation celebrated its bicentennial.

1978

In 1978, Carter pardoned Vietnam War draft evaders.

Chapter 5

MOVING FORWARD

1980–1989

While Betty Friedan's *The Feminine Mystique*, which provided the impetus for a second wave of feminism and significantly spurred the women's movement, was published in 1963, it wasn't until nearly two decades later that Mountainside felt its impact. In January 1980, Marilyn Hart was sworn in as the first woman ever to serve on the borough council. Hart, a professor at Kean University, came in first in a field of four candidates and served for twelve years. Down the hall in the municipal building, the police department also felt the ripples of this national tidal wave when, in 1989, it appointed its first female police officer, Dorothy Sullivan. Progress in other aspects of life moved much more rapidly, or so it would appear.

1980

Marilyn Hart was sworn in as the first female council member on January 3, 1980, and the Senior Citizen Housing Advisory was formed. Police Chief Edward Mullin retired on July 1 after thirty-two years of service. Mullin, fifty-six, was born and raised in Mountainside. He started his tenure with a five-man force and one patrol car. By 1980, twenty officers using sophisticated equipment composed the squad. William A. Alder was appointed chief of police on July 1.

The Mountainside municipal building had a new lease on life. Eugene Lord moved his State Farm insurance offices from Springfield into the seventy-year-old building. According to the *Mountainside Echo*, Lord had bought the building two years earlier at auction and proceeded to launch an extensive renovation project "that began as a business venture and ended as a labor of love."

The One and Only

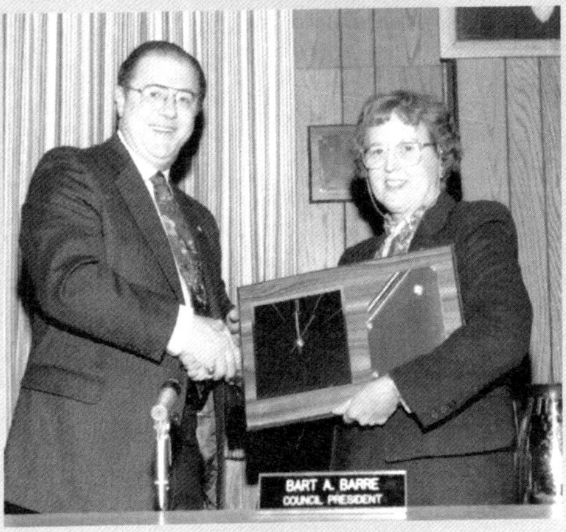

Marilyn Hart leaving office. *Courtesy of Classic Studio, Westfield, New Jersey.*

Probably the farthest thought from the mind of young Marilyn McGuire was that one day she would be a groundbreaker of sorts. Her family moved from Jersey City to Mountainside in the early 1930s and settled on Beech Avenue. Nearly half a century later, when she was campaigning for a seat on the borough council and residents asked, "Who's Marilyn Hart?" she quickly responded, "I'm Marilyn McGuire Hart, and I grew up in Mountainside."

Hart was elected in 1979 and served for twelve years, the first and only woman ever to sit on Mountainside Borough Council. Convinced that there wasn't any prejudice against her as a female during those dozen years, she does laughingly reveal that, now and then, others thought of her ideas as "kooky." For instance, when she proposed an outdoor sign on which to post town activities, she met with opposition. "So I went around and took photographs of towns that had such signs," she reminisced. "When I was about to present the evidence, one of the council members joked, 'Here's Marilyn's show and tell.'" The sign became a reality as a result of a donation to the governing body. Known by insiders as "Marilyn's sign," it turned out to be a valuable and practical presence in town, and a larger replication still stands on the corner of New Providence Road and Route 22 East.

Marilyn McGuire Hart is unique in her attainment of membership in a kind of "boys' club," yet she is one of many who was brought to Mountainside as a youngster and decided to raise her own children here. She continued to reside here with her husband after their children—Michael, Ellen and Allison—left the nest.

As a couple, the Harts hold a second record. Following Marilyn's years of service on the borough council, her husband, David, was elected to the council, making them the only husband-and-wife team to be members of this governing body.

1981

In 1981, Helen Rosenbauer served as senior citizen coordinator, a newly created position. The board of education decided to close Beechwood School at the end of the 1981–82 school year. Enrollment had dwindled from 1,114 in 1972–73 to 607 in 1980–81. The Vail-Deane School, a private school located in Elizabeth for many years, would lease the Beechwood School building.

1982

Regional high school enrollment was expected to decline through the 1980s. The peak of Union County Regional District enrollment reached 5,722 students in 1972–73. In 1982, it stood at 3,952.

Frederick Wilhelms Jr., former mayor, was elected to the board of trustees of the Vail-Deane School, which would open in September in the Beechwood School. Wilhelms was mayor from 1964 to 1970 and president of the board of education from 1956 to 1962. He received a bachelor's of science in engineering from Lafayette College in 1943. He and his wife, Jeanne, have three children—Linda, Frederick III and Christopher J.

Mountainside Active Retirees was established.

Table 2. Population Over 65 Years of Age

Year	Total Population 65+	% of Population 65+
1950	129	6.3%
1960	201	3.2%
1970	626	8.3%
1980	863	12.1%
1990	1,318	19.8%
2000	1,644	25.0%

Voters rejected the proposal of a community center, and construction of the 5.5-mile missing link of Route 78 was expected to begin this year. For the first time, all 495 district students were housed in one building: Deerfield School. The Vail-Deane School began its occupancy of the Beechwood School building.

Mabel Young won the Mabel G. Young Good Neighbor Award, which would be given annually to a resident who "helped to make

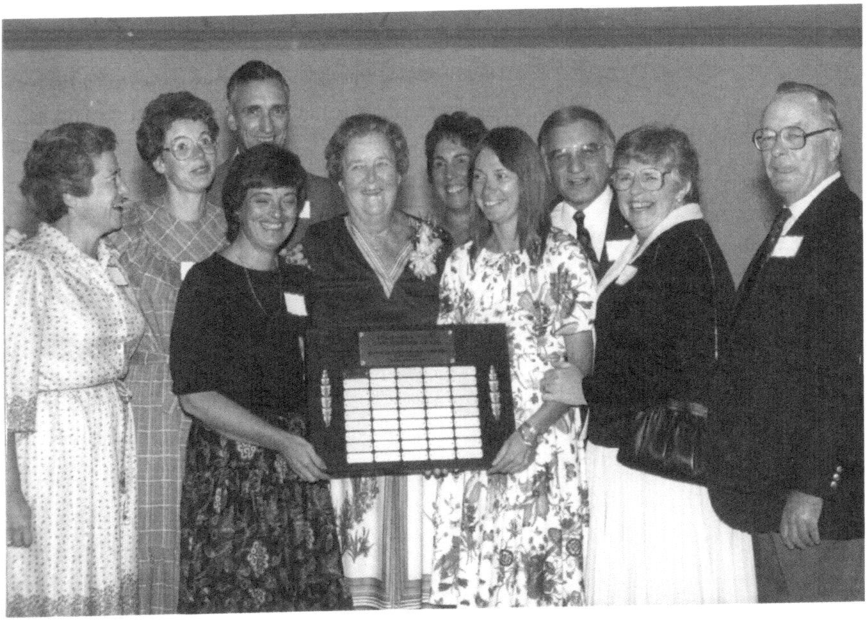

The 1982 Mabel G. Young Good Neighbor Award Committee. *From left to right*: Helen Borchert, Sandy Burdge, Tom Knierim, Peg Wilson, Mabel Young, Doris Julian, Sue Winans, Bill Biunno and Jeanne and Fred Wilhelms. *Missing*: Betty and Bill VanBlarcum. *Courtesy of the Mountainside Recreation Department.*

Mountainside a fine place to live." Young was a former teacher in the borough and was also active in Meals on Wheels, the Republican Club, the Community Presbyterian Church and the Mountainside Music Association.

The Nike site was to hold stables. The former missile installation area would undergo a state-funded $5.5 million renovation, beginning in March, to be completed by 1984.

1983

On March 24, 1983, artist and resident Harry Devlin won a recognition award from the New Jersey Historical Commission. "I was curious about old houses, and I saw many of them going to ruin," said Devlin at the time. It became his aim to "make people aware of the beauty of this vanishing heritage." Many of the homes that Devlin so beautifully depicted are no longer standing. His purpose was to preserve those homes through his paintings, one of which featured the Hetfield House.

The Republican Municipal Committee selected Bruce A. Geiger to run in the June primary for mayor. Tom Ricciardi, mayor for twelve years, would not run again. The Democratic candidate was Robert DiBella.

The *Mountainside Echo* commemorated its twenty-fifth year.

1984

Bruce Geiger was sworn in as mayor on January 3, 1984, succeeding Thomas Ricciardi. The month of April was dedicated to Marine Captain James Thomas Egan, who was captured shortly after his plane was shot down in South Vietnam on January 21, 1966.

The Badgley House, the oldest building in Mountainside and located near Trailside Museum, burned down on May 2 in an apparent case of arson. The house served as the first area Sunday school until about 1825.

Officials from the local and county governments and from the Children's Specialized Hospital broke ground on May 14 for a fitness trail, a three-quarters-mile course featuring twenty-eight exercise stations, including ten for the hospital's handicapped. At the time, planning for the $46,000 course was already more than one year in the making.

Mayor Geiger appeared on NBC *Nightly News* on August 16 in an interview profiling him as "a small business man in Union County." Geiger and his brother, Frank, owned Geiger's Cider Mill and Restaurant.

Representatives from the Historic Preservation Committee made several presentations to seek assistance in saving the historic Hetfield House, also known as the "Dutch Oven House." Built around 1755, the structure stood a chance of being demolished if it was not moved from its Route 22 West site.

1985

In 1985, the Historic Preservation Committee was in the process of incorporating as a private organization that would focus on preserving historic sites in Mountainside.

The borough spent $70,000 on moving the Hetfield House. It was expected to be used as a museum and for storing borough records. The move took two hours and fifty-seven minutes from its site next to Dasti's Mountainside Inn on Route 22 West (now Arirang Hibachi Steak House) to its new location near the library.

The fitness trail was completed and opened on June 22, 1985.

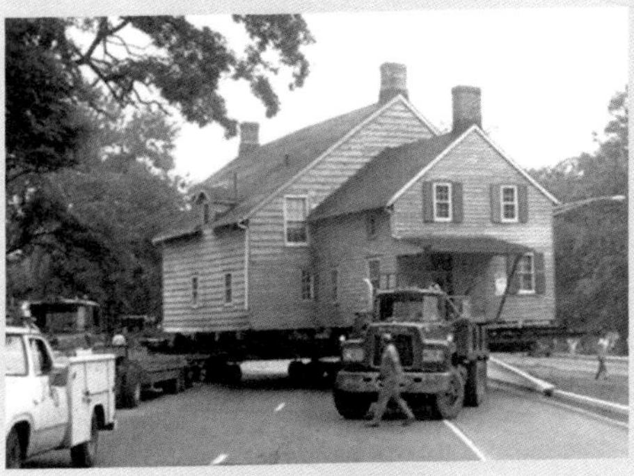

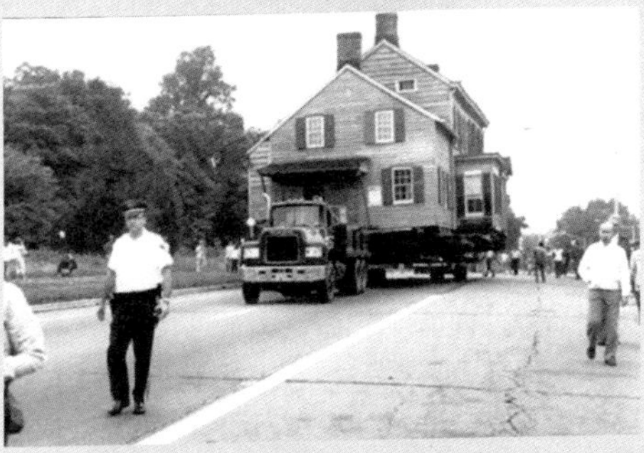

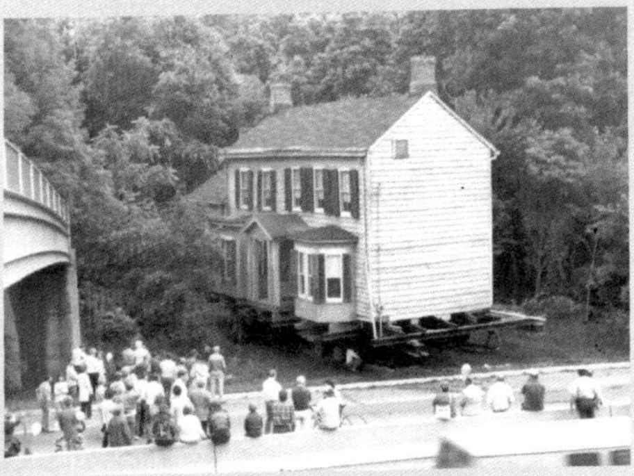

Moving Day

June 29, 1985, was a typical day for Fred Ranalli, of Mullen and Ranalli, Inc. of Mount Holly, who began moving houses when he was thirteen years old and had been doing it for about thirty years. All went according to plan. Even muddy areas near Route 22 were no deterrence for the work crews transporting the Deacon Andrew Hetfield House to its new location adjacent to the library. Ranalli said that any inconveniences were "about par for the course."

Not so for the denizens of Mountainside. This was a day that would go down in the annals of town history. The house that was being transported a half mile away was one of the oldest in the area, and the Mountainside Historic Preservation Committee, headed by Fern Carter Hyde, was determined to save it.

When Walter Kuczynski and his son, Robert, purchased the house in June 1984, they intended to raze it and clear the area to make room for a manufacturing building, not realizing the historical significance of the house. The Historic Preservation Committee intervened, requesting that the Kuczynskis delay the start of their project until a way could be found to save the house. "They were very cooperative about it," said Hyde. The details, including the funds needed, took about six months to finalize before the move could take place.

Early that morning in June 1985, steel beams were placed under the house; then a hydraulic lift set the structure on several dollies. According to an article in the

Courier-News *of July 1, 1985, the house "weighed 115 tons, traveled 3mph, closed Route 22 and attracted hundreds of curious onlookers."*

The house was towed from its foundation on Route 22 West onto the highway, one of the busiest in the state, and then westward toward Constitution Plaza. Because of the overpass just before New Providence Road, crewmen had to carefully guide the building off the highway through a wooded area east of the library that was still muddy from recent rains. Once in its new location, the Hetfield House sat on a new foundation and underwent an updating of its plumbing and heating systems. Structural damage from the move was minimal. In fact, it is reported that only one pane of glass was broken during the relocation. (See chapter 1 for additional information on the Deacon Andrew Hetfield House.)

Opposite: Moving the Hetfield House. *Courtesy of the Mountainside Historic Preservation Committee.*

1986

The Hetfield House was dedicated in 1986. Three hundred people, including actress Celeste Holm, Assemblywoman Maureen Ogden and William Hetfield, a descendant of the Andrew Hetfield family attended the ceremony, as did the Kuczynski family, who bought the house and would use the property where it formerly stood for a manufacturing facility. Also in attendance was Walda Rosencrantz, who operated the Dutch Oven Antiques shop at the house for nearly fifty years; she traveled from Connecticut to the ceremony. Longtime resident Walter Heckel donated use of his flatbed truck for a stage. It was decorated with 192 red geraniums.

Route 78 was completed.

1987

Deerfield Olympics of the Mind qualified for the Northern Regional League Tournament in 1987. The team then headed for the World Olympics of the Mind Tournament in Michigan after a successful showing in the state tournament. The seven-member team was the first to qualify since 1983.

A state mandate for recycling glass, aluminum and newspaper was initiated. Governor Thomas H. Kean signed the Mandatory Source Separation and Recycling Act into law on April 20. It required everyone to recycle at least these three materials, plus leaves. Businesses were also required to recycle cardboard, as well as corrugated and high-grade office paper.

A tornado struck Mountainside and caused damage to Evergreen Court and Old Tote Road. Over one hundred trees in town and in Echo Lake Park were downed. The majority of the borough was without electricity.

Union County Regional High School District celebrated its fiftieth anniversary. Jonathan Dayton opened its doors in 1937 to students from Berkeley Heights, Clark, Kenilworth, Mountainside, Garwood and Springfield. Three additional schools—Arthur L. Johnson in Clark, Governor Livingston in Berkeley Heights and David Brearley in Kenilworth—later opened because of increased enrollment.

Construction of the 5.5-mile missing section of Route 78 was completed and opened in August. The segment cost about $111 million and took nearly four years to build. The link connected the 18.8-mile stretch from Springfield east to the Holland Tunnel and another section that ran from Berkeley Heights west into Pennsylvania.

The Mountainside school district joined fifteen towns in Morris and Union Counties in an effort to pool resources to reduce the cost of special education.

Residents were asked to compost leaves as the Edgeboro landfill would no longer accept them.

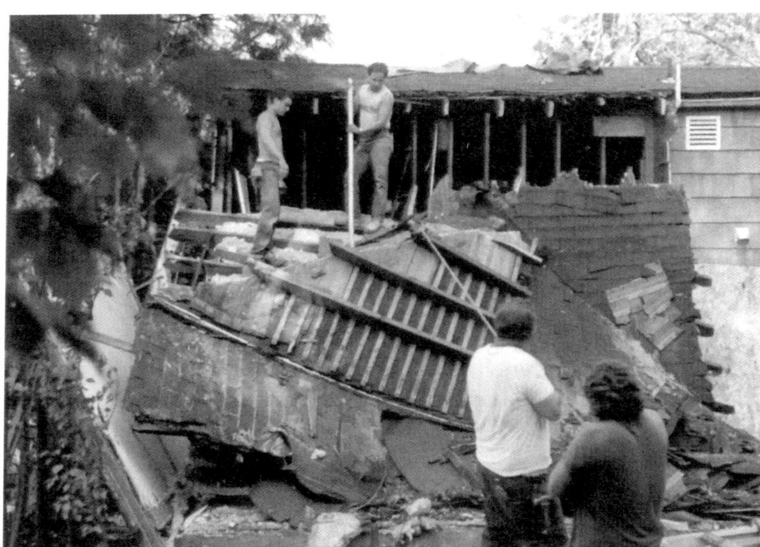

The 1987 tornado damage to the home of Trisha and Bob Yurochko. *Courtesy of Trisha Yurochko.*

Toto, Are We in Kansas?

The following are Trisha Yurochko's recollections of the July 1987 tornado that tore through Mountainside and, more specifically, struck the Yurochko house on Evergreen Court.

> *My son Michael was twelve at the time. He and I were at the Plainfield Country Club for the women's golf opening. Bob* [her husband] *was out in western Pennsylvania visiting his father and brother. The weather got so bad that the golf outing for the day was cancelled. As we headed home, we found that all the traffic lights were out, so Route 22 was all backed up.*
>
> *As I turned up Birch Hill to reach our house on Evergreen Court, I saw wires down and a felled tree across the street. Our section was all blocked off. One of the volunteer firemen said, "You can't bring your car here." I could see a tree down at a neighbor's house. Our next-door neighbor had lost part of his chimney. Then I saw that a big tree had landed across the whole back of our house. It turned out that we had a total of seven trees down. We were definitely the worst hit. Someone on the street said, "It sounded like a locomotive coming through."*
>
> *I went in and turned off the electricity and the water because I was afraid of fire and pipes bursting. I asked a fireman to go in and turn off the gas. Almost every room of the house had some damage to it. The volunteer fire department was really fantastic. In addition to everything else they did, they used a chain saw to cut down a lot of the trees resting on the house to take the pressure off.*
>
> *The first night or two we stayed with our neighbors. Then someone in the neighborhood was going away for a few days, so we stayed in their house and moved to a motel after that. A week later we had a trailer on the front lawn of our property. We lived in the trailer for nearly five months. We got back into the house two days before Christmas.*

It should be noted that excitement was not new to Bob and Trisha Yurochko. On August 10, 1974, their son, Michael, was born in an ambulance en route to Overlook Hospital.

1988

Robert Viglianti was sworn in as mayor in 1988.

Friends of the Mountainside Rescue Squad began a fund that would lead to the purchase of a second ambulance.

Borough librarian Joanna Chen announced her retirement from the post she had held for eighteen years. Alice Cronin was named the library's new chief administrator.

Manor Care Nursing Home held its grand opening, with physical fitness personalities Jack and Elaine LaLanne on hand as guest speakers.

The board of education noted Deerfield's highest enrollment in four years. The rescue squad celebrated its fiftieth anniversary.

1989

In 1989, Marilyn Hart became the first woman to serve as borough council president.

The planning board ruled against any type of multiple housing but approved a site plan calling for alterations to a Route 22 building to accommodate the borough's first sperm bank.

The borough flew the American flag at half-mast to protest the U.S. Supreme Court's decision that protestors may burn, mutilate or otherwise desecrate the American flag.

The National Register of Historic Places accepted the Hetfield House onto its roll.

Beyond Mountainside's Borders

1980

Ronald Reagan was elected president in 1980, and the United States broke diplomatic ties with Iran.

1981

In 1981, scientists announced the discovery of Acquired Immune Deficiency Syndrome, or AIDS. Reagan nominated Judge Sandra Day O'Connor, fifty-one, of Arizona, as the first woman on the U.S. Supreme Court.

1982

In 1982, John W. Hinckley Jr. was found not guilty by reason of insanity in the shooting of President Reagan.

1983

In 1983, Sally K. Ride, thirty-two, became the first U.S. woman astronaut in space as a crew member aboard the space shuttle *Challenger*.

1984

Reagan was reelected president in 1984 in a landslide, with 59 percent of the vote. The Bell System was broken up.

1985

In 1985, British scientists reported the opening of an enormous hole in the earth's ozone layer over Antarctica.

1986

The space shuttle *Challenger* exploded after its launch at Cape Canaveral, Florida, in 1986, killing all seven aboard. Dick Rutan and Jeana Yeager made the first nonstop flight around the world without refueling.

1987

The stock market crashed nearly 23 percent on Black Monday, October 19, 1987. Reagan said that the Iran-Contra policy went astray and accepted responsibility. Prozac was released for use in the United States by Eli Lily & Company.

1988

George H.W. Bush was elected president in 1988. Saudi militant Osama Bin Laden founded the Islamist Al Qaeda network in Afghanistan.

1989

In 1989, the Berlin Wall fell, and an Exxon Valdez oil spill occurred in Alaska.

Chapter 6

CELEBRATION

1990-1999

Planning for the centennial of the borough and progress in areas such as the renovation of Borough Hall and downtown were deemed positive efforts.

However, Democrats failed to make inroads onto the borough council, and Mountainside's one and only female member retired.

1990

In 1990, after thirty years with its own parochial school, Our Lady of Lourdes merged with two other nearby churches—Holy Trinity and St. Helen's, both in Westfield—to form Holy Trinity Inter-Parochial School. It was set to open for the 1991–92 school year.

The fifty-two-year-old rescue squad planned to enlarge its building at a cost of $285,000. In 1990, it responded to between five and six hundred calls each year and logged 1,500 man hours on the job. Twenty steady volunteers and ten who served part time made up the squad.

The Trailside Nature and Science Center celebrated its fiftieth anniversary. It opened on May 3, 1941, as a place to become familiar with plants, wildlife and geology common to the 1,945-acre reservation.

Emily Hoffarth died at the age of eighty-five on May 10. She was the first library director and a longtime volunteer in the borough.

Westfield contractors were denied permission to build town houses at 940 Mountain Avenue because the borough's zoning restricted the area to single-family dwellings.

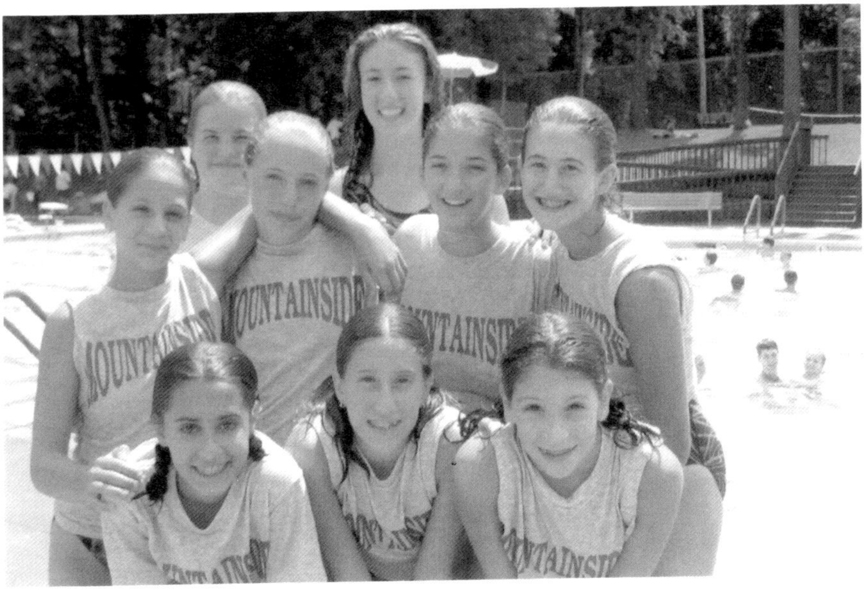

Swim team, 1990s. *Courtesy of the Mountainside Recreation Department.*

The Children's Specialized Hospital celebrated its 100th anniversary on June 8 with a gala centennial birthday party. It opened in 1891 as Children's Country Home and began as a summer retreat for kids living in the tenement slums of cities. In 1990, it had sixty acute rehabilitation beds and twenty-five long-term-care beds.

Charles J. Honecker, the first borough police chief, died on August 7 at the age of ninety-one. He had lived in the borough for seventy-five years, twenty-four of which he served as police chief. His duty began in 1934, when the position and department were created. Honecker learned of most of the calls when his wife turned on a "beacon light" in a tree at the family's Mountainside home.

The "Firemen's Coat of Arms" on the front of the Mountainside Volunteer Fire Department was dedicated to the memory of the late Glenn M. Bass. Bass was twenty-two years old and a volunteer firefighter when he died in a car accident in 1989. His father, Manfred, designed and erected the sculpture as a tribute to the "strength and security" of the department. The memorial, which separates the fire truck bays from the administrative offices, stands approximately ten feet tall by five feet wide and is two feet deep.

1991

In 1991, after 122 years of educating the young, the Vail-Deane School was forced to close due to declining enrollment and increased operating costs.

1992

Former police chief Edward Mullin died in 1992. He was Mountainside's third chief from 1970 to 1983. Fern Hyde, a member of the Public Assistance Board and the Mountainside Historic Preservation Committee, also died. Hyde "saved" the Hetfield House while chairwoman of the committee.

Local Democrats placed one of their own on the ballot. Steven Brociner received 1,082 votes, while Republican Ron Romak garnered 2,046. The latter would fill the council seat vacated by Robert Wyckoff, who resigned to become Department of Public Works director.

The Marriott Corporation progressed with its plan to construct a multifaceted senior citizen retirement complex. The facility would encompass a 4.3-acre parcel of land at 1350 Route 22 and accommodate 103 living units and 24 personal-care units for senior citizens.

An unresolved issue at the end of the year was the future of the old Mountainside School on Route 22. Would it be renovated or razed? Most officials said razed, sometime, in conjunction with back burner plans to renovate Borough Hall.

Officials also continued to seek a solution to a left-hand turn at the intersection of New Providence Road and Route 22. The most popular was to put in a left-hand signal, giving motorists an unchallenged opportunity to make a left onto the highway, the borough's main thoroughfare. The least popular was the state's reputed plan: tear up the highway and surrounding property to create an overpass system.

1994

In 1994, Union County Regional District #1 gave in to political pressures and agreed to cooperate with an inquiry about dissolving the district. The county's first sanctioned deer hunts in Watchung Reservation were scheduled for January 14–15 and January 21–22; 110 participants were selected by lottery.

Mountainside Democratic Club announced two candidates for the November council election: Karen MacQueen and Henry Knaz. MacQueen had run in 1993 with Eli Hoffman and pulled a shocking 44 percent of the vote against William "Tex" Jackson and Keith Turner.

The old Mountainside School building was razed to accommodate the $2.9 million plan to renovate and put an addition on Borough Hall. The plan included fulfilling state mandates to comply with the Americans with Disabilities Act, as well as a one-floor addition to the police department. A 4,500-square-foot police building was scheduled for the site of the former Echobrook School.

1995

In 1995, Sony Theater was proposed for the site of Echo Lanes, Tower Steak House and office buildings on Route 22 East. It would be a 3,000-seat facility with parking for 968. The board of adjustment approved Sony's plans to construct a multi-screen theatre.

The deer population in Watchung Reservation would be cut by 80 percent in five years if a hunt were approved. While private citizens performed the 1994 thinning effort, police officers from Union County would carry out the 1995 hunt. The recommended deer-population management plan stated that the Division of Parks and Recreation should be authorized by freeholders to reduce the herd to an "over-wintering density of 20 deer per square mile." In 1995, the deer population was estimated at 300, which translated to 100 deer per square mile. Freeholders approved the deer hunt proposal; 590 deer would be killed at an estimated cost of $38,350, or $65 per deer.

Mountainside Center was upgraded with interlocking concrete-paved sidewalks, Victorian-style streetlights and an improved system of traffic lights at the intersection of Mountain Avenue and New Providence Road. A grant from Union County would cover most of the cost for the $300,000 project.

Mountainside celebrated its centennial.

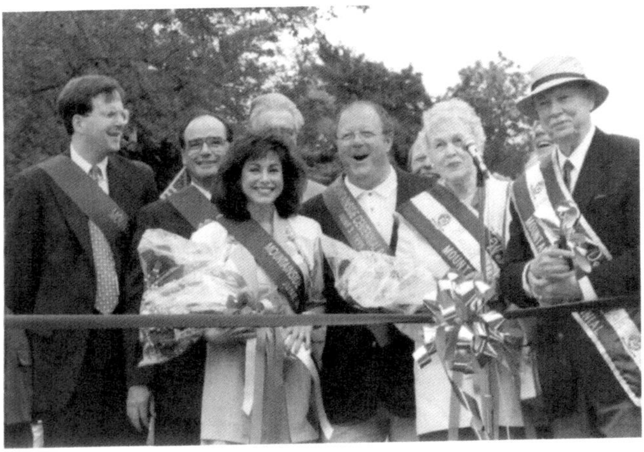

Dignitaries at the centennial parade. *From left to right*: Assemblyman Richard Bagger, State Senator Donald DiFrancesco, mistress of ceremonies Hela Young, Mayor Robert Viglianti and grand marshals Wende and Harry Devlin. *Courtesy of Quality Portraits, Mountainside, New Jersey.*

Happy 100th Anniversary, Mountainside

Like other celebratory events, careful planning was a part of the borough's really big birthday. Committee chairs selected those most suitable for the jobs at hand. Unlike most weddings, bar mitzvahs, birthdays and communions that last a day or perhaps a weekend, bells and whistles sounded around Mountainside for more than six months during 1995. Beginning with April's Gala Ball at the Berkeley Plaza in Berkeley Heights, reminders that this was a special year were pervasive.

A beautiful, sunny Saturday, June 3, was the setting for the revelry of a town parade. Marchers started in downtown Mountainside at Mountain Avenue and New Providence Road, crossed Route 22 and moved on to the terminus at Deerfield School, about two miles away. The State Department of Transportation had already posted an electronic sign, warning highway drivers to expect delays, since Route 22 traffic would be stopped at five-minute intervals to permit parade participants to cross from south to north of the borough.

Local dignitaries, as well as mayors from surrounding towns, county officials and state representatives, kicked off the hoopla in the center of town. On Central Avenue near Our Lady of Lourdes Church, mistress of ceremonies Hela Young, Miss New Jersey 1970, television hostess for the state lottery and a Mountainside resident, introduced groups of marchers to the onlookers. Author Wende Devlin and painter Harry Devlin served as grand marshals of the parade. A family picnic on the grounds of Deerfield School rounded out the day's events.

June 12 was the day for Mountainside's second annual golf outing at Echo Lake Country Club, also a part of the year's observance of the centennial. A Heritage Day Fair lasting an entire weekend in September marked the culmination of this monumental occasion.

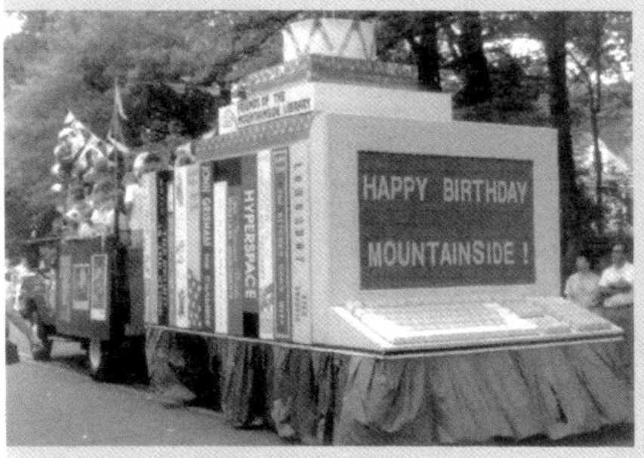

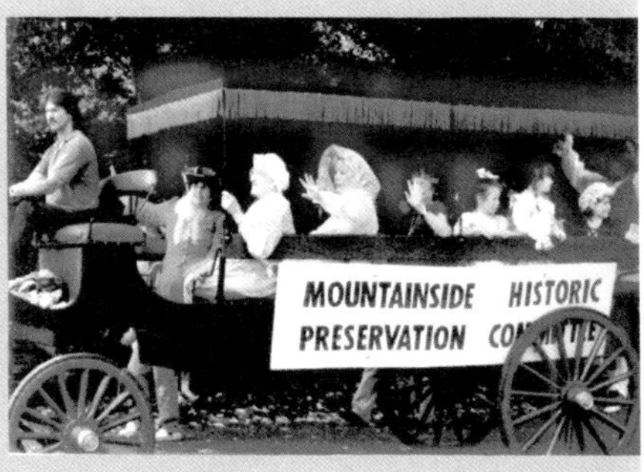

Above, left: Friends of the Library float. *Courtesy of Bobbi Weeks.*

Above, right: Historic Preservation Committee float. *Courtesy of Quality Portraits, Mountainside, New Jersey.*

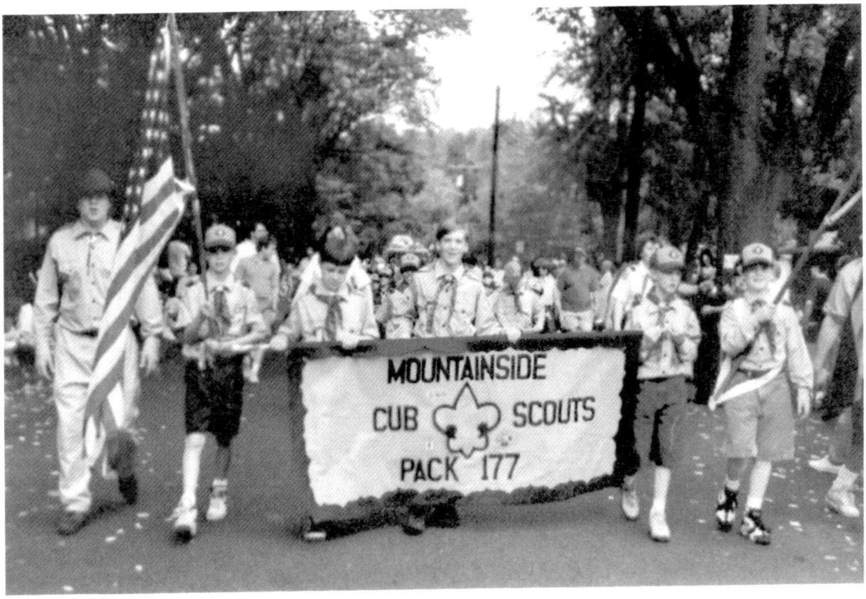

Cub Scouts, Pack 177. *Courtesy of Quality Portraits, Mountainside, New Jersey.*

1996

The Union County Regional School system was dissolved on May 14, 1996.

Sony opened a ten-screen theatre on Route 22 as the newest member of the borough's corporate community.

A third police headquarters was built.

1997

A two-hundred-pound black bear made a surprise visit to Mountainside on May 12–14, 1997. It was tracked to Deerfield School, prompting an evacuation. Members of the borough police and the New Jersey State Division of Fish, Game & Wildlife used peanut butter and a tranquilizer dart to help capture and return him to Sussex County.

Deerfield added computers to its classrooms on September 11, signifying a new era of technology in the borough.

Governor Livingston dropped "Regional" from its name on September 20, recognizing the dissolution of the Union County Regional High School District. Governor Livingston, a product of the four-school, six-town district, was absorbed by the Berkeley Heights school district. Mountainside would continue to send students to Governor Livingston.

Renovations to Borough Hall were completed by September 22. A room on the top floor would be available to private and public organizations for a nominal fee.

GLHS Highlanders marched off with two major band championships on November 8–9. Band Director Daniel Kopcha, who had headed the band for twenty-six years, led the musicians to a first place in the Atlantic Coast Championships and the Group II Open Championships, the latter held at Giants Stadium. Participants for this event came from fourteen states. The Highlanders band was made up of fifty-two students from Berkeley Heights and Mountainside.

The *Echo-Leader* printed its first issue on November 20, a result of the merger of the *Mountainside Echo* and the *Springfield Leader.*

1998

In 1998, the borough council abolished the board of recreation commissioners in favor of an official Department of Recreation.

On July 9, Lieutenant James J. Debbie Jr. was named chief of police. He had served as acting chief since the retirement of William Alder on March 1.

The Lightning Wheels, thirteen athletes from the Children's Specialized Hospital, set thirty-four national records and collected enough points to earn the trophy of the number one wheelchair team in the country at the National Championships for Wheelchair Sports in Bellevue, Washington.

The Computer Aided Dispatch (CAD) system was initiated. Police officers could electronically submit reports from police cars to headquarters and check suspects for any outstanding tickets or active warrants nationwide automatically.

1999

In 1999, residents began ice-skating in the rink proposed in 1998.

Chief School Administrator Gerard Schaller took to the Deerfield School roof as a challenge to his students to read at least two thousand books during "Read Across America" month.

Mountainside resident Claire Butler earned a gold medal in archery at the United States Senior Olympics. More than twelve thousand senior athletes competed in eighteen sports; over three hundred participated in archery.

Beyond Mountainside's Borders

1990

In 1990, the Americans with Disabilities Act barred discrimination against people with mental or physical disabilities. The U.S. Supreme Court overturned the law banning flag burning. President Bush signed the Clean Air Act, mandating a variety of pollution-reducing changes in the automobile and fuel industries.

1991

In 1991, the Union of Soviet Socialist Republics was dissolved, and a cease-fire ended the Persian Gulf War. United Nations forces were victorious.

1992

In 1992, Bill Clinton was elected president, the North American Free Trade Agreement (NAFTA) was signed and Bush and Yeltsin proclaimed a formal end to the Cold War.

1993

In 1993, members of Al Qaeda bombed the World Trade Center in New York City, killing six. Clinton signed the Brady Bill regulating firearms purchases.

1994

In 1994, four were convicted in the World Trade Center bombing.

1995

In 1995, the bombing of a federal building in Oklahoma City by Timothy McVeigh killed 168.

1996

Clinton was reelected president in 1996, and he appointed Madeleine Albright as the first female U.S. secretary of state.

1997

In 1997, Timothy McVeigh was sentenced to death for the Oklahoma City bombing.

1998

In 1998, Clinton was impeached in the House over perjury. The Senate acquitted him in 1999. Seventy-seven-year-old John Glenn, the first American to orbit the earth, returned to orbit in the space shuttle *Discovery*.

1999

In 1999, the world awaited the consequences of the Y2K bug, with more drastic millennial theorists warning of Armageddon.

Chapter 7

THE NEW MILLENNIUM

2000–2007/8

Advances in computer technology precipitated unwarranted concern for Y2K problems. Instead, the September 11, 2001 terrorist attacks ushered in a new era of security, surveillance and reduced personal freedoms.

2000

In 2000, freezing temperatures allowed all to enjoy the town's first ice-skating rink on the tennis courts adjacent to Borough Hall. Robert Viglianti was sworn in for his fourth term as mayor on January 4, and the planning board and zoning board (board of adjustment) merged into a twelve-member board.

Channel 35 began broadcasting full time.

First-aid squad president Kit Carson put out an urgent call for additional volunteers. Enrollment in 2000 was thirty-five, but only twenty-five were active participants.

Kindergarten became a full day by a four-to-one vote of the school board, making the children's day just about an hour and a half longer.

Friendly's, a local landmark and gathering place since February 1, 1970, closed on March 26.

The 2000–01 school year anticipated eighty-three new kindergarten children, but September's actual enrollment was fifty-nine.

Arthur Brahm retired to Montague, New Jersey. Born and raised in Mountainside, Brahm had been both a volunteer and chairman on the Historic Preservation Committee. During his military service, he met and

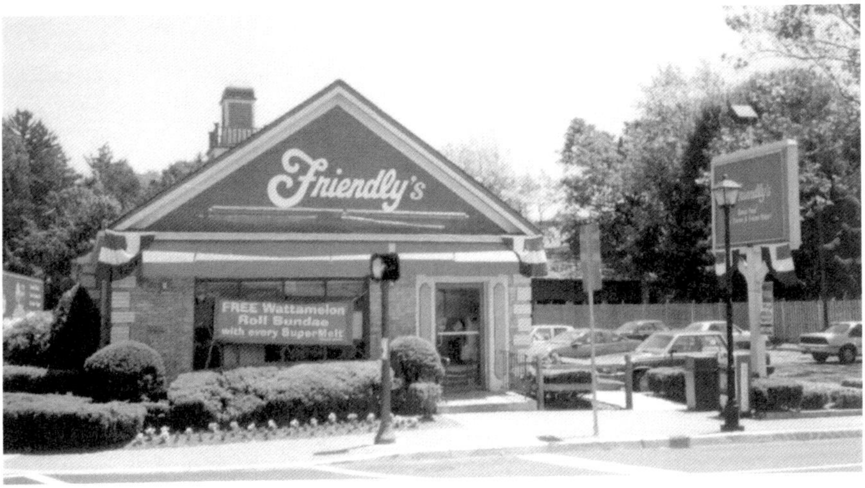

Friendly's, a mainstay in downtown Mountainside, closed after thirty years. *Courtesy of the Borough of Mountainside.*

served with Elvis Presley. On May 16, Brahm received a Joint Legislative Resolution from the New Jersey General Assembly, honoring his "remarkable span of community service."

2001

A demographic study conducted by the board of education in 2001 revealed an increase in the number of young families moving to Mountainside. The board suggested that more programs were needed for the borough's families. The district planned to reopen Beechwood School and make improvements to Deerfield. On April 7, voters approved a $9.3 million bond referendum to expand Deerfield and reopen Beechwood schools.

Little League fields needed outdoor lighting, and New Jersey "Field of Dreams" grants were obtained in 2000 to fund the project. Residents debated the merits of the borough council's intention to allocate $75,000 to install lights in a field near Deerfield. They raised questions about Title IX and gender equality in sports. Some residents claimed that the field would be used only by boys. The council made a public announcement that all athletes, regardless of gender, would have an opportunity to play on the renovated and soon-to-be-lighted fields.

Reflecting an aging trend, the latest 2000 census data revealed an increase in the borough's elderly population, which had been rising since 1990. Senior citizens—ages seventy-five and older—composed 13 percent of

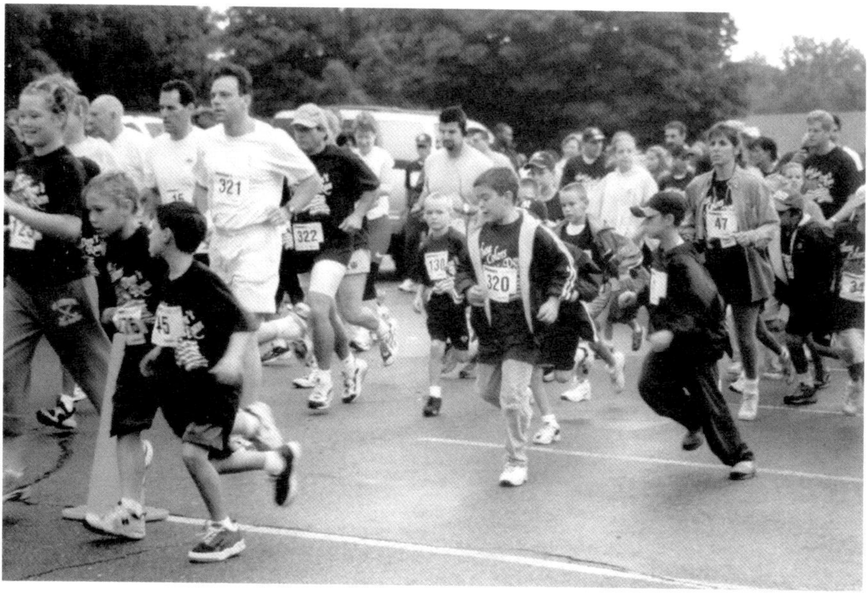

Cop Trot, 2001. *Photo by Maureen Giannone.*

Mountainside's population. The median age increased to 46.4, compared to 44.5 just ten years earlier.

Renovations to the library allowed for a new media room.

On September 11, in the wake of the terrorist attacks on the Twin Towers of the World Trade Center, four firemen and one truck were deployed to Goethals Bridge in Elizabeth. Police and fire departments were put on full alert, and the rescue squad remained on standby to supply mutual aid to surrounding communities. Houses of worship gathered residents together. Schools took extra steps to ensure the safety of their children.

Cub Scout Pack 177 raised over $900 and donated it for the fire department's first defibrillator in remembrance of September 11. The council announced its application to Union County for a Field of Dreams grant of $100,000 to fund improvements at Echobrook Field.

Citing lack of volunteers, the borough council announced its plans to enter into an agreement with the Atlantic Ambulance Corporation in order for paid EMS workers in town to cover calls between 4:00 a.m. and 4:00 p.m., Monday through Friday.

Author/artist Harry Devlin died of lymphoma at the age of eighty-three at his home on November 25.

September 11

Shortly before 9:00 a.m. on September 11, 2001, Police Sergeant Allan Attanasio and his wife were getting their two-year-old daughter, Jenna, ready for her first day of preschool at the Community Presbyterian Church when news of a plane crashing into one of the Twin Towers in Manhattan interrupted the regular television program they were viewing. Forced to tear themselves away from their television to be on time, the Attanasios drove their older daughter, Nicole, to Deerfield School and then took Jenna to her school. No sooner did they arrive than Sergeant Attanasio's beeper sounded. "That's how quickly things started moving," he recalls.

That was the beginning of Attanasio's six-day stint assisting the New York fire and police departments in their rescue and recovery work following this infamous event in American history. Attanasio, a borough police officer by profession, was called in this instance because he also is a volunteer in the Mountainside Fire Department.

"On 9/11, the county mutual aid system activated units from the entire county," he explained. The units reconnoitered at a staging area at the Goethals Bridge. "Everybody was setting up at the different exits and entrances of NYC to handle overflow that the FDNY couldn't accommodate," says Attanasio. Union County units were slated to respond to any fire calls on Staten Island.

Four men from Mountainside—Gary Cantagallo, Kevin Rogers, Vinnie Munoz and Attanasio—joined an engine from Plainfield and became part of the backup at the bridge in Elizabeth. As units were needed, they were sent over the bridge into Staten Island. When the Plainfield engine was next to go over the bridge, a call came from FDNY indicating that they needed additional units to go to the Staten Island ferry docks, where a temporary morgue was being set up. The Mountainside and Plainfield engines were sent to the docks.

Attanasio remembers that day as a "hurry-up-and-wait type of thing. Everybody was expecting huge numbers of bodies to be coming over on the ferries. We were there a total of twelve hours on the first day; nothing was coming over. Nobody was being found."

The Mountainside and Plainfield engines were redirected to Manhattan to assist with recovery. While the engines were being loaded onto the ferry, Building #7 collapsed. FDNY command then stopped

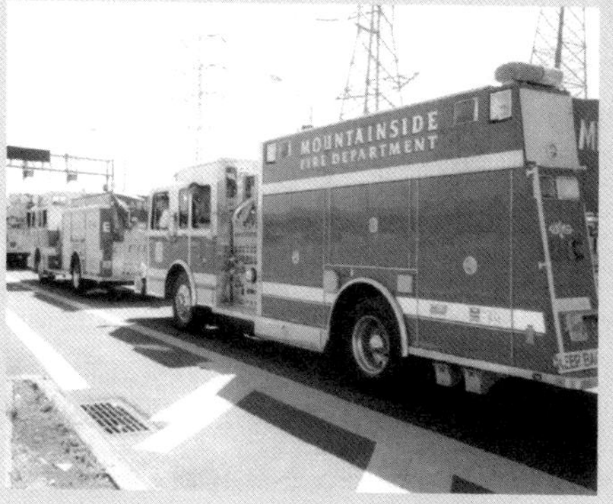

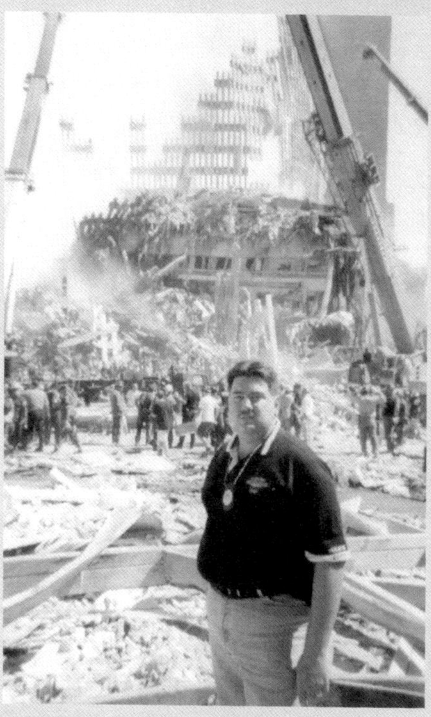

additional responding units for fear of trapping more rescuers until all involved buildings were stabilized.

The next day, the New Jersey Police Benevolent Association, loaded down with donations of food and beverages that filled two tractor trailer trucks, headed toward the Holland Tunnel with the two vehicles and a lunch trailer. Restrictions on trucks through the tunnel were already being enforced, so the cortège proceeded to the George Washington Bridge down through Manhattan to a relief area at Moore and West Streets. Here the New Jersey police volunteers fed New York and Port Authority police.

"Each local had six or seven guys cooking food and assisting with digging through the rubble," Attanasio reminisces. "Twenty-four hour shifts, manning the relief center and digging. During the first four or five days we were hand-digging with buckets—five-gallon buckets sent from Home Depot—a bucket-brigade line."

By the sixth day, hopes of rescue faded, and a recovery effort began. "Volunteers were using backhoes to load flat-bed and dump trucks, bringing everything over to Fresh Kills in Staten Island," continues Attanasio. "There were officers there going through the remains trying to find whatever they could: identification, body parts, anything."

In Manhattan were Chief James Debbie, Sergeant Allan Attanasio, Detective Corporal Kenneth Capobianco, Officer Thomas Norton and Officer Steve DeVito, while volunteers in Staten Island were Sergeant Andrew Sullivan, Corporal Rich Latargia, Officer Donald Amberg, Officer John Philippakos and Officer Jeffrey Stinner.

Attanasio, who says that he had never related to other earth-shattering events that people spoke of like Pearl Harbor or the Kennedy assassination because he was too young to witness them, is certain that "every officer who was anywhere near Ground Zero knows exactly what he was doing every single minute of the time."

Following 9/11, the three things he recalls most vividly are:

> *First, whenever a policeman or fireman's body was found in the rubble, everything, everything stopped. There was silence. Then there were the notes that the children wrote and delivered to those that were working. They were touching. Finally, there was the tremendous support of the public. All you had to do was walk down the street and people would quietly say "Thank you."*

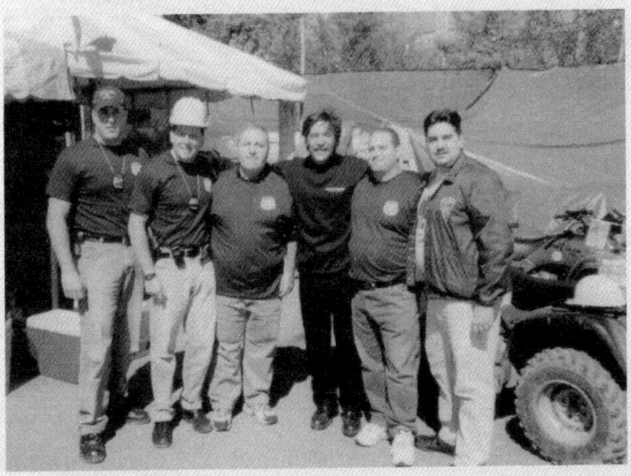

Above: Newsman Geraldo Rivera thanks Mountainside's volunteers at Ground Zero. *From left to right*: Officer Thomas Norton, Officer Steve DeVito, Chief James Debbie, Rivera, Detective Corporal Kenneth Capobianco and Sergeant Allan Attanasio. *Courtesy of Allan Attanasio.*

Previous page, top: Mountainside Engine #4 behind Plainfield Engine #4, waiting on the New Jersey side of the Goethals Bridge on September 11, 2001. *Courtesy of Allan Attanasio.*

Previous page, bottom: Sergeant Allan Attanasio in front of World Trade Center Tower #1 on September 12, 2001. *Courtesy of Allan Attanasio.*

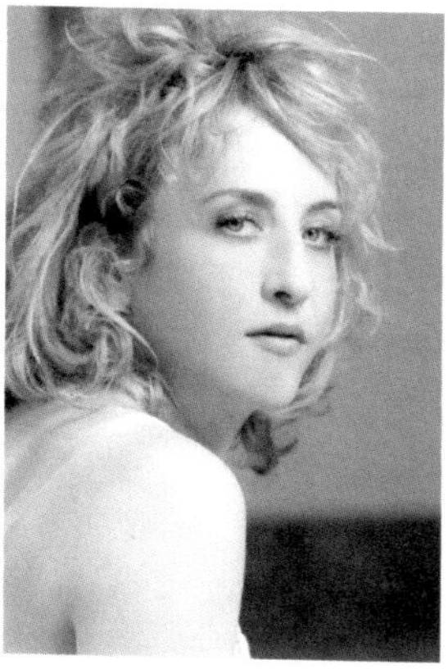

Born and raised in Mountainside, Bitty Schram played Sharona Fleming on USA's *Monk* for nearly three seasons and garnered a Golden Globe nomination in 2004. *Courtesy of Linda Schram.*

2002

In 2002, the borough council agreed to allow sidewalk cafés in front of restaurants. Hela Young, former Miss New Jersey and borough resident who announced the New Jersey lottery numbers every night for twenty-four years on New Jersey Network, died.

Boy Scout Troop 177 collected thirty-seven torn and discolored flags from residents to properly dispose of through dignified ceremonies. For the first time in sixty-two years, the police department added a motorcycle as part of its squad of vehicles.

Actress Bitty Schram, former Mountainside resident, got the female lead in the USA TV series *Monk* with Tony Shaloub.

2003

In 2003, the vehicle of off-duty police lieutenant Todd Turner, age forty-two, was hit by another driver in Mountainside. Turner died a few days later. He was promoted posthumously to the rank of captain on August 19.

A new street at Mountain and Woodland Avenues was named Little Court in honor of Outlook Drive resident William Little III, killed in the line of duty in Vietnam in 1969.

2004

Beechwood School reopened in 2004. It would house kindergarten through grade two. After meeting with four different architects, officials looked forward to construction of a community center on the Barnes Tract on Mountain Avenue. The council hired a firm for the preliminary stages of planning at a cost of $8,000.

J&M Market on Mountain Avenue closed its doors after more than thirty-five years of business.

Egan Court, located off New Providence Road, was dedicated in honor of Major James T. Egan Jr. (listed MIA on January 21, 1966). LeRoy Blessing, who served with Egan in the marines, Egan's sister and his former fiancée attended the ceremony held on May 31, his birthday.

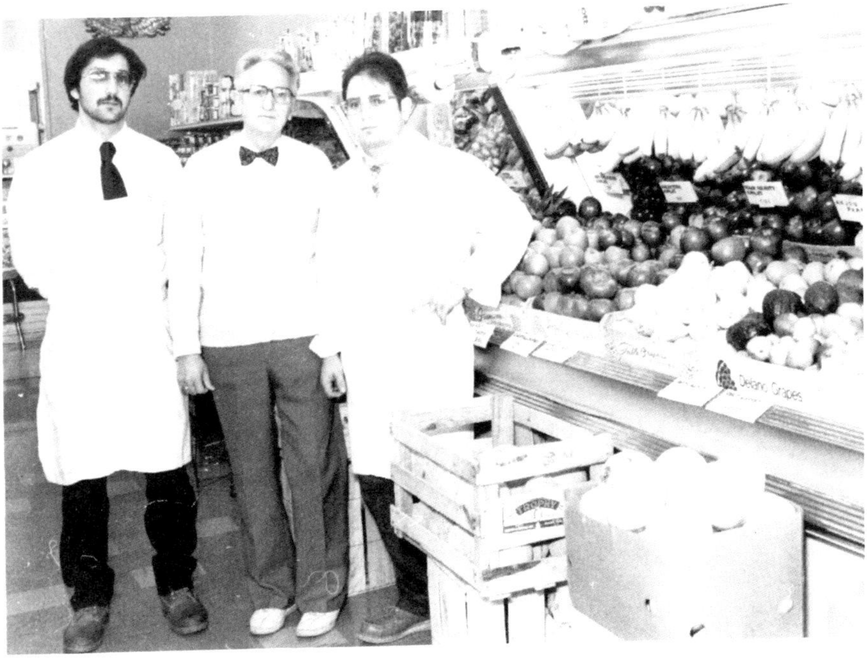

A 1978 photo of Ray, Frank Sr. and Frank Jr. DeRosa in front of produce at J&M Market. *Photo by Frank DeRosa.*

Plans for the community center were halted. The master plan needed revision to comply with new rules for affordable housing that would become law in 2005. A town clock was planned, and fundraising began for the $30,000 price tag.

2005

The council began considering an ordinance to prohibit residents from feeding deer. The threat of disease both to humans and the deer, as well as an increase in automobile accidents, was becoming a growing concern for Mountainside residents. The council soon passed an ordinance prohibiting the feeding of wild animals.

Mountainside saw a decrease of about 2.3 percent in school taxes in 2005 as a result of funds awarded to Mountainside after the dissolution of the Regional School System. Recreational director Susan Winans announced plans to retire in the fall. She held this post for thirty-one years.

The state's uniform crime report published for 2004 revealed that crime overall was down in the borough. In 2004, sixty-eight crimes were reported as opposed to eighty-nine in 2003.

Mountainside Lends a Hand

Emergencies beyond local perimeters on occasion signal a clarion call for good neighbors to lend a hand. Such was the case in late August 2005, when computer models placed New Orleans in the center of the growing Hurricane Katrina. Mandatory evacuation on August 28 of the city, 80 percent of which is below sea level, and a direct hit on August 29 drew nationwide attention. Breaking levees, stranded residents, rising water, subsequent fires and looting drew immediate response from police and fire departments from around the country. Louisiana alone could not handle what New Orleans mayor C. Ray Nagin described as "the storm that most of us have long feared."

Detective Donald Amberg, then a ten-year veteran of the Mountainside Police Department, volunteered to be part of a Union County group—a riot and control team—that accompanied police from all over the state to assist in keeping the peace in the city of New Orleans. In the second of three groups from New Jersey to assist in search, rescue and recovery, Amberg made the twenty-eight-hour drive to the Big Easy in a Scotch Plains marked police car. "We drove straight through," he recollects. "Men from Union and Middlesex counties in twelve vehicles were sworn in at Baton Rouge federally so we had law-enforcement powers."

Following the onset of the hurricane, there were over six thousand calls to 911 pleading for rescuers. "When we got down there, the number was down to three thousand, but the police couldn't get to all of them," says Amberg. "They would hand us lists of calls and say, 'This is your job for the day. Just follow up on them.' We would do twenty to thirty a day. Most callers said, 'We're trapped in the attic. The water's rising. We can't get out.'"

Water levels made driving treacherous, often too high for cars to get through. "We were put on military trucks to search through the houses and mark where the bodies were found," recalls Amberg. "The mortuary detail would come back to pick them up. Then we would have to go out there and provide cover for that detail. There was a lot of crime and corruption going on. People were shooting because they didn't know who was approaching—help or looters."

Amberg recalls that he couldn't get into some of the houses. "We had to go in through the roof," he says. "Had to cut a hole to get in.

The people were living there with lanterns and flashlights. People moved up as high as possible. They were used to the storms and would ride them out. That's what killed some of these people. A lot of them drowned. Rescuers would find claw marks on the ceilings near the bodies; they were trying to break through the ceilings. It wasn't pretty; that's for sure."

He remarks that the temperature early in September reached 108 degrees. Houses that appeared vacant had been shut up for two or three weeks, following the order to evacuate. "The first thing you'd do when you break down the door is take a step back and let the stale air come out. The smell was horrible. As gruesome as it sounds, you might then find bodies covered in mold."

Amberg remembers the devastation: houses in the middle of roads, cars on houses, houses on houses, hungry animals everywhere drinking the sick water and eating remains of other animals and getting sick; workers becoming ill. "One of the guys from our first deployment was very ill. We ended up having to fly him out."

Workers would return to Bonnabel High School in Kenner where they were being housed in the gym to decontaminate themselves at the end of each day. It was a two-week mission for Amberg, who says that all wanted to stay longer to help out, but he concludes, "You did what you could. The job wasn't done and wouldn't be for quite a while. I think what we did was a good thing—for the people, for the animals, for the

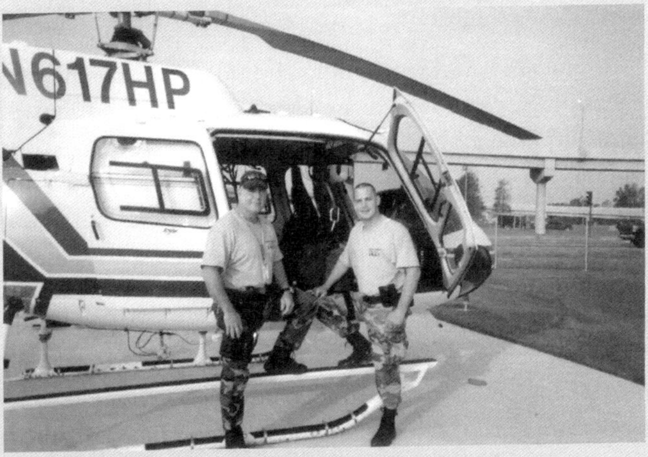

Detective Donald Amberg with Detective James Weinberg of the Union County Prosecutor's Office preparing to help during Hurricane Katrina. *Courtesy of Donald Amberg.*

police departments. One of the guys from New Jersey brought a puppy back. I brought memories and some pictures."

The world stands out on either side
No wider than the heart is wide;
Above the world is stretched the sky
No higher than the soul is high.
—Edna St. Vincent Millay

The human heart is about the size of one's fist. In Mountainside, hearts seem to be much larger. In times of travail the local human spirit has risen to meet whatever needs present themselves, whether they are nearby or miles away.

Witness the reaction and response of resident Debbie Hoffman following Hurricane Katrina in late August 2005. When a former colleague's daughter told her about a group of children from New Orleans who had been displaced and taken in by the Milton School in Lafayette Parish, Hoffman took action.

"What can we do to help?" inquired Hoffman. Milton School principal Suzie Kebodeaux related the plight of the seventy-six evacuees and their families who had lost everything in the storm and were in need of everything, including school supplies, money for extra desks and chairs for the classrooms they were to temporarily share with a student body of seven hundred.

In addition to family and friends, Hoffman approached the student council of Deerfield School, which her own two children attended. With the help of student council advisor Linda Shanahan, she put a plan into motion. Mountainside students collected notebooks, backpacks and other school supplies and raised over $4,000 to send to their counterparts in Louisiana. An eighth-grade teacher at the Milton School later described how her new students' faces "lit up with wonder" as they received the school supplies. Mountainside's Hoffman says, "I kept in touch with the principal down there for over a year; she was really grateful. She sent pictures, and the kids helped in putting together a PowerPoint thank you to the kids of Deerfield." Hearts seemed to be overflowing with kindness and gratitude in both sections of the nation.

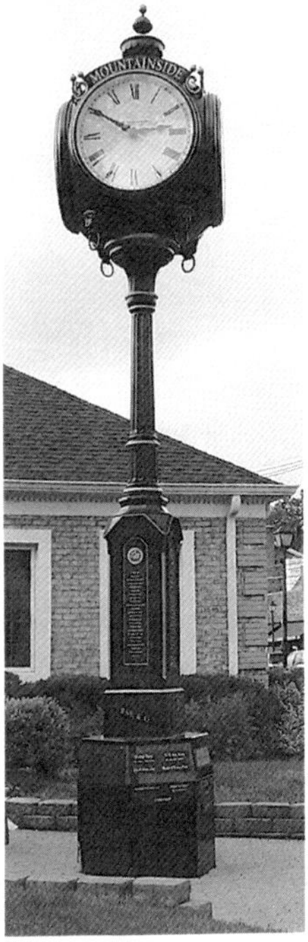

The Downtown Clock stands in front of Valley National Bank, the former site of Friendly's. *Photo by Maureen Giannone.*

Borough officials put together a plan that would meet affordable-housing requirements but stay true to the character of the community. The site of this new housing project would be the Barnes Tract on Mountain Avenue.

Dedication of a town clock was held on July 9. The clock was located in front of Valley National Bank on Mountain Avenue, the former site of Friendly's. The bank donated the land, as well as $5,000, toward the purchase of a clock. Other businesses were requested to donate $1,000 to offset the cost. Residents could purchase a nameplate on the clock for $250; for a donation of $350, residents would receive a nameplate plus a miniature of the clock for their own use. Any extra money would go to the rescue squad. Donald and Bob Maxwell, owners of Maxwell Furniture Restoration, donated a metal English-style bench to be placed next to the clock.

2006

In 2006, as a result of declining volunteerism in numerous areas, the rescue squad was forced to employ paid ambulance service from Atlantic Ambulance to cover daytime requests for aid. Its own eighteen members would continue to respond to calls between 6:00 p.m. and 6:00 a.m. on weekdays and provide twenty-four-hour service on weekends. During this year, the squad received over six hundred calls for assistance.

Borough Clerk Judith Osty retired after more than fifteen years of service. Martha DeJesus succeeded her.

The borough council unanimously passed a No-Knock Registry to prevent unwanted solicitors from knocking on the doors of residents. A "No Solicitation" sign had to be visible on the exterior of the house. By the beginning of October, 56 of Mountainside's 1,200 homeowners had registered.

Two water slides were opened at the Mountainside Community Pool, replacing two of the diving boards.

Miriam Bein resigned after sixteen years as library director. During her tenure, Bein oversaw the demise of the manual paper card catalogue and the

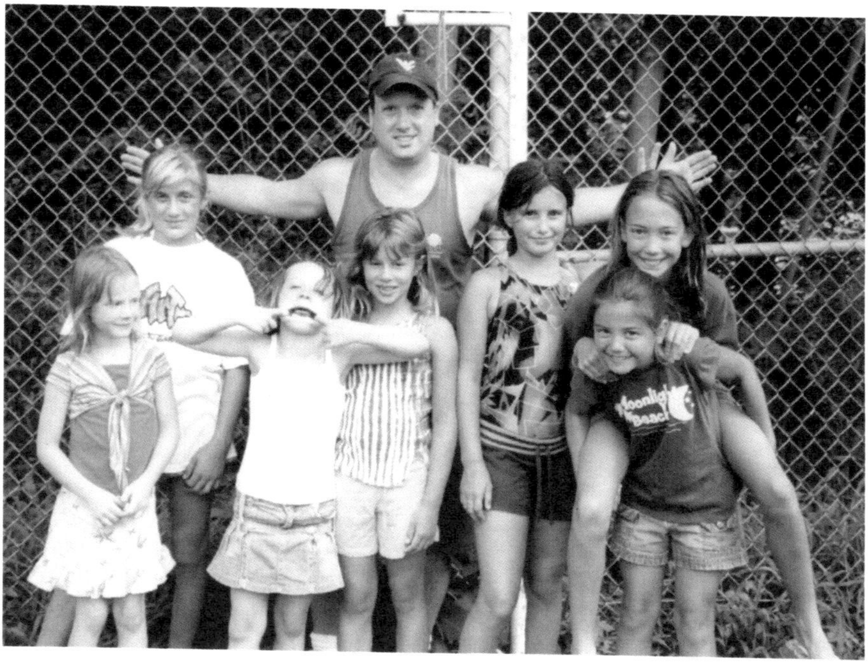

Scott "Snoopy" Laudati and friends, summer 2006. *Courtesy of the Mountainside Recreation Department.*

incorporation of wireless Internet connections, a big-screen movie system, a dozen Internet work stations and several computer databases to keep pace with technology.

2007

In 2007, Robert Viglianti became the longest serving mayor in office in Union County. He had held that position for twenty years, after serving ten years on the borough council. Among the accomplishments of his administration, as noted by the *Echo-Leader*, were "the inclusion of Mountainside as a full member of the Rahway Valley Sewerage Authority; heading the charge for county de-regionalization, which resulted in a lawsuit gain of $8.6 million for the borough; and the renovation of Borough Hall."

After forty-four years of standing on Route 22, the seventy-foot-tall Mountainside Christmas tree was lighted for the last time. Originally planted by the Lion's Club, the tree had been deteriorating in spite of attempts to save it.

The borough council validated a ninety-eight-year-old ordinance banning ice cream trucks from the borough. In 1909, the ordinance read, "No person

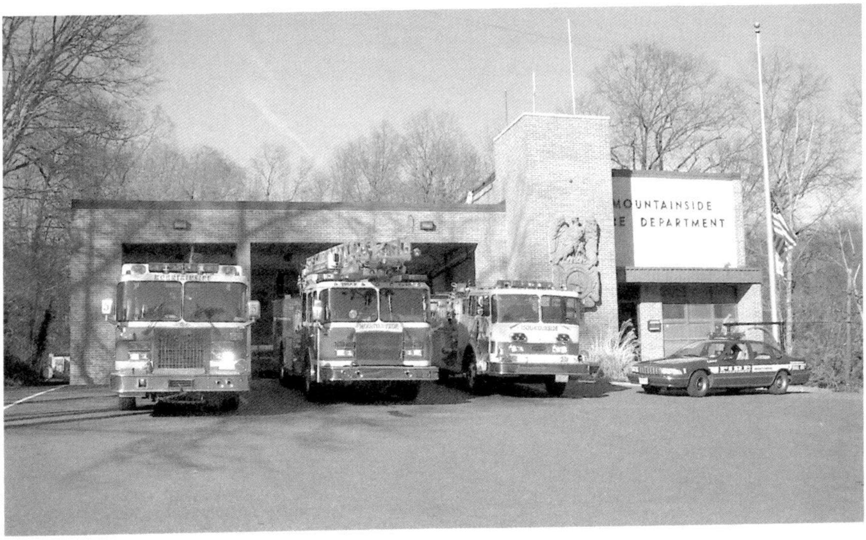

Firehouse, 2007. *Courtesy of the Borough of Mountainside.*

shall, within the limits of the borough, ring any bell or blow any horn or make any public outcry at or for any public sale, auction or venue or to advertise any goods, wares or merchandise for sale." Twenty-first-century rationale for excluding such sales vehicles included their taking away business from volunteer organizations and safety measures.

2008

In 2008, the *New Jersey Monthly* magazine ranked Mountainside number sixteen of the top one hundred places to live in New Jersey. It was the highest ranked municipality from Union County.

Mountainside's Christmas tree on the corner of New Providence Road and Route 22 was cut down in September.

Beyond Mountainside's Borders

2000

In 2000, Al Qaeda bombed the warship USS *Cole* in Yemen, killing seventeen. George W. Bush became president; the election was the closest in decades.

2001

In 2001, Al Qaeda destroyed the World Trade Center and damaged the Pentagon using hijacked planes. A fourth hijacked plane crashed eighty miles outside Pittsburgh. Bush ordered a sustained war on terror. Oklahoma City bomber Timothy McVeigh was executed.

2002

In 2002, North Korea admitted to developing nuclear arms in defiance of a treaty. AIDS deaths were projected to skyrocket; the United Nations announced that the toll could reach an additional 65 million by 2020 if preventative measures were not expanded.

2003

In 2003, North Korea withdrew from a treaty on nonproliferation of nuclear weapons, and the space shuttle *Columbia* exploded, killing all seven astronauts on board.

2004

In 2004, the 9/11 Commission Report identified U.S. intelligence and policy failures that allowed the September 11, 2001 terrorist attacks to take place. Bush was reelected president.

The U.S. media released graphic photos of American soldiers abusing and sexually harassing Iraqi prisoners at Abu Ghraib prison. These images sparked outrage around the world.

The United States' final report on Iraqi weapons found no Weapons of Mass Destruction.

2005

In 2005, cancer replaced heart disease as the number one cause of death for people ages eighty-five and under. The number of deaths from both, however, had fallen.

2006

In 2006, Saddam Hussein was convicted of crimes against humanity by an Iraqi court and was hanged in Baghdad. The International Astronomical Union voted to redefine the solar system, and Pluto lost its status as a planet. It was reclassified as a dwarf planet.

Chapter 8

THE SUM OF THE PARTS

Community Components

Greek philosopher Aristotle (384–322 BC) may have been the first to assert the belief that the whole is greater than the sum of its parts. Several hundred years later, the Apostle Paul proffered the same idea in his Epistles. In this case, it illustrated cooperation among the human, the divine and the cosmic. Paul's words: "I did the planting, Apollos the watering, but God made things grow…We are fellow workers with God." Known as *synergy*, the concept comes from the Greek "syn-ergo," meaning working together. Used in a religious context for centuries, it wasn't until early in the twentieth century that the term began to be used in a broader, non-theological sense.

Clearly, a painting by Monet or Degas has greater value than the paint and canvas used to make it. A house, likewise, is worth more than the pieces of wood, sheetrock, wiring and roofing materials used in its construction. So also a community—while needing law enforcement, a fire department, a governing body and various other groups—evolves into so much more when the human factor, including energy, caring and talent, is added into the process. Like the painting and the house, the community has a value above and beyond its extrinsic components. Nonetheless, it is these "extrinsics" that provide the mainstay, foundation and impetus for the desired product to grow and prosper. Mountainside has been fortunate over the years to have community components that work well individually and synergistically.

Mayor and Borough Council

While the names, faces and meeting locations have changed over the years, the form of government in Mountainside has remained much the same. From the first election on October 22, 1895, at Beaman's Blacksmith Shop (behind what is now 899 Mountain Avenue), a mayor and council, elected at large—that is, to represent the entire community—still make up the governing body.

Initially, the mayor and six council members met at Klopf's Mountainside Hotel on what is now Route 22. (To commemorate that historical era, in September 1970, during the borough's Diamond Jubilee, the council met in the very same building, now the local Elks lodge.) Meetings moved to the Willow Grove School in 1904. When construction readied the "new" Borough Hall (now the Lord Building), the council held its first meeting there on January 1, 1910. In addition to council meeting rooms, this building housed police headquarters and the tax collector's and clerk's offices. A second-floor auditorium provided space for meetings of civic organizations, as well as for a variety of community social functions.

A 1957 fire damaged Borough Hall. Repairs were made, and an addition to the rear of the building was constructed. Nonetheless, in 1964 council meetings moved to Echobrook School because of the better facilities. Then Beechwood School became the site of meetings until 1976, when the Borough Council entered into an agreement with the board of education to purchase the newer section of Echobrook School (the part built in 1936) and turn it into a municipal complex. The council has met at this location since then.

A mayor and six councilmen form the governing body. The mayor is elected for a four-year term and the councilmen for three, with two elected each year. The mayor does not have a vote in town matters unless there is a tie. He is, however, given veto power. The council can overrule a veto with a two-thirds vote.

While not a member of the council himself, Borough Attorney John Post has been an integral part of the workings of the government for nearly four decades. In his annual letter to residents in 2008, Mayor Robert Viglianti revealed the impact Post has had on policymaking:

> *John Post is an individual who for thirty-five years has contributed legal advice that has had a major impact on the quality of life for all of Mountainside. John and his law firm have led Mountainside through*

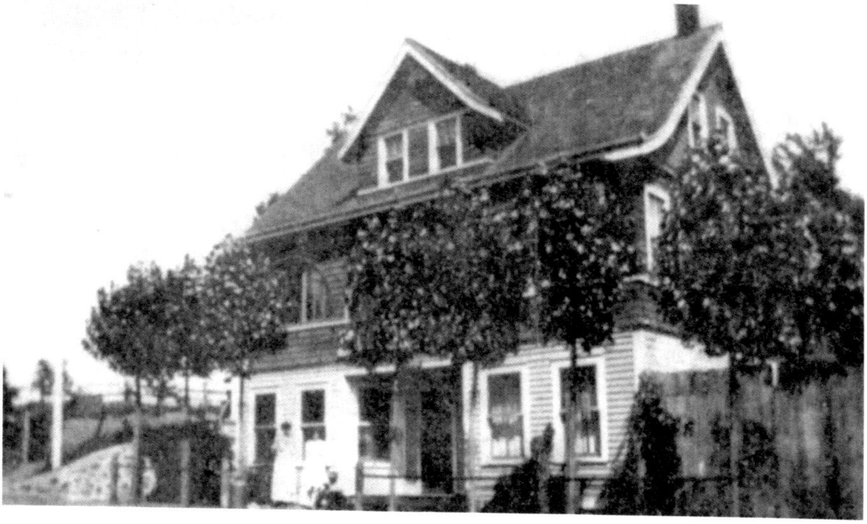

A local news article highlighted Mountainside's secession from Westfield, becoming its own borough. Mountainside Borough Council meetings were held in Klopf's Hotel until 1904. It is the current site of the Elks Club. *Courtesy of Eleanor Pfeifer.*

three major legal actions that, if lost, would have had very negative effects on our community. John led Mountainside throughout a major legal confrontation to obtain Mountainside's membership in the Rahway Valley Sewerage Authority. He led us up to the New Jersey Supreme Court to win over 8 million dollars from the breakup of the Regional High School District. Recently, through John's efforts, we successfully won a decision that prevents very high-density housing from being built in town; this would have changed the character of our community. As a resident I know that John has always represented our community, his community, with a higher level of zeal that only a resident would have.

Municipal Court

Ordinance Number 151 abolished the police or recorder's court on December 31, 1948, and established a municipal court of the borough of Mountainside on January 1, 1949. Before this enactment took effect, the title of the official in charge was police recorder. Thereafter, the titles of magistrate and judge were used. Presiding over the years were:

Police Recorder Albert J. Benninger	January 1, 1947–December 31, 1948
Police Recorder Alan Thompson (At the meeting of February 8, 1949, his title became Magistrate Alan Thompson.)	January 1, 1949–December 31, 1954
Magistrate Jacob R. Bauer	January 1, 1955–December 31, 1967
Judge Jacob R. Bauer	January 1, 1968–December 31, 1975
Judge Robert A. Ruggiero	February 2, 1976–2000 (deceased July 2000)
Temporary Judge Bart Barre	January 1, 2000
Judge Bart Barre	January 1, 2001–December 31, 2003
Judge James DeRose	January 1, 2004–present

Mr. Mountainside

If Elmer and Emily Hoffarth hadn't gotten lost near Route 22 and practically stumbled into Mountainside—where they subsequently bought a house on Evergreen Court in 1940—the town would have been without two of its greatest contributors. Emily became the first full-time librarian and was instrumental in building the library on Constitution Plaza. And Elmer, well, he did just about everything else.

Having worked in real estate and as a heating contractor, truck driver and park policeman, in 1932 Elmer joined the receiving department of Chevrolet in Tarrytown, New York, before transferring to the General Motors plant in Linden in 1937. Nine years later, when he resigned his position, Mountainside's borough tax collector was retiring, and Hoffarth was hired to fill the vacancy.

Not only was Hoffarth the first full-time municipal employee in Mountainside's history, but also, within a short time, he was appointed assistant borough clerk and treasurer. In 1958, he became borough clerk, a position he held until 1972. As if this wasn't enough to keep the man busy, he took on the jobs of custodian of school funds, court clerk and business administrator.

In his spare time, Elmer Hoffarth was a Boy Scout leader, a volunteer fireman for twelve years and, in 1961, the first president and a charter member of the Rotary Club. Sandwiched in between was a twelve-year stint on the board of education and a strong hand in acquiring property on which the Deerfield and Beechwood schools would be built.

Probably what most Mountainsiders of the second half of the twentieth century remember Hoffarth for was his portrayal of Santa Claus during the holiday season. This forty-five-year annual event began on Evergreen Court, where nearby residents would string lights around a fir tree on a front lawn at the end of the street. Then Hoffarth would emerge from the wooded area and present candy canes to the children. He would ask the youngsters to form two lines—the bad children on one side, the good on the other. Very few, needless to say, stood in the former line. "They were all so happy," he recalled in a *Star-Ledger* interview in 1994. "They were all so anxious to get close to me."

Just weeks before he was to ride in the lead car in the Centennial Parade on June 3, 1995, as a tribute to his decades of service to borough government and to the community, Hoffarth died at the age of eighty-seven. The late Thomas Ricciardi, who was mayor while Hoffarth was clerk, remembered him as a "very fine and strong administrator and leader. He did his job very well." Robert Viglianti, mayor at the time of Hoffarth's death and a neighbor as well, remembers him as "a strong supporter of Mountainside. He really believed in the community. He was quite colorful, too. As the borough clerk, he'd tell the mayor and the council what to do."

Judge Robert A. Ruggiero

Nineteenth-century British statesman and prime minister Benjamin Disraeli once said, "Justice is truth in action." An individual who personifies this belief is former municipal judge Robert A. Ruggiero, who presided over the borough's court for twenty-five years until his death in 2000.

Ruggiero, whose tenure in this position was the longest of any other judge in Mountainside history, arrived in town in 1963 with a wife, two sons and a law practice. It was not long before the people of the borough recognized his positive manner and his sense of civic pride. Ruggiero

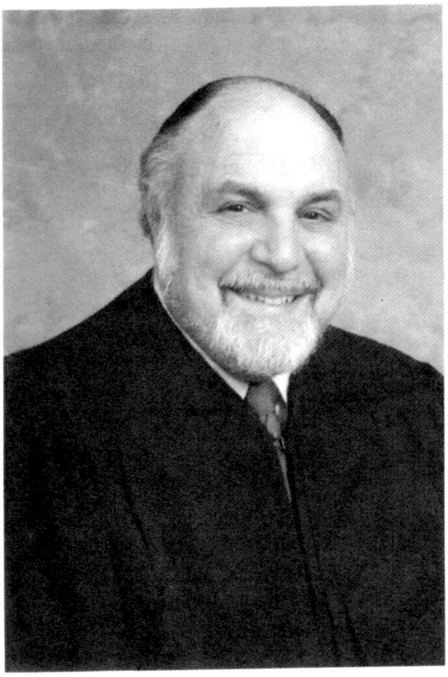

Judge Robert A. Ruggiero, circa 1997. *Courtesy of Diane Ruggiero.*

co-founded the Mountainside Pop Warner Midget Football League, and he served as a council member from 1967 through 1972; during this time, he also served as a member of the planning board and as police commissioner. Because of his many contributions to the police department of Mountainside, in 1969 Ruggiero was awarded an honorary silver lifetime membership in the Police Benevolent Association. Later, as a volunteer teacher, he shared his love of painting with patients with Alzheimer's disease at SAGE Spend-A-Day, operated by the Summit Area Association for Gerontological Endeavor.

With a major highway running through it and major portions of two Union County parks within its boundaries, Mountainside's municipal court has always been kept busy with cases involving nonresidents, as well as its own citizens. In 1987, Ruggiero noted that in addition to the four to six hours a week he spent in court, he required several additional hours to read and review local and state laws involving cases over which he was about to preside. He felt that part of his responsibility was "to discover the relevant background of a citizen who has been charged with an offense so that a speedy trial can take place." Ruggiero said that the penalties he handed down were neither extreme nor lenient. "I try and call it as it is," he said. "You do what has to be done."

Ruggiero's wife, Diane, calls him "a fair and good man." Sons Charles, a veterinarian, and Peter, head of a food service company in the Caribbean area, were always proud of what their dad did. Nevertheless, Diane recalls that once, when they were teenagers, she warned her sons to stay out of trouble and set an example because of their dad's position in town. Peter responded, "I wish I had a normal father like everyone else." Well, they didn't, because he wasn't, and we are better off as a result.

Police Department

Although Mountainside was established in 1895, it wasn't until nearly four decades later that the borough council created a full-time, paid police department and appointed a police chief. Since 1934, five department members have held this position.

So began the borough's law-enforcement detail, gradually expanding to match the community's growing population. Between 1941 and 1989, reserve police officers augmented the force by responding to all police and fire emergencies. To date, a total of seventy-six officers have been part of the Mountainside Police Department, and currently twenty-two officers serve the borough.

The department kept pace with twentieth-century strides in communication and technology. Radio equipment in individual cars in 1941 eliminated the need to check at a pole-mounted red light at police headquarters for emergency notification. Then, in 1944, a teletype at police headquarters allowed information on statewide crime to be received directly rather than via surrounding districts. By 1992, the department

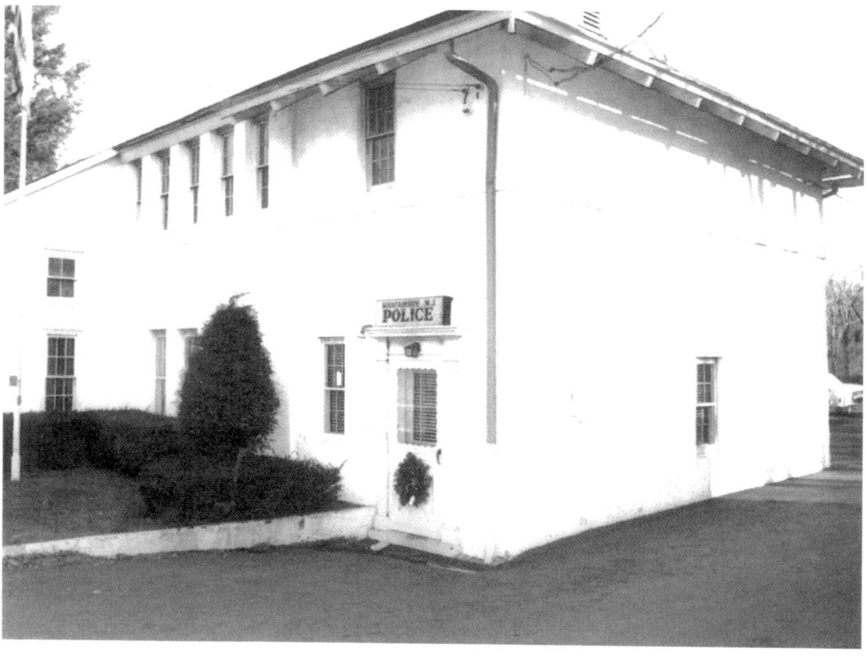

Mountainside's first police headquarters. *Courtesy of the Mountainside Police Department.*

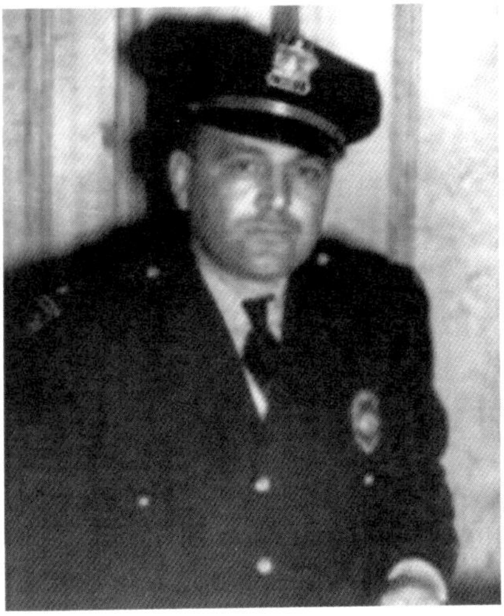

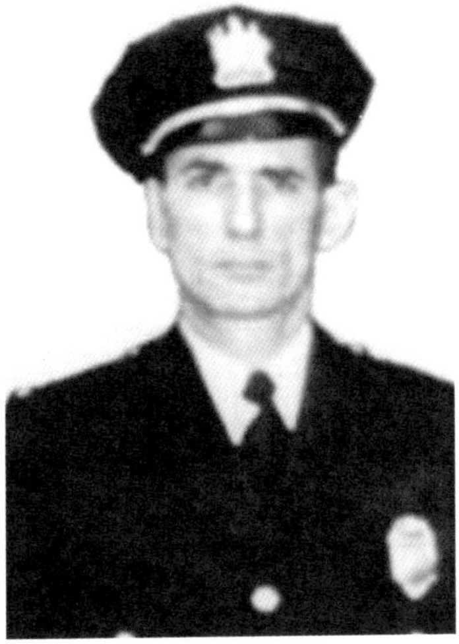

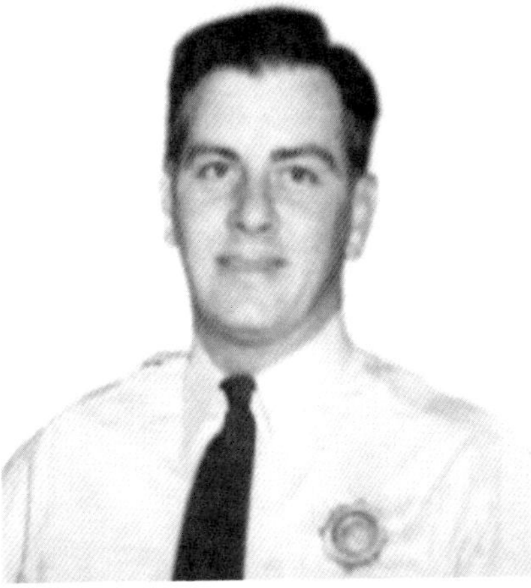

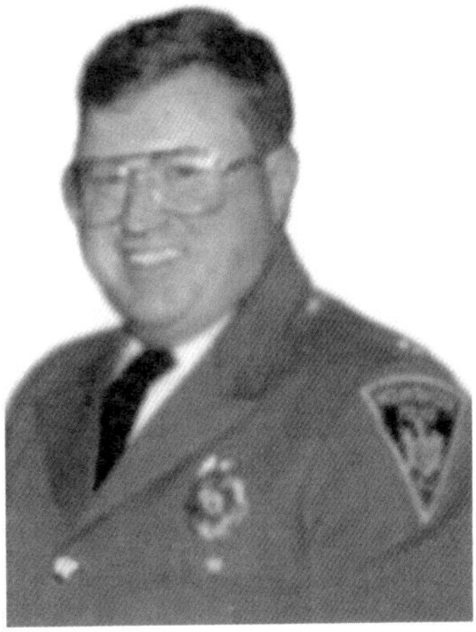

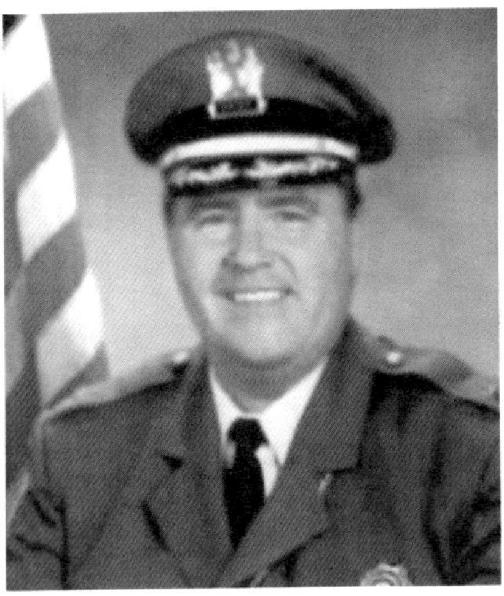

Police chiefs over the years. *Left to right, top row*: Charles Honecker (1934–1958) and Christian Fritz (1958–1970); *middle row*: Edward Mullin (1970–1983) and William Alder (1983–1998); *bottom row*: James Debbie Jr. (1998–present). *Courtesy of the Mountainside Police Department.*

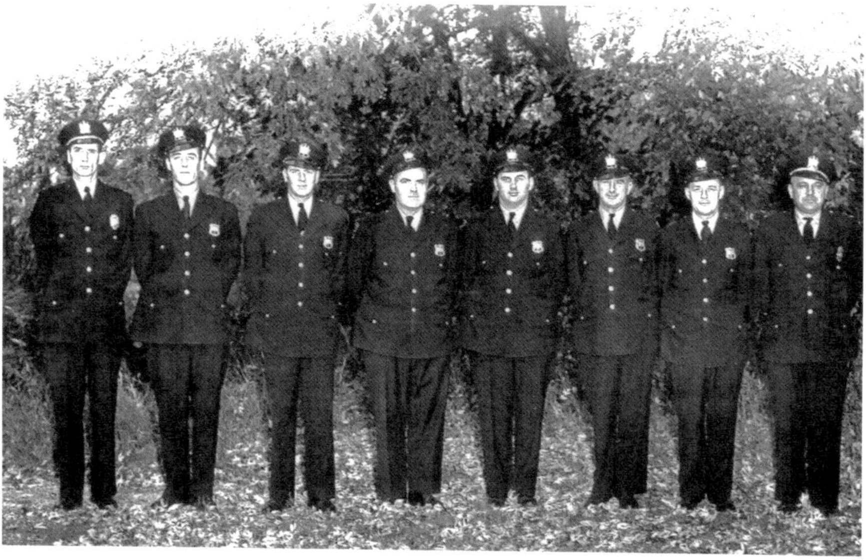

Police department, 1950. *From left to right*: Sergeant Christian Fritz, Patrolman Charles Doyle, Patrolman Edward Mullin, Special Patrolman Emmit Dugan, Patrolman William Leneham, Patrolman Harry Boyton. Special Patrolman Jack McCrea and Chief Charles Honecker. *Courtesy of the Mountainside Police Department.*

had discontinued the use of police call boxes, which had been located on utility poles throughout the borough. Further advances included mobile computers in patrol cars, a live-scan fingerprint system at police headquarters and a computerized accident-diagramming program on the computers. Our hi-tech society has further allowed handwritten reports to become computerized, mug shots to become digital and police cars to have GPS installed so that headquarters can monitor the locations of the cars. The dispatcher uses the GPS to enter a borough address and have its exact location display so that he may direct responding patrol cars more accurately to the location.

Over time, Route 22 grew from a lightly traveled suburban highway without a center divider to a major, national thoroughfare with its share of motor vehicle accidents, traffic violations and criminal activity. Located between two major New Jersey cities, Newark and Plainfield, and two major national centers, New York and Philadelphia, the majority of the arrests made resulted from Route 22 car stops rather than resident violations. In response, the Mountainside Police Department created additional units and enforcement programs.

Formed in 1964, the Detective Bureau is responsible for criminal investigations, maintaining evidence and criminal files, fingerprinting and

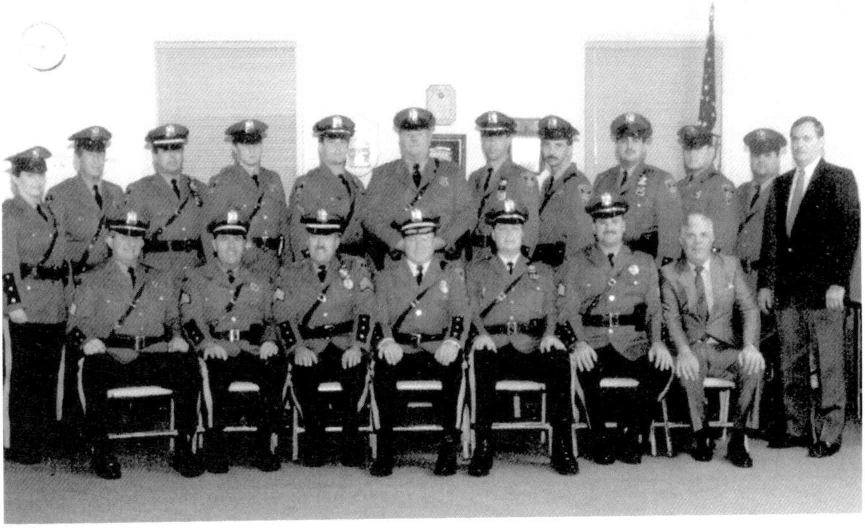

Police department, 1992. *Courtesy of the Mountainside Police Department.*

conducting background checks on police and firearm permit applicants. Prior to this date, patrolmen conducted all follow-up investigations. Detectives are also members of the Union County Investigators Association, the New Jersey Narcotic Enforcement Officers Association, the Union County Juvenile Officers Association and the Union County Terrorism Task Force.

In addition, officers are members of various county crime-fighting forces, facilitating cooperative efforts among surrounding municipalities when the infraction reaches beyond the borough's borders. For example, officers assigned to the Essex/Union County Auto Theft Task Force work together to combat a growing auto-theft rate. In 1994, Union County reestablished a county-wide tactical team, named the Union County Emergency Response Team. At present, Corporal Kenneth Capobianco is a member of the Union County Prosecutor's Computer Crimes Task Force, and Sergeant Allan Attanasio is part of the Union County Arson Squad. Within the borough, the department maintains a six-member major accident investigation team, three Drug Abuse Resistance Education officers, two physical fitness officers, several firearms instructors, a Homeland Security liaison officer and a motorcycle squad.

A bit of déjà vu occurred in 2000, when motorcycles (last used in the 1920s and 1930s) were reinstated. The lease of a Harley-Davidson police motorcycle and, in 2002, the donation of a used police motorcycle by BMW of North America let the squad easily maneuver in highway traffic. The department maintains a motorcycle instructor, and all officers assigned to the squad attend a forty-hour Police Motor Officer Safety Course run by the department, which also trains motorcycle officers from surrounding departments.

Nearly a decade into the twenty-first century, Mountainside operates five marked patrol cars, a marked special-duty truck and three unmarked patrol cars, all with state-of-the-art lighting, radio and video equipment and computers, as well as first-aid kits, oxygen units and other medical and emergency gear.

Mountainside's finest have offered assistance outside the borough. During the 1967 Plainfield riots, department members joined with other municipal, county and state officers in quelling the disturbances. Following the 2001 terrorist attacks on the World Trade Center, a group of officers aided New York City and New York/New Jersey Port Authority Police. In 2004, Police Officer Steve DeVito was activated and deployed by the New Jersey Army National Guard to serve in Operation Iraqi Freedom. In 2005, Hurricane Katrina offered yet another opportunity for local law enforcement to venture beyond the borough's boundaries when officers volunteered to bolster the ranks of the New Orleans Police Department.

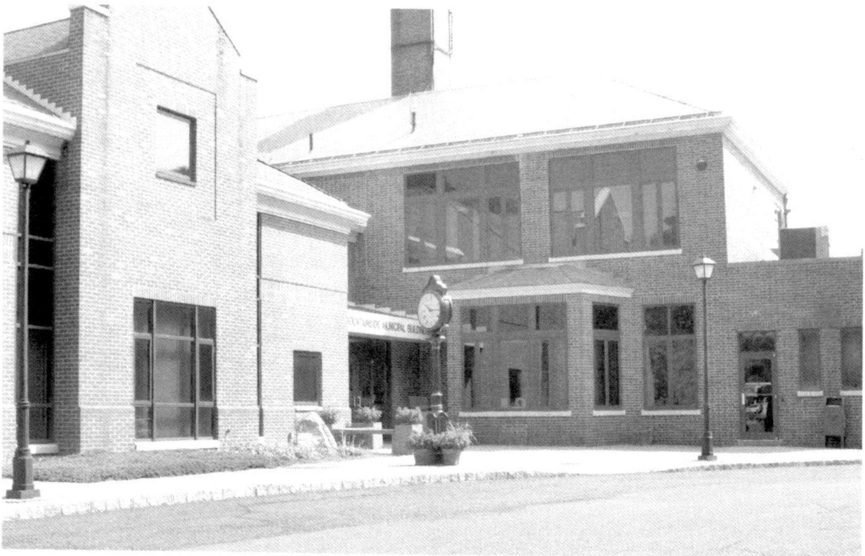

Current police headquarters. *Courtesy of the Borough of Mountainside.*

Police Cases of Note

Now and then, local police work attracts widespread area interest. Such is the circumstance of the following two Mountainside cases.

On patrol on Prospect Avenue on January 14, 1975, Officer Jack Yerich was approached by four youths who had spotted a body at the base of the water tower. Yerich notified Mountainside Police Headquarters, which in turn contacted the Union County Police, since the 150-foot water tower is on county property. Yerich, joined by Detective Jerome Rice, found the body, later identified as fifteen-year-old Gregg Sanders.

Both went to the family home on Sunny Slope Drive to inform Gregg's parents. No one responded to their knocks on the door. While checking the property and looking through the windows, the two policemen saw a man's body lying on the floor by the back door. So as not to disturb a possible crime scene, the officers went in through the front of the house by breaking a window. They found the body of a woman on the living room floor. Both victims, the parents of Gregg Sanders, had been murdered with an axe.

After a search through the rest of the house, the police found a suicide/confession note that Gregg had apparently written and signed. Underneath the desk in his room was a little doorway that led to a crawl space above the first-floor porch. In this hideaway was a mattress, narcotics and alcohol bottles.

Following interviews of friends and teachers, police discovered that Sanders had been reprimanded only days before by a teacher at Pingry, the private school he attended. The conclusion was that the pressures were becoming too great for the teen to handle; he was feeling that he had failed to attain the expectations that his parents had set for him. He killed them so they would not have to deal with the burden of his suicide.

A missing-person investigation in 1989 led to the involvement of Interpol, an organization of police agencies throughout the world that assist when a crime pervades multiple countries. On July 30, Lin Hsieh, co-owner of the Pagoda Restaurant, where Raagini Restaurant now operates, left her restaurant at 2:00 p.m., after telling the manager that she was going to help a friend who was having domestic problems. The next day, when she failed to return to Pagoda and didn't show up at home, her husband reported her missing. While she had driven her car and had about $100 in cash, most of her remaining property was still at her house. The situation appeared suspicious. Both she and her car were entered into the National Crime Information computer as missing.

On August 1, the Mountainside Police Department received a phone call from the Fort Lee (New Jersey) Police Department stating that they had found the burned remains of Hsieh's vehicle in their city. They determined that the fire had been intentionally set: it was arson.

The Mountainside Police began checking phone records from the Hsieh house and discovered that in the recent past several calls had been made to Queens, New York. On August 4, Mountainside detectives, along with NYPD detectives, went to the location in Queens to which the calls had been made. After a series of interviews with the occupant, the police determined that this former employee had been having an affair with Hsieh.

After checking his credit card statements, they found that he had purchased two airline tickets to Taiwan. Interpol then intervened and determined that, indeed, Hsieh was not a missing person at all. The attractive Asian woman whose photograph and story had made the front pages of numerous East Coast newspapers was merely in the process of leaving her husband and her life in the United States. She and her lover wanted to start life anew in Taiwan. There was no crime, and the case was closed. Nonetheless, press coverage put Mountainside on television screens and news pages.

Volunteer Fire Department

The thirty-three-member (as of 2007) volunteer fire department that protects nearly 2,500 residences, two nursing homes, a major movie theatre and numerous industrial facilities and responds to accidents on the borough's 2.7-mile stretch of Route 22 is a far cry from the bucket brigade first organized in 1910 by a group of foresighted individuals led by Robert Laing, Charles B. Heckel and Henry C. Weber.

A used chemical engine, bought by Laing for thirty-five dollars, was drawn by Henry Weber's horse and buggy until 1918, when the department purchased its first truck, a Thomas Flyer, an engine containing two seventy-gallon chemical tanks. It wasn't until 1944 that the town had two trucks capable of being used simultaneously. Upgrading vehicles continued, as well as adding a third fire engine and brush units: two smaller trucks used primarily for their maneuverability in smaller and off-road areas. These are four-wheel-drive vehicles, of which there are only four in Union County at the present time.

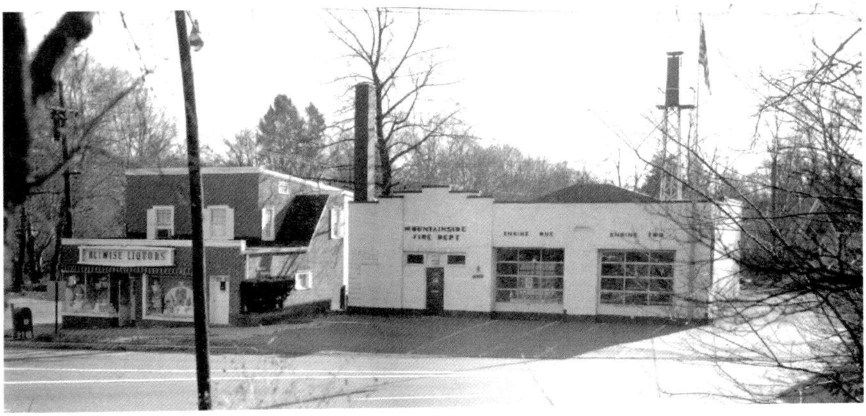

Mountainside Volunteer Fire Department, 1975. *Courtesy of John Sharkey.*

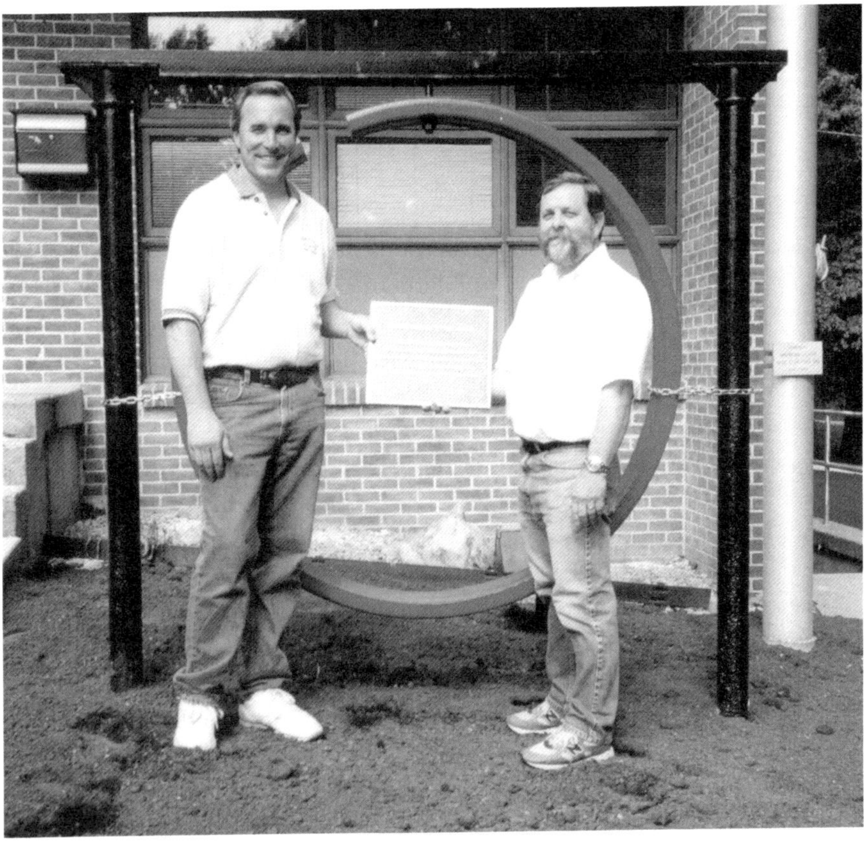

Scott Daniels, chairman of the Mountainside Historic Preservation Committee, presents a plaque to Dan Clark, president of the fire department, upon the return of the gong to the firehouse, October 2001. *Courtesy of the Mountainside Historic Preservation Committee.*

The first firehouse was part of Borough Hall when it stood on Route 22 near the intersection of Mountain Avenue. In 1934, the fire department moved into a garage at the rear of Borough Hall when its original space was converted into the first police headquarters. Then, in 1944, the borough passed an ordinance that allocated $9,000 for the purchase of a garage several hundred feet from Borough Hall. Originally a Hudson car showroom and then a gas station, the facility was transformed into a functioning firehouse after many hours of work by department volunteers.

The burgeoning population, industrial growth and increased traffic on Route 22 during the 1950s and '60s were the catalysts for renewed efforts in the area of fire safety. In the late 1960s, the borough council purchased one acre of land off Route 22 on New Providence Road. The location provides easy access to areas both north and south of Route 22. Groundbreaking ceremonies for a nine-thousand-square-foot firehouse were held on April 6, 1974. Move-in day was April 5, 1975. The dedication of the new three-bay building with ample room for six vehicles, three offices and a second-floor all-purpose room took place on June 7, 1975, signaling the advent of a new era in fire protection.

Back in 1915, the Garwood Volunteer Fire Department had donated a gong to Mountainside. An old railroad tie sounded with a sledgehammer, it was used to alert volunteers of their immediate need at the engine company until 1933, when a siren was installed. By the early days of World War

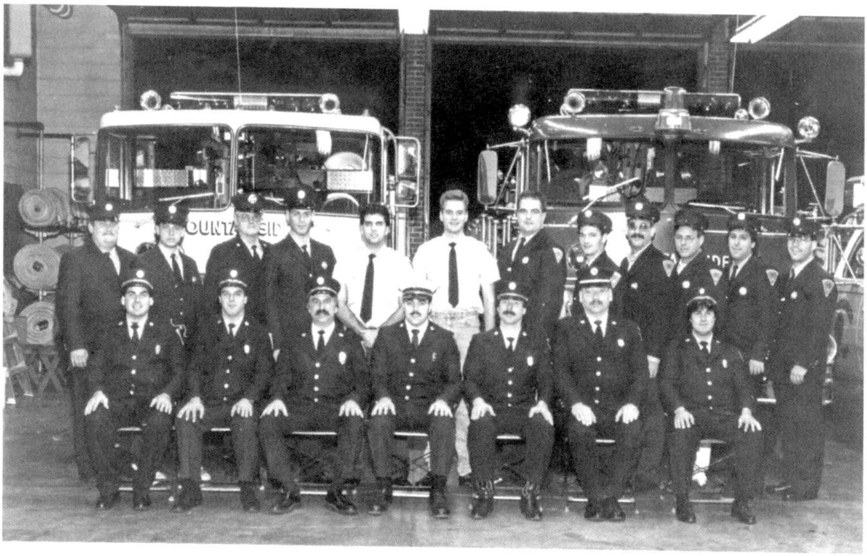

Fire department members in the mid-1990s. *Courtesy of Borough Hall.*

II, when metal was scarce, the gong was slated for the scrap heap. Joseph Linden, a borough fireman, saved it and installed it at the entrance to his driveway at 1260 Cedar Avenue. After buying the property years later, Mr. and Mrs. Lawrence Jacobsen donated the gong to the fire department. It was restored and, in 2001, returned to its old home in front of the firehouse on New Providence Road.

During the early years, a telephone-bell alerting system called firemen to duty. It was replaced with a Plectron radio in 1964. At a signal from the radio, the volunteer knew to report to the firehouse. Over the years, the device became more sophisticated. Each fireman then had a more traditional radio on the Plectron that was activated by a voice message from police headquarters, giving the type of fire and its location. Sometime later, the radio became detachable and the firefighter could take it with him. Today, a pager is carried by each volunteer.

With the growth of both the town and the use of Route 22, the number of calls answered by the volunteer firefighters has also increased. In 1944, the department responded to forty-seven calls; in 1971, it responded to sixty. Currently, over three hundred pleas for assistance come in during the year.

Women in the Department

In 2006, after nearly nine years in town, Candice Fiorenza decided to volunteer for the Mountainside Fire Department. "I like to help people," she says. "As a dental assistant I help people, so being a firefighter goes with the territory."

While a probationary member of the department, during which time she attended Monday night meetings and drills, Fiorenza completed a sixteen-week training program at the Union County Fire Academy in Linden. Before training, only exterior tasks are assigned to the probationer. "Once you've finished Fire Fighter I, you are off probation and can go inside," she reports.

Female firefighters perform the exact same duties as their male counterparts. "You have to be in top physical condition. It's very strenuous," says Fiorenza. "I've always worked out. I've always been very athletic." This mother of four emphasizes that there is no prejudice in training or at work: "First and foremost, I do my job. If I need help, I ask. It's as simple as that."

As for her unscheduled absences from the homefront, Fiorenza has a tag with a little fire engine attached. "In the middle of the night if I'm called to a fire, I hang the tag on the door. My children know where I am, and they're proud of me."

Fire Department Veteran Kevin Rogers Describes Protocol

We're on call 24/7. The chief, assistant chief, and two deputy chiefs carry portable radios with them all the time and keep fire gear in their cars. When the police dispatcher pages, the chiefs head straight for the fire scene and inform the dispatcher that they are on their way.

The dispatcher waits three minutes, then puts out another page. Other department members, including four other officers, head for the firehouse.

Mutual aid—assistance from surrounding fire departments—is called for when the officers deem that a house fire warrants additional manpower [Mountainside is surrounded by paid departments: Cranford, Westfield, Summit and Springfield].

The ability to fight a large fire with one department is not usual. You get pretty exhausted; you need to rehab. There is a tremendous amount of work following a fire as well.

Rescue Squad

Using a donated, converted hearse housed in an adapted garage behind the old Borough Hall (now the Lord Building), the Mountainside Rescue Squad began providing emergency medical services in 1939. Prior to that date, when emergencies occurred, a policeman, usually on motorcycle, responded to the call. If a trip to the hospital was needed—it would have been Muhlenberg in Plainfield—the injured person would be transported by automobile, sometimes in an upright position despite the type of injury. A group consisting primarily of volunteer firemen decided to organize a first-aid unit. Though its mission remains unchanged, the surroundings and equipment have undergone vast transformations.

By 1940, volunteers were responding to calls in their first authentic ambulance, a second-hand 1936 Packard. The year 1948 saw the arrival of a modern and fully equipped vehicle, a Cadillac Meteor. The squad continues to conform to technological progress in its purchase of state-of-the-art vehicles and equipment.

Today, the ambulances are more than a means of transportation. While the volunteers still provide immediate first aid and a means of travel to a hospital, paramedic units introduced by Overlook Hospital in the early 1980s assist in life-threatening emergencies. The ambulances become

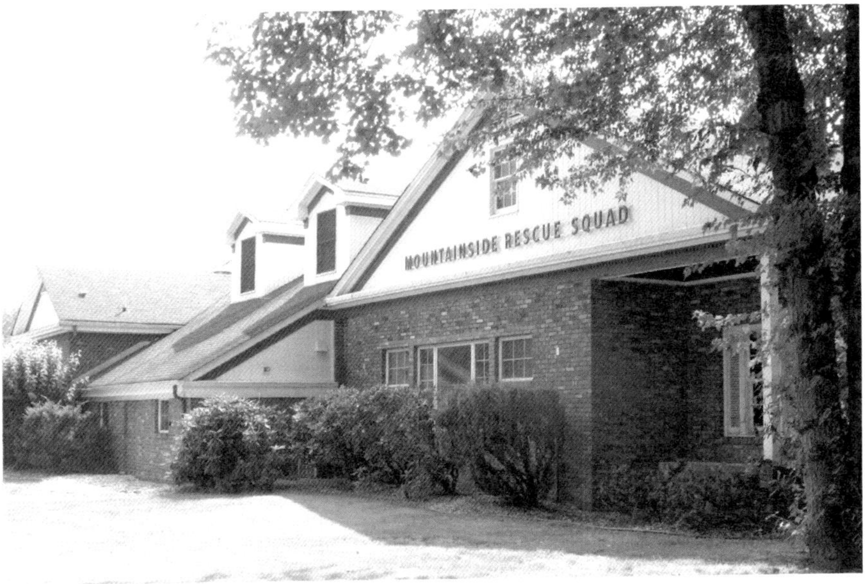

The rescue squad building, 2000. *Courtesy of the Borough of Mountainside.*

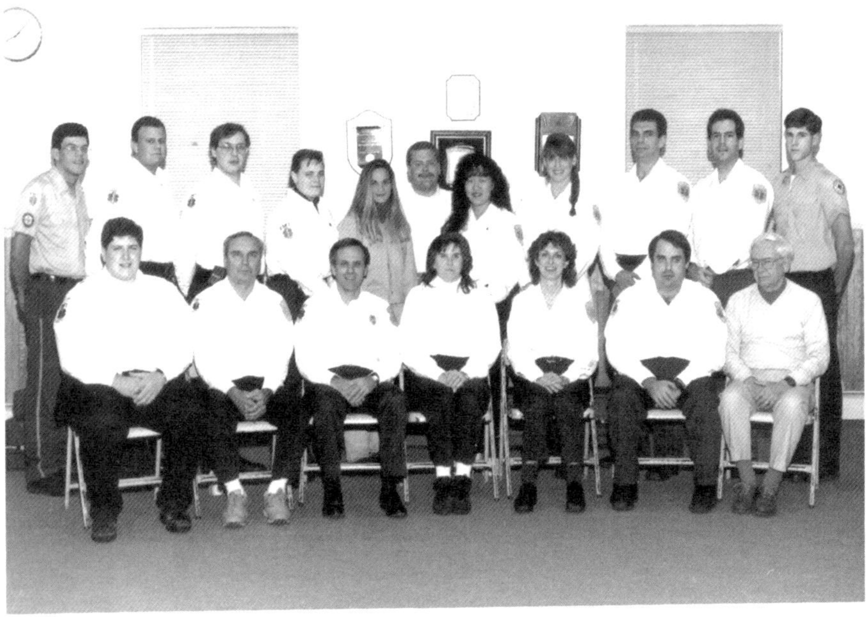

Mountainside Rescue Squad members, early 1990s. *Courtesy of Borough Hall.*

emergency rooms on wheels, with personnel—i.e. the paramedics—trained to administer drugs and injections, perform tracheotomies and otherwise stabilize a patient until arrival at a local hospital. Defibrillators, placed in service in the 1970s, enhance the process, as do radio contact with the nearest hospital and direct contact with emergency room doctors while en route.

"Home" for the squad is the 1960 building on Route 22 between New Providence Road and Borough Hall. A 1991 addition at a cost of $285,000 was the most significant municipal project of that year. The building houses two ambulances, a meeting room, a training area and sleeping quarters for the eighteen active members, ten of whom are women.

Membership is open to those age sixteen and older. One can be certified at the age of seventeen. Residence within five miles of the squad building is mandatory, although those who work in town are permitted to serve during their normal working hours. Due to the decline of volunteers, however, Atlantic Healthcare from Overlook Hospital now stations an ambulance nearby and responds to weekday emergencies.

Increased traffic along Route 22, growth of the senior population and the emergence of six medical-related facilities in the borough (two outpatient surgery centers, a dialysis center, Children's Specialized Hospital, Manor Care and Brighton Gardens) have caused the number of calls to multiply over the years. Eight calls were received in 1939 and fifty-eight in 1945; in 2000, the rescue squad responded to over six hundred pleas for assistance.

Volunteer firemen often supplement the crisis team, particularly when there is a possibility of a fire during an automobile accident or when there are victims trapped in a car who need to be extricated. Likewise, squad members often accompany the fire department to calls, treating fire personnel injured while fighting a fire; they also monitor firefighters' vital signs and treat non-life-threatening injuries to victims of the fire.

Retired volunteer Kit Carson, veteran of thirty years on the rescue squad, recalls the "numerous appreciative people" during his tenure. He believes that not only is this "a great avenue for community service but a wonderful means of acquiring medical knowledge for oneself and one's own family."

Mayor Robert Viglianti praised volunteers in his annual letter to the borough in January 2008:

> *Looking at the Squad building, you will see a plaque with the name John Keuhler. John was not only a founding member of the Squad but was also a member of the Fire Company. For years he was the only person permitted*

> *to hold both roles. His wife Ruth also served on the Squad for many years. When one talks about the Squad one can never forget the tremendous service given by Mary Steiner and Helen Hay. For years these two ladies were the daytime, weekday squad. In more recent years Kit Carson gave many hours of service to our community.*

Though the physical size of the community may be relatively small, the diversity of cases that the rescue squad handles runs a wide spectrum. Longtime member and former president Kit Carson recalls several critical calls during a two-week period in the early 1990s, each of which resulted in a fatality:

> *In the first, a car in the east-bound lane on Route 22 hit the center divider, bounced over into the west-bound lane, landing on the front windshield of a vehicle in the west-bound lane. Not only was the driver of the first vehicle killed but the bittersweet aspect was that the family was riding with a baby who had been adopted only a day earlier.*
>
> *Three days later a van went off the road into a tree. The driver was killed. Several days after that a car careened off Route 22 and was lodged between two trees. Although the fire department offered additional assistance, the incident itself caused one death.*
>
> *Only a few days after, a call came from Watchung Reservation. While riding on a trail near Surprise Lake, a man had fallen from a horse. The squad was forced to drive the ambulance a half mile on the horse trail in order to approach the victim. The horse had suffered a heart attack and in the process of collapsing had thrown its rider to the ground.*

EDUCATION

Though Mountainside gained its independence in 1895, its first red-brick schoolhouse was built in 1900 at the cost of $3,448 by the combined boards of education of the town of Westfield and the borough of Mountainside. It wasn't until 1904, when the boards separated, that the school officially became the Mountainside Grammar School. It had two classrooms, two smaller rooms, two teachers with a combined salary of $1,000, an estimated budget of $1,163 and fifty students. Remodeled twenty years later, the school then had two more classrooms, two lavatories and a furnace. The building was located on the site of the present police headquarters.

In 1930, voters approved the purchase of one and a half acres of land adjoining the old schoolhouse. Five years later, with a Public Works Administration grant from Washington, taxpayers approved the projected $87,273 to build a new school adjacent to the old structure. Called the Echobrook School, it utilized the entire new structure, as well as space in the old building. By 1945, the school budget was $49,047, teachers' salaries were a total of $32,529 and 170 children attended classes.

In 1950, the borough purchased a twenty-two-acre site at $1,000 per acre on Central Avenue for a school, and construction began on Deerfield School. Opening in 1951, it was a one-story building with a new architectural feature: each classroom had an outer door leading to the play area. Additions in 1957, 1963 and 1968, as well as two portable classrooms in 1966, accommodated the growing school population.

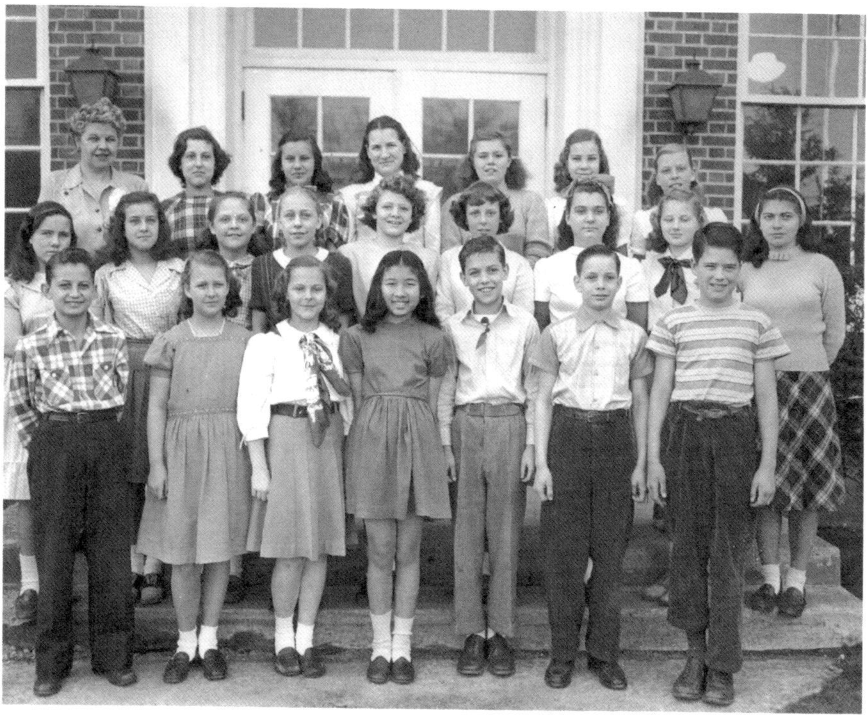

Miss Featherstone with students at Echobrook School, circa 1948. *Courtesy of the Mountainside Public Library.*

In 1954, the borough acquired property for a third school. That autumn, voters defeated a referendum for a new elementary school; however, the proposal passed the following year, and Beechwood School on Woodacres Drive was ready for occupancy in 1959. It would hold kindergarten through third grade, while Echobrook would house only fourth and fifth grades; the sixth, seventh and eighth grades remained at Deerfield. Over the next decade, realignment of the grade configuration among the three schools continued until the age of Echobrook and the noise of the nearby traffic made it increasingly difficult to maintain a sound educational program in the Route 22 building.

The phasing out of Echobrook began in 1973, when a Municipal Building Advisory Committee was formed. It recommended using the building as a municipal complex. The school officially closed in June 1974. A ten-year agreement was reached in 1975 between the council and the board of education for leasing Echobrook for borough purposes. The building was then renovated in the mid-1980s and finally demolished in 1995 to make way for renovations to Borough Hall, which was located in the addition to the original building.

Reorganization of the grade structure took place in 1976, with grades kindergarten through three calling Beechwood home and grades four through eight situated at Deerfield, and again in the early 1980s when the Deerfield building became overcrowded and fourth-grade classes were transferred to the Beechwood location.

A significant drop in school population necessitated the closing of Beechwood as a school for Mountainside residents in June 1982. By September of the same year, however, the Vail-Deane School, in Elizabeth since 1869, had leased the Beechwood building; it stayed there until 1991. For the next decade, Deerfield was Mountainside's sole functioning school, while the Beechwood building was occupied by both the Union County Educational Services Commission and the Morris-Union Jointure Committee at various times.

Then, in 2002, projected enrollment figures red-flagged the board of education to take Beechwood School back for the community. Construction to upgrade the facility began, and in January 2004 it reopened for the borough's students. Since that time, pre-kindergarten classes through second grade are housed at Beechwood, and grades three through eight call Deerfield home.

Union County Regional High School System

When Mountainside was part of the township of Westfield, and for decades after its incorporation, secondary students attended Westfield High School. In this case, there was consistency. However, in other Union County towns without their own high school, students might be shuttled from one high school to another. Often, when one of the receiving neighboring high schools reached maximum capacity, any one of these Union County towns was turned away and was forced to find a new educational venue for its students.

Because of this, in 1935 the municipalities of Berkeley Heights, Clark, Garwood, Kenilworth, Mountainside and Springfield formed the Union County High School Regional District #1 in order to provide stability and continuity for its high school population. Jonathan Dayton Regional High School was built in 1937 to accommodate students from these six towns. (Jonathan Dayton [1760–1824] was the youngest signer of the Constitution and later Speaker of the U.S. House of Representatives and a U.S. senator from New Jersey.) As the county's school population increased, three more schools were added to District #1: Arthur L. Johnson (1869–1955, first Union County superintendent of schools and a founder of Union County College) in 1956; Governor (William) Livingston (1723–1790, a signer of the Constitution and governor of New Jersey from 1776 to 1790) in 1960; and David Brearley (1745–1790, a signer of the Constitution and New Jersey Supreme Court justice from 1779 to 1789) in 1965.

Funding for the district's operation and later for construction of the other schools was apportioned among the six municipalities based on their tax ratables. From the outset of the system until 1960, Mountainside teenagers attended Jonathan Dayton. In 1960, Mountainside joined Berkeley Heights in sending students to the newly built Governor Livingston High School. This continued for seven school years, at which time overcrowding at GL forced Mountainside students to attend Jonathan Dayton for their freshman year. Each class for the next three years then completed high school at GL, known familiarly as their "home" school.

Bursting seams at GL served as a catalyst for another change. In the early 1970s until 1973, the borough's high schoolers all received their educations at Jonathan Dayton. This continued until 1993, when David Brearley High School in Kenilworth closed and its students were sent to Dayton. All incoming Mountainside freshmen at that time were sent to GL. (Anyone from Mountainside at JD was able to choose whether to stay there or complete his education at GL.) Since that period, every high school student has attended Governor Livingston High School.

By the early 1990s, Mountainside was contributing approximately 15 percent of the district's budget. Its governing body became concerned that the borough's per student share was disproportional to the shares of the other towns. In early 1994, with Mountainside as a catalyst, all participating communities except Garwood began the process to dissolve the regional district. Finally, on July 1, 1997, the Union County Regional District was dissolved. However, litigation continued for the next four years concerning the contributions of Mountainside and Garwood, the two towns not housing a high school within their borders. Each had invested in capital improvements to the buildings within the regional system, as well as to the original building costs of each school. The New Jersey Supreme Court ordered an equitable distribution of the liquid assets of the now dissolved Union County Regional District. Mountainside continues to send high school students to Governor Livingston High School, paying on a per student basis.

Anna Matko Reviews a Half Century in the Borough

Nonagenarian Anna Matko chose Mountainside as home not once but twice. In 1959, she and her husband, George, built a house on Barton Drive and moved in with their children, Susan, George Jr. and Betty.

Shortly after, George Sr. was transferred to Texas. The Barton Drive home was sold, the family was uprooted and off they went. The move was short-lived, and back came Anna and Susan in 1962 to buy another house. "There was no question about it," says Anna, who turned ninety-two in August 2008. "We wanted Mountainside because of the school system. I must tell you this because it's very important," she interjects without missing a beat. "A week from Wednesday [May 21, 2008] is my seventy-fifth high school [Hillside] reunion. It's at L'Affaire." (She was hoping to see her classmate Martha, who now lives in Scotch Plains, as well as "a Hillside fellow.")

Born in Newark and raised in Hillside, Anna taught at the Hurden-Looker Elementary School in Hillside for ten years before marrying in 1944. "Then I had three children and stayed home for twenty years. Married women didn't work in those days. I taught Sunday school."

With her oldest going off to college, Anna decided that extra money would certainly help out, so she put her name on the substitute list at Echobrook School. The very next day, she was called to fill in for three days. "It was a stroke of luck that one of the teachers was Jewish, and it was Rosh Hashanah, and there I was."

The following summer, she was called for an interview. She remembers, "Dr. Hanigan came to my house to interview me because I had told the secretary I didn't have a car that day." How unusual—a superintendent of schools making a house call! Anna taught for thirteen years in Mountainside. "I always taught third grade. They never put me back, but they never promoted me either," she jokes.

Twenty years had passed since Anna taught at the Hurden-Looker School. "In Hillside we had a free milk program, and we collected clothing for some of the children. Every boy had to wear a white shirt and tie," she recollects. "If he didn't have a tie, they'd give him a paper tie." Times had changed. Children had changed. "One of the first things I said to my class in Mountainside was 'I'm going to teach you manners.'" Apparently, that sat well with her students because she still receives Christmas cards from numerous former pupils.

Anna remembers the new buildings and additions and the school closings, and she credits a former mayor with saving Beechwood School. "Thank God for Fred Wilhelms," she posits. "He wouldn't sell the property, and the Board of Education also was forward-looking, maintaining the building as an educational facility." Anna retired in 1983 after twenty-three years in education.

Ninety-two-year-old Anna Matko thinks fondly about many of her former colleagues. One in particular is Joan Krystow. "Joan and I used to team teach," she says. "She had math because she's a Cornell graduate. I did the social studies. She and I made a great team."

Board of Education

The board is composed of seven members elected by the voters. Two members are elected the first year, two the second year and three the third year. All terms run for three years. Each year, the board presents a school budget based on a careful study of the schools' needs for the following year. Following a public hearing where questions are answered about the line items, the public votes on the budget during the annual School Budget Election.

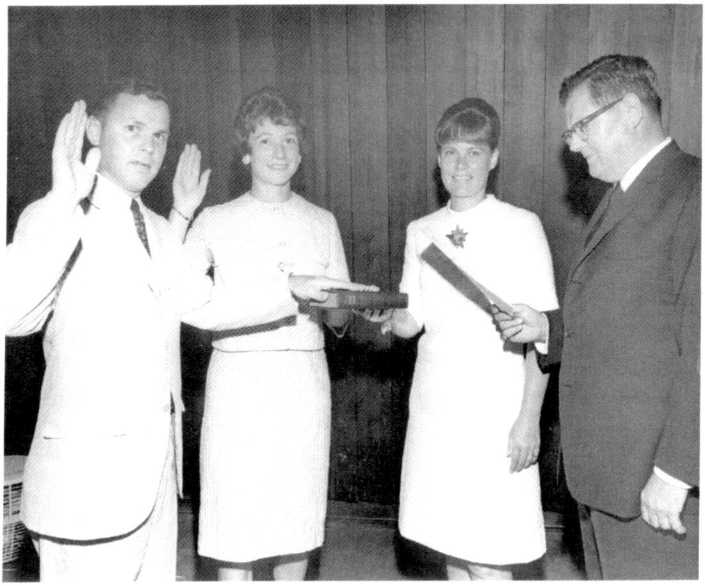

The oath of office administered to new members Donald L. Jeka and Gloria S. Johnson. Don's wife, Yvonne, holds the Bible as Board Secretary John McDonough officiates, July 11, 1967. *Courtesy of the Mountainside Board of Education.*

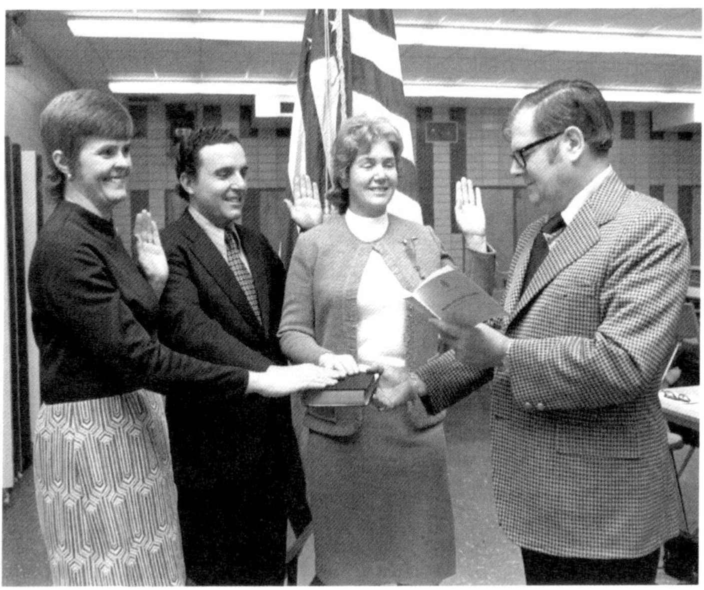

Board Secretary John McDonough administers the oath to new board of education members Patricia Knodel, Irvin Krause and Gertrude Palmer, February 20, 1973. *Courtesy of the Mountainside Board of Education.*

Pat Knodel

Pat Knodel has had a hand and a voice in the borough's educational system for more than fifty years. Starting as a teacher at Deerfield School shortly after it opened in 1952, Pat taught for three years before starting her own family of eight children. When they were on the road to adulthood, she then spent a total of twenty-nine years on Mountainside's board of education.

In 1971, when she ran for a seat on the board of education, only 6 percent of the members of New Jersey's local school boards were women. By the late 1980s, the number of females participating was up to 24 percent. Pat's candidacy always seemed to have an impact on voter turnout in Mountainside. She says, "In elections, controversy brings out voters. It stirs their interest in education. The turnout whenever I ran was usually about 30 percent of those eligible to vote."

She continues, "Mountainside has been fortunate to have many citizens willing to serve as members of the board of education. All believed in providing our Mountainside students with a quality education, although they sometimes disagreed on the best way to operate the school system efficiently. But this healthy disagreement has resulted in alerting the public to the importance of education and has produced a voter turnout often double the state average."

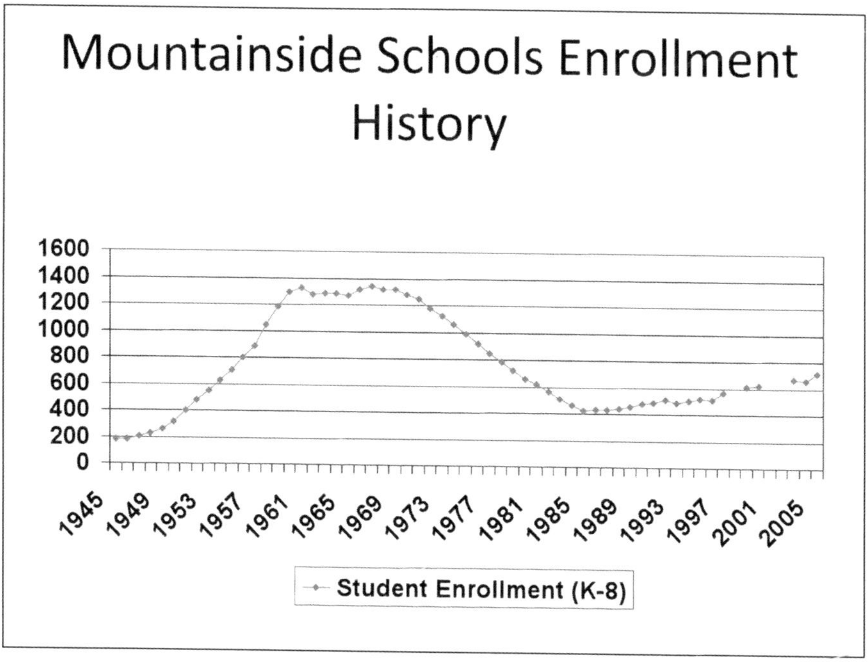

Religion

Strikingly dissimilar in appearance, the three houses of worship in Mountainside have amazingly kindred intents and goals, as do the parishioners who attend the respective services. Each of the Christian houses seeks to round out and complement the lifestyles of those in the community.

Mountainside Gospel Chapel

By far the oldest, Mountainside Gospel Chapel began as a Sunday school in a private home (the Badgley House) in 1821 and then moved to a schoolhouse in 1825. (Known later as the Bee-Hive, this building served the community for both religious and secular instruction.) The midafternoon, multigenerational Sunday school continued until 1862, when according to a church history written by Dewey Knoll, who was born on his family's farm on Central Avenue and was a lifelong member of the church, "Sunday school was discontinued because of the displacement of many of its members and to the effects of the Civil War." In 1871, it was reorganized as the Locust Grove Union Sunday School and met in a new schoolhouse set back from Springfield Road, now Route 22, near today's location of the Mountainside Community Pool.

A donation of land by Kate B. High in 1893 gave the nondenominational congregation a permanent home. Known as the Locust Grove Union Chapel, it was dedicated in 1901, and the first evening service was held in the new chapel at that time. Circuit, or traveling, pastors preached until 1909, when the first pastor was engaged to preach on alternate Sundays. In 1911, the name was changed to the Mountainside Union Chapel. When Route 29 was widened in 1929 to incorporate a westbound lane, the chapel location became an island. The building remained in the center island until 1973, when state plans to again widen and improve the highway, known as Route 22 by then, forced the congregation to move.

The state eventually demolished the original structure and converted the Route 22 site to a highway department service area. Before that destruction, two of the chapel's original stained-glass windows, a large wooden cross and the bell were rescued. All now reside in the current building on Spruce Drive, the land for which was donated by the Conrad (owner of Oak Tree Florist on Route 22) and Hoppe (original owners of Hotel 29) families. Groundbreaking was in September 1972, and the new $600,000 building on Spruce Drive was dedicated on April 28, 1974.

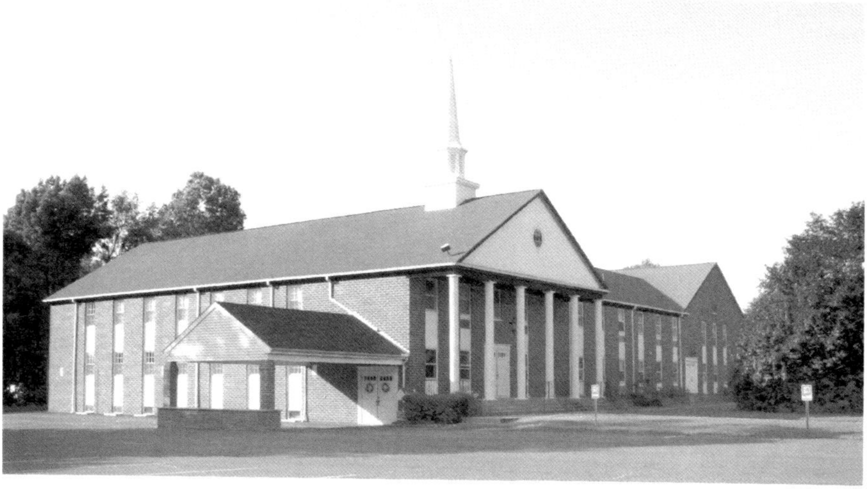

Mountainside Gospel Chapel. *Courtesy of Mountainside Gospel Chapel.*

Until 1959, the Sunday school and the chapel were separate entities with a superintendent presiding over the former. The Sunday school had been totally self-supporting. In fact, on occasion it contributed to the support of the chapel. In addition, the Sunday school maintained an extensive missions program, collecting money for missionaries and sending its own missionaries out to the mission field. Among those Mountainside-resident missionaries were Lois Knoll Gothman, Robert Curtiss and Carol Rumpf. In 1959, the chapel assumed jurisdiction over the Sunday school. Each February, parishioners celebrate the founding of the Sunday school.

Sandy Goense Wilson, secretary at the chapel and lifelong Mountainside resident, recalls her childhood:

> *If you wanted your kids to go to Sunday school, a bus rented by our church from Somerset Bus Company would pick them up. My mother would let us* [the Goense children] *wait at the end of the driveway so we could get the bus even though the Chapel was only down the street. She used to laugh because often we'd ask her if we could go sleep over at a friend's house on Saturday night so we could ride the bus longer on Sunday morning.*

Programs for the youth have always been important for the Mountainside Gospel Chapel. For several decades near the end of the twentieth century, three different groups met weekly. The Tree Climbers included children and dads who met on Sunday afternoons for Bible study and recreational outings. The Pioneers Girls' Club and the Boys' Brigade met with volunteer leaders to work on badges earned by providing services to the community. Camping experiences in the summer months rounded out the diversified activities. Junior and senior high school youth groups still meet once a week.

The Vacation Bible School is a major outreach method. Designed to teach the basic Christian tenets, it attracts children from not only surrounding communities but also the shore and western New Jersey. MOPS (Mothers of Preschoolers) brings women together for monthly Bible study, crafts and socialization. Their youngsters are divided into age-related groups and are occupied in activities simultaneously.

A Thanksgiving food drive and a Christmas White-Gift Sunday are two of the charitable projects of the chapel. The latter, where all gifts are wrapped in white so that all are equal in the eyes of the Lord, are distributed to prison fellowship, needy families and soldiers in hospitals.

In 2006, Mountainside Gospel Chapel counted one hundred families as part of its membership.

Community Presbyterian Church

Following World War II, Mountainside's farmlands began to be replaced by single-family houses. One of the developers near Deer Path set aside a four-and-a-half-acre piece of property as a clean-fill site because it was the lowest piece of property on which he was working. He named the street Meeting House Lane. According to Reverend Christopher Belden, pastor of the Community Presbyterian Church since 1986, "The contractor said he would give this property to a religious group, but it had to be one of the mainline Protestant denominations." So a group of men, led by Walter Rupp, conducted a door-to-door survey, attempting to determine whether another church was needed in the community and what type was preferred.

"The largest number was interested in a Presbyterian church," says Belden, "so the canvassers approached what was then the synod of New Jersey with their request to start a church in Mountainside."

A Presbyterian church was founded in 1954. The Reverend Delwyn Rayson, who assisted in organizing the church, was selected as the first pastor. On April 25, he conducted the first worship service at Deerfield School; 120 adults and 30 children attended. Members continued to worship at the school auditorium until the construction of a church building to house

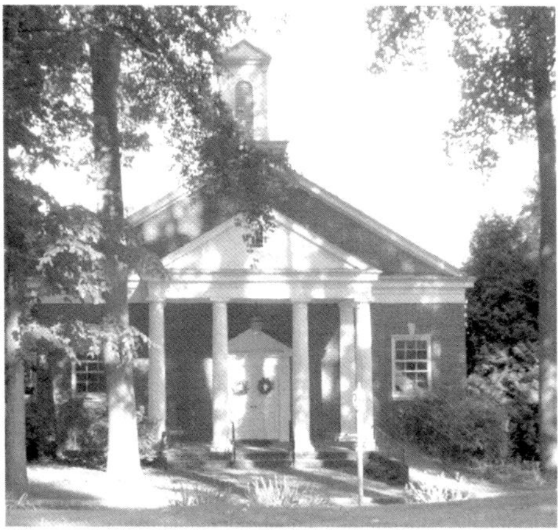

Community Presbyterian Church. *Courtesy of Mountainside Gospel Chapel.*

the congregation of 205 was completed. In 1956, the building was ready for occupancy, and on November 4, barely two years after it all began, the congregants held their first Sunday morning service in the new church. Membership had grown to 400 by that time.

Sunday school classes began shortly thereafter. The grade schoolers were housed in the church basement, but there wasn't room for the high school section. Jeanne and Fred Wilhelms, members of the church, held four levels of classes in their home each Sunday for over two years. In October 1960, when a new addition for the Christian Education Program was ready for occupancy, the entire Sunday school convened in the new building.

Reverend Elmer A. Talcott became the pastor early in 1961 and served until 1986. He remembers that Henry Grassman, who gave the land to the Presbyterian Church, wanted a colonial church to blend in with the community, including cedar shingles on the roof rather than tile. Miles Goodrich made all the furniture for the sanctuary, including the pulpit, the baptismal font and hymn rack and the bookcases for the church parlor.

Talcott describes his early years at the church:

> *The Kennedy era was an era of hope. When JFK died, I said, "We have to go to church." We had an 8:00 p.m. service that evening. Louise Armstrong, a professional singer from Westfield, called and said, "I have to sing. I'll sit in the balcony, if I have to." Walter Legovias, a violinist, also called. He wanted to play. The church was jammed that evening.*

The Community Presbyterian Church, like other religious institutions, has seen ebbs and flows in membership. Reverend Belden's analysis of such trends follows:

> *Following the social unrest of the '60s, church membership in most denominations has been sliding. People have become "unchurched" as our*

society has become more secular. The church, like the community, goes through cycles. There's another factor in congregations of our size: I call it "the bump in the snake." You get groups of kids; then they go off to college; membership shrinks. It grows again. In a larger congregation there is enough of a mix of ages so it averages out. In a small congregation you get these lumps.

In 1976, the church added a new wing consisting of a garage and a choir room. By 1970, the church membership had grown to 638, and by the turn of the century, well over 300 parishioners were counted among those attending services at the Community Presbyterian Church.

The Sunday school program, which now extends from nursery school age through eighth grade, is still functioning, as is a preschool, which was also started in the 1950s. It welcomes seventy-five children between the ages of two and a half and five years of age each school year. It is open to those of all faiths and, according to the pastor, is "a big mix" of ethnicities and religions.

Annual events include a food drive at Thanksgiving to benefit the needy in the area and housing the homeless for a week in the summer. "In the winter," says Reverend Belden, "we help other churches. In the time I've been here we've become much more involved in ministering to the homeless. I think that's been a problem that's been growing in Union County for the last twenty years, and we've been trying to respond to that."

Recollections on Community Presbyterian Church on the Occasion of its Tenth Anniversary
Walter Rupp, Founding Member

It all really began before most of our young community was aware of it, but the first productive meeting was held in Borough Hall on February 12, 1954, with representatives of the Synod, National Missions, and several residents of Mountainside who were members of other churches in surrounding communities. This meeting was initiated by Tom Hyde of the planning board.

Mountainside at that time boasted of 1,300 families. The first step, of course, was to see whether or not the people would support a new church, and if so, what kind? Obviously, house-to-house canvassing was called for, and in a little over a month some 1850 people were visited. Omitting those who chose to make no change—which included 513 Catholics, 28 of the Jewish faith and 155 from the highway chapel—there were 457 who said they would definitely support a Presbyterian church…With these results in, it was "full speed ahead."

Two major events involving every member of the church were high points of 1957. Our decision to adopt a German refugee family was by far the most significant and rewarding. George and Kati John and their two daughters, Angelika and Heidi, arrived in this country and became our sole responsibility. What fun it was helping to get them settled in a little house on Summit Road, gather together some possessions and get George situated in a suitable job. These people were like a fresh breath of air. They helped themselves more than anyone helped them and became our fast friends and good neighbors in no time at all. They were a welcome addition to our church and to our community as well.

The other project was precipitated by our need to stop sloshing in the mud in the back parking lot and get at least some crushed stone put on it. Empty coffers brought us to consider a single additional fundraising effort. A Smorgasbord dinner was planned for which we would sell tickets to the public and which would personally require the involvement of each of our four hundred members, either with a donation of food or labor—and, in most cases, both.

Countless hundreds of Swedish meatballs rolled out of our downstairs kitchen and into freezers until the big night—June 15. Salads and casseroles by the dozens were prepared. To put it mildly, it surpassed our wildest dreams!

June 15 was the hottest night of the year, and the Smorgasbord at the Community Presbyterian Church was the hottest affair in town. Everyone enjoyed it, but probably none as much as the actual workers. The words "church smorgasbord" will bring a reminiscent chuckle from any who were involved to this day. After expenses, we cleared over a thousand dollars for our parking lot.

Our Lady of Lourdes

In the mid-1950s, local Catholics were blazing a parallel path in establishing a new church. Until that time they were part of the parish of St. James in Springfield. Ten acres of land on Central Avenue purchased from Henry Weber, whose family had farmed in the area for many years, would be the site of Our Lady of Lourdes. Until the church was built, parishioners worshipped in the auditorium at Deerfield School. On March 17, 1957, Father Aloysius Carney, pastor of St. James, said the first Mass for what was then known as the Mission of St. James.

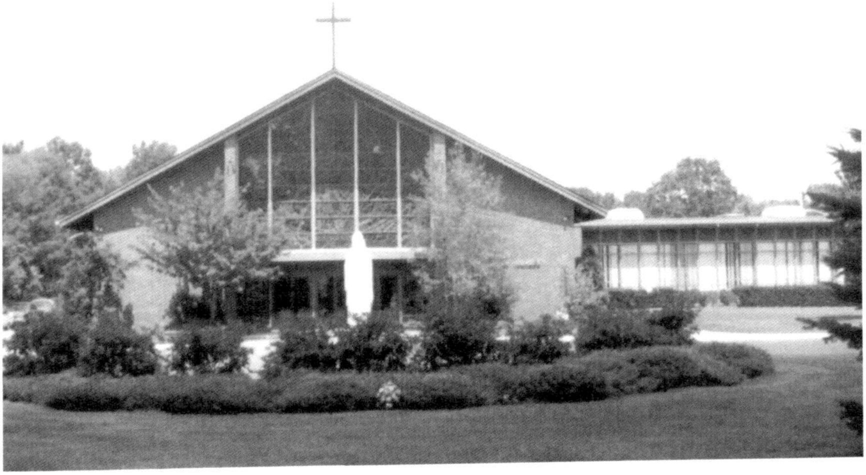

Our Lady of Lourdes Roman Catholic Church. *Courtesy of Mountainside Gospel Chapel.*

Longtime resident Loretta Ryan tells of the casual manner in which she became an officer of the Rosary Society when it was founded in 1957:

> *Gertrude Suski called me and said, "We'd like you to be president of the Rosary Society. Actually we picked you and we picked Kitty Ziegler. We'll put your names in a hat, and whosever name is drawn will be president. The other will be vice-president." That's how Kitty became president, and I became vice-president.*

This women's group met at the Elks Club until the church was ready in 1961. Fashion shows, fish and chips dinners and pancake breakfasts were instituted way back then.

In 1958, the Archdiocese of Newark established a yet unnamed parish in Mountainside and appointed Father Gerard J. McGarry as the founding pastor on December 13, 1958. Archbishop Thomas A. Boland asked that Father McGarry select a name for the new parish. Because 1958 was the centenary of Our Lady's appearance at Lourdes in France, Father McGarry requested that the new church be named Our Lady of Lourdes.

McGarry immediately began plans for building a church, a school and an all-purpose building. A one-day drive on December 6, 1959, by 180 men of the parish raised more than $230,000 in pledges toward the estimated $600,000 cost of the structure. Several days later, the parish was incorporated.

Religious instruction and preparation for sacraments were conducted in the Deerfield auditorium after the Masses. Confessions were held in an adjoining locker room. A census conducted in February 1959 counted 573 families in the new parish.

Groundbreaking ceremonies took place on Sunday, May 15, 1960. It is known that Father McGarry worked closely with Alphonso Alvarez, the architect, and strove for two key notes in the modern-style structure: simplicity and utility. Construction began on July 7. The first Mass in the new structure was said on July 23, 1961, by Father McGarry. The official dedication ceremony was on September 9, 1961. In the early days, the rectory and convent were located at 1220 and 1222 Wyoming Avenue, respectively. By early 1965, 830 families were registered in the church.

In his notes on the beginnings of the parish, Father McGarry recalled the first Christmas in the two-week-old church as

> *exhilarating, with Masses at midnight and in the morning* [in the Deerfield school auditorium]. *An organ was hired from Altenburg's* [piano house in Elizabeth], *and the choir of St Mary's Academy* [Mount St. Mary's in Watchung] *sang for us. A Christmas manger was made by George Benninger (who became our first custodian). The altar used in the auditorium was designed by Mrs. Gloria Johnson* [a local artist]. *On Christmas we distributed 759 Communions. (One priest; no Eucharistic ministers then.)*

Joan Bieszczak and Linda Esemplare recall that Father McGarry designed and made the original wooden cross that hung above the altar in the new church starting in 1961. In addition, when he came to the church, McGarry donated a statue that became known as the pilgrim statue because it was—and still is—a traveling statue. It resides in someone's home for a week and then travels to the home of another parishioner. The cabinet for the pilgrim statue was made by Joan's husband, John.

In September 1961, four classrooms were opened to children in grades one through four. An additional grade was opened each successive year until the parochial school comprised eight grades. Thirty years later, the school merged with two Westfield churches, Holy Trinity and St. Helen's, to form Holy Trinity Inter-Parochial School

When Father McGarry retired in 1978, Monsignor Raymond J. Pollard was appointed his successor and continued as pastor until he retired in 1995. Monsignor Richard Groncki served Our Lady of Lourdes for a short period until Father Patrick J. Leonard came on board as the fourth pastor in 1996. In 2003, Father John McCrone, who had been ordained at Our Lady of Lourdes in 1982, became the fifth pastor of the church. In 2007, Our Lady of Lourdes had a membership of 1,125 families.

Mountainside Public Library

Started in 1934 at Borough Hall through the efforts of Mrs. Henry C. Weber with several shelves built by a resident, a bookcase purchased from a thrift shop for fifteen dollars and donated books, the Mountainside Public Library underwent a number of transformations during the mid-twentieth century on its way to becoming the quality institution it is today. A move to a classroom in the Echobrook School building on Route 22 in 1938 and then to the basement of the building in 1941, each providing larger quarters, still did not fill the needs of a growing community.

Forced to close for a time in 1940 due to sporadic help, the library was not yet municipally funded and continually faced financial crises. Maintained through membership fees, fundraisers and donations, it depended also on its inclusion in the Community Fund budget for sustenance. In 1941, with an average daily circulation of twenty-five books, the board of trustees requested that the borough allocate funds for book purchases and the librarian's wages (which by 1949 were $600 per year). This arrangement continued for the next twenty years. The library was then a privately operated institution, by which the borough council was not obligated by law to give any specific amount of money for its maintenance.

As early as 1945, when the library housed 2,500 books and free space was dear, the board of trustees began to discuss a free-standing library building, as well as further financial assistance. The discussions went on for well over a decade. In 1961, voters approved a public referendum that transferred the responsibility of operating the library to the municipality. State law mandated a specified number of dollars for the maintenance of the library. In 1966, construction on a new building started. The dedication of the 10,343-square-foot library was held on February 12, 1968.

By 1970, the library boasted eighty periodicals, two local and two national newspapers, a collection of over 24,000 books with an average daily circulation of 360 and almost five thousand registered library members. The latest tally counts over 53,000 volumes, more than one hundred subscriptions to newspapers and magazines and nearly eight thousand DVDs, videos, compact discs and audio books to complement technological advances of the late twentieth and early twenty-first centuries. Internet services, interlibrary loans and adult and children's programs are examples of the services that round out the library's offerings.

Occupying a wall in the adult reading area is the Harry & Wende Devlin Collection, a museum-like celebration of the lives of two of Mountainside's most prominent residents. Writers and artists, the Devlins are known not only in their own community but also in the literary and art worlds for their children's stories, books on architecture and illustrations.

Friends of the Library, which started in 1959, is a support and fundraising group of volunteers that has supplemented library offerings with speakers from the New Jersey Council for the Humanities, guest authors, book discussion groups, Shakespeare summer theatre productions and programs geared to various age levels from babies and preschoolers to youngsters—and beyond.

The 2006 budget of $620,000 is a far cry from the fledgling one-room operation of the late 1930s that relied on contributions for survival. A paid staff of twelve, including three full-time employees, must have been unimaginable to Emily Hoffarth, Mountainside's first full-time librarian, who ran the original library for many years as a one-woman force.

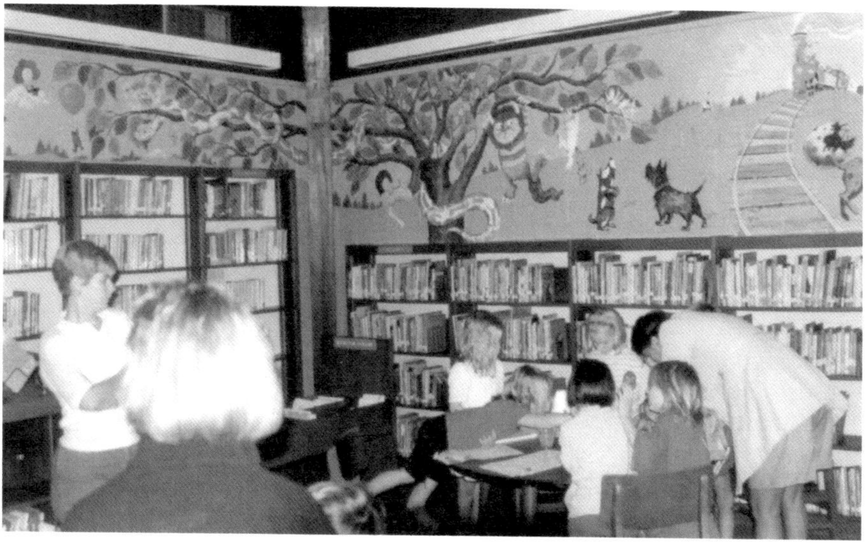

A library mural highlighting some favorite children's literature. *Courtesy of the Mountainside Public Library.*

The Librarian "Who Came to Dinner"

Like so many of the "pioneers" of the mid-twentieth century, Emily Hoffarth arrived in Mountainside with her husband and two young daughters, leaving the familiarity of city life and facing the unknowns of a future in central New Jersey. In 1940, when General Motors transferred her husband, Elmer, from Yonkers, New York, to its plant in Linden, Emily sent everything on ahead except for the clock above the mantle and the children's goldfish. She remembered "sitting in the car with the clock clutched to me and the goldfish slopping all over and tears streaming down my face. The goldfish died and the clock never ran again, but we survived the ordeal and found Mountainside to be one of the nicest places we could have asked for."

The original town library was located in a small room in the basement of Echobrook School, and in 1946, when the librarian left, Emily was recommended to fill in until a full-time librarian could be hired. And that is the beginning of Mountainside's version of Moss Hart and George S. Kaufman's *The Man Who Came to Dinner*.

With Elmer becoming Mountainside's first full-time employee as the borough tax collector and treasurer in 1949, and Emily the first full-time librarian in 1952, the couple became even more entrenched in local workings and history. Emily added to her agenda traveling between Deerfield and Echobrook schools with a portable library to meet students' educational needs. Because of transportation difficulties, it was not considered safe to have children make the trip to the library, which was located on then Route 29. "Most of the children have good books at home," Mrs. Hoffarth said in 1952, "but they prefer to use the library books even though some of them are battered and worn." Hoffarth added story hours for the lower grades in the early 1950s, and at the beginning of the school year in 1951, each class had a regularly scheduled library period each week.

In 1957, the New Jersey Board of Education awarded her a professional librarian certificate. Years later, when it was time to move to a modern, free-standing facility on Constitution Plaza, Emily remarked, "You really feel like a mole coming out of the old library. Now the sun is like a benediction."

The city girl from Yonkers took root in the growing soil of Mountainside and blossomed with her family. She found it a "generous, warm-hearted town." Emily Hoffarth, who passed away in 1990 at the age of eighty-five, was the interim employee who stayed on the job for twenty-five years.

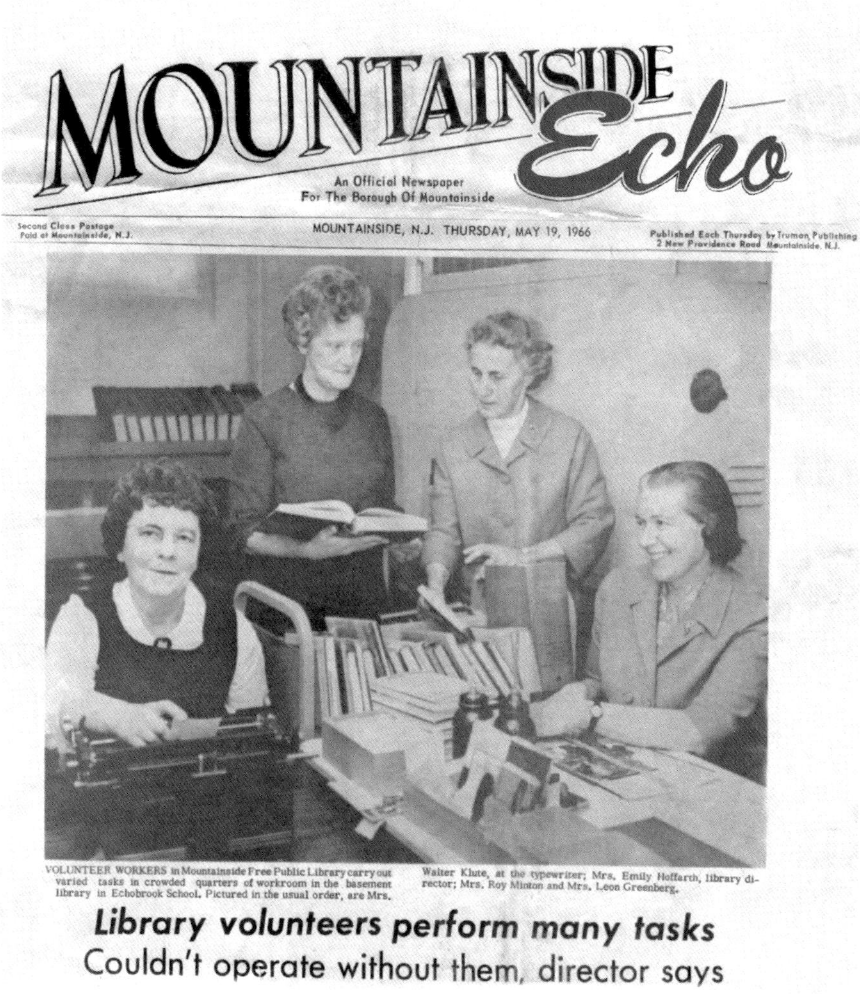

MOUNTAINSIDE Echo

An Official Newspaper
For The Borough Of Mountainside

Second Class Postage
Paid at Mountainside, N.J.

MOUNTAINSIDE, N.J. THURSDAY, MAY 19, 1966

Published Each Thursday by Truman Publishing
2 New Providence Road Mountainside, N.J.

VOLUNTEER WORKERS in Mountainside Free Public Library carry out varied tasks in crowded quarters of workroom in the basement library in Echobrook School. Pictured in the usual order, are Mrs. Walter Klute, at the typewriter; Mrs. Emily Hoffarth, library director; Mrs. Roy Minton and Mrs. Leon Greenberg.

Library volunteers perform many tasks

Couldn't operate without them, director says

A copy of the *Mountainside Echo* paper highlighting library volunteers in the crowded quarters of a workroom in the basement library in Echobrook School in 1966. Pictured are Mrs. Walter Klute, Mrs. Emily Hoffarth (library director), Mrs. Roy Minton and Mrs. Leon Greenberg. *Courtesy of the* Mountainside Echo.

The Storybook Pair

It's exceedingly difficult to tell where the fictional and artistic lives of Harry and Wende Devlin left off and where their personal and family lives began; the two aspects were so deeply intertwined. The couple, who met at Syracuse University and married in 1941, became for Mountainside and much of the world outside its boundaries the epitome of a picture-perfect relationship in both business and marriage.

Seven children and an assortment of animals—including geese, poodles, a cat and a donkey—created a jubilant and lively environment around the Devlin three-acre enclave on the Westfield/Mountainside border. While the parents painted and wrote children's books together in their studios, the neighborhood youngsters delighted in playing with the Devlin offspring where there seemed to be loads of time for nurturing, encouragement and just plain fun. "It was just an environment steeped with joy and artistic celebration," son Jeffrey recalls.

Harry, who started as a navy artist and later worked as a cartoonist while Wende painted portraits of children, joined his wife to create a cartoon strip, *Full House*, based on their life with their brood of seven. The name of the comic strip changed to *Raggmopp* when a poodle, based on the Devlins' dog, joined the cast of characters.

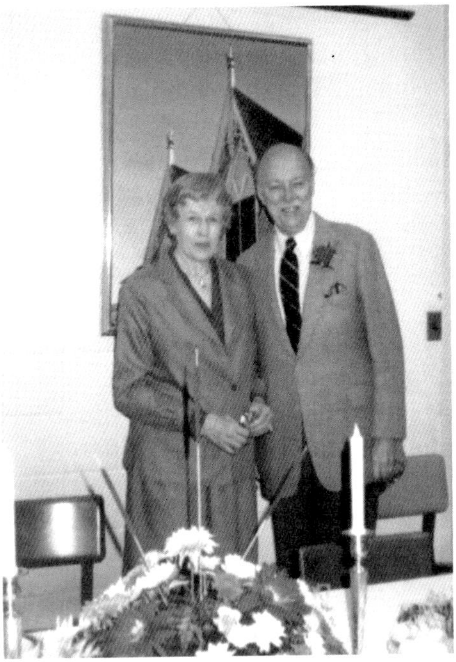

Wende and Harry Devlin, September 30, 1984. "The Friends are honoring Harry Devlin because he has enriched the lives of us all by so willingly and generously giving of his time and talent to the community life and spirit of Mountainside." *Courtesy of Friends of the Library.*

In 1963, the pair began their collaboration on twenty-eight children's books. She wrote the stories; he illustrated and edited them. *Old Black Witch*, their first joint venture in literature, became a children's classic. It also broke new ground. During the '50s, children's editors were influenced by a trend that promulgated only stories in which nothing bad happened. "They wanted what we call 'angel fluffs'—nobody got hurt, nobody fell down, nobody said anything that wasn't politically correct," Harry said.

The Devlins' tale was about an enraged witch who rode her broomstick through a window and a little boy who wasn't afraid and took her antics in stride. "We sent it to the leading children's editor in New York. She sent it back with a letter longer than the

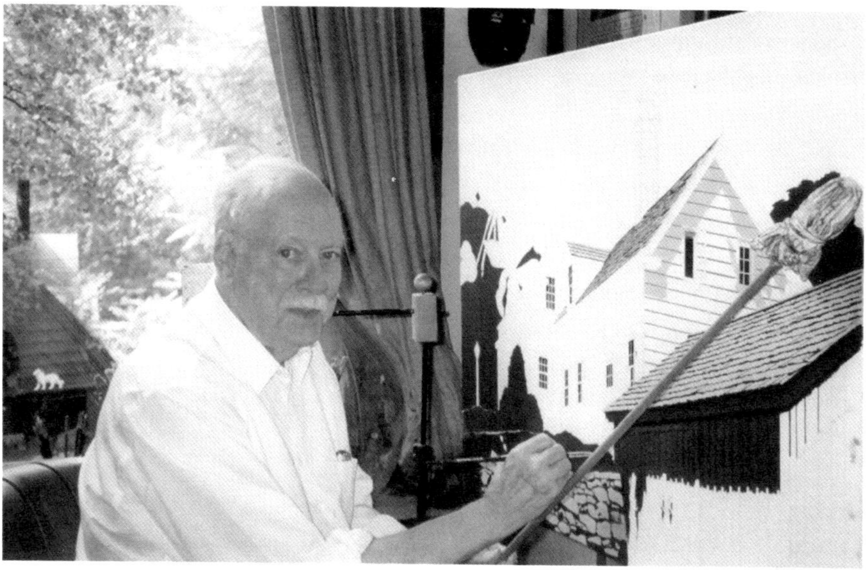

Harry Devlin painting in his studio, 1998. *Courtesy of Wende Devlin Gates.*

book," Wende said in 1992. The editor didn't like the broken glass and, more than that, the witch's language. "'Giblets!' sounded too much like a swear word to her," Wende added. Subsequently, a friend showed the manuscript to the editor-in-chief of *Encyclopedia Britannica*, who printed it. By 1992, 1.5 million copies had been sold. "It put the kids through college," Mr. Devlin said.

The writers later launched the Cranberry series of children's books. These and others provided fodder for American moviemakers of the late twentieth century. *How Fletcher Was Hatched*, a story about a hound dog who feels forgotten after the little girl who loves him turns her attention to a brood of hatchling chicks, was selected by former first lady Barbara Bush to read on her literacy campaign. In winning the little girl back, the hound shows how love triumphs against all odds.

Both the Devlins were portrait painters. Wende's talents also lent themselves to still life, while Harry "saved" American architecture by preserving our heritage of structures and style on canvas. He used many of these paintings to illustrate his books *To Grandfather's House We Go* and *What Kind of House is That?* In 1989, he published *Portraits of American Architecture: Monuments to a Romantic Mood*, a book filled with his paintings of old homes accompanied by his own text.

Wende and Harry Devlin played active roles in promoting the arts in New Jersey, always available to speak and judge at art and literary events while continuing to paint and write. In 1995, they served as grand marshals of Mountainside's centennial parade. The couple observed their sixtieth wedding anniversary in 2001. Shortly after, Harry died at the age of eighty-three. Wende passed away nine months later at eighty-four. Daughter Wende Gates remarked on the couple's sharing of their lives and professions by saying, "I think my mother wanted to celebrate her sixty-first anniversary with my father. She wanted to be with him." Mountainside remains grateful to the longtime residents for sharing their lives with the community.

ORGANIZED RECREATION

With checks of $100 each from the Deerfield Student Council and the Mountainside Music Association, a $400 donation from the Newcomers Club and promised funds from the town budget, the first recreation commission became a reality on June 11, 1963. An ordinance calling for a board of seven commissioners—all to serve on a voluntary basis without compensation—was passed. Planning for a six-week summer program to be held at Deerfield School began immediately.

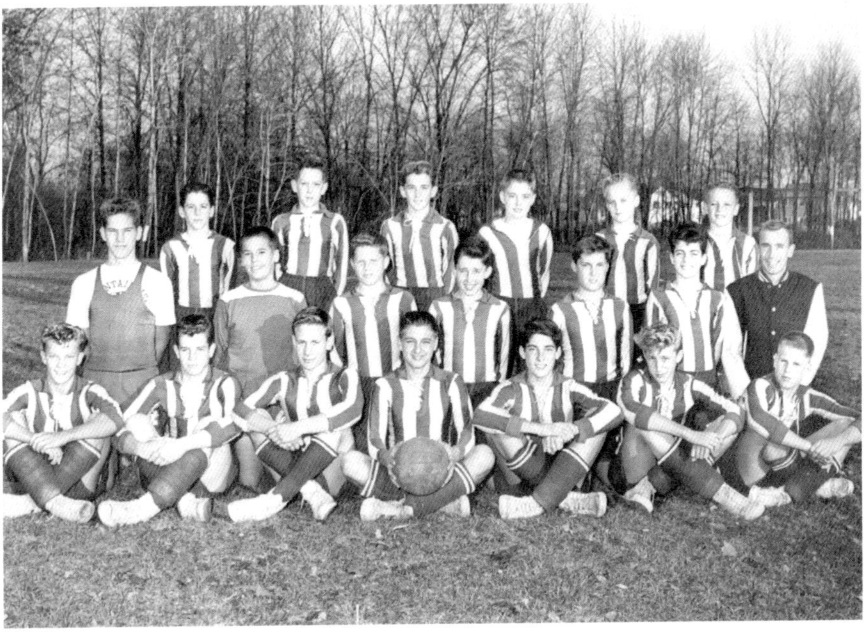

The 1960 varsity soccer team, with Coach Ollie Dean. *Courtesy of Richard Benninger.*

When the playground opened on July 8 with Joseph Pucillo at the helm, along with two other paid supervisors, more than five hundred boys and girls from first grade through high school attended. Morning activities consisted of athletics, including softball, horseshoes and volleyball, while afternoons focused on specialty events, such as a variety of arts and crafts, instruction in baton and golf and quiet games and storytelling. An article appearing in the *Westfield Leader* late in the summer reported that youngsters at the playground made handcrafted gifts for patients at Children's Specialized Hospital: stuffed clowns from brightly colored scraps of cloth and piggy banks designed from plastic jugs were turned over to Martha VanWert, hospital executive director, for distribution to the children.

Off to a strong start with Richard F. Collins as commission chairman, the group had tennis courts ready near Deerfield School at a cost of $665 for lining and installation before the summer ended. Activities such as canteens and gym nights on Friday evenings, as well as square dancing at an entrance cost of twenty-five cents, soon followed.

Following a successful first summer playground season in 1963, Mayor Orlin E. Johnson presented certificates to two sixteen-year-olds for volunteer supervisory work. Susan Winans, of Outlook Drive, and Dorothy Locke, of Garrett Road, received commendation that they had "served with initiative and sincerity and furthered the cause of good government and community service in Mountainside."

By the autumn of 1964, the recreation commission recommended to the borough council that "serious consideration be given to construction of a municipal pool," according to a story in the *Elizabeth Journal* on October 17 of that year. Response to a questionnaire indicated that more than six hundred families favored such a pool and would join. And so the Mountainside Community Pool opened on Saturday, July 30, 1966. (See the next section for additional information on the evolution of the pool.)

During the Vietnam years, the immediate family of someone on active duty with the armed forces was entitled to free membership in the pool. That protocol is still followed.

The late '60s saw the introduction of Saturday morning basketball and weekend ski trips throughout the winter months. In 1970, Jim Green became the first paid recreation supervisor; Nancy Pollack replaced him in 1971, followed by Sue Winans in 1974. Each of the three held part-time positions. It wasn't until 1975 that Winans became a full-time recreation director. Winans, who served in this spot until 2005, recalls that "the '70s were dominated by tennis: children, adults, lessons, tournaments, parties,

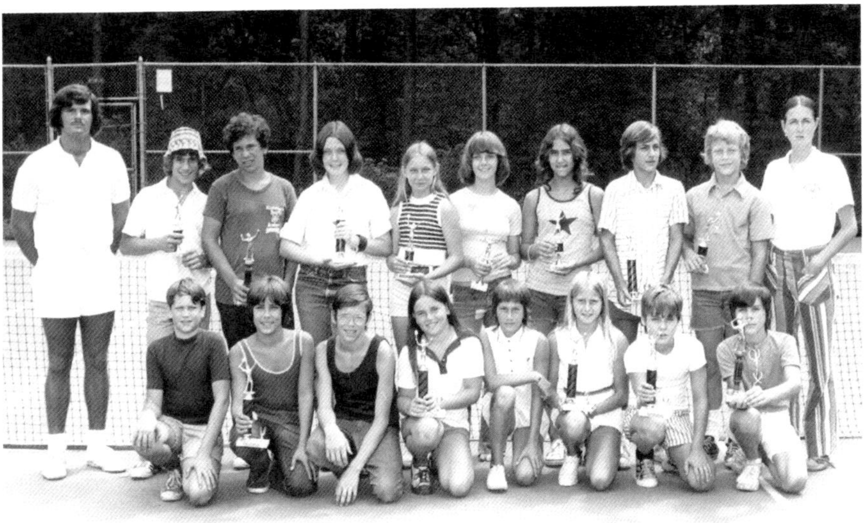

Tops on the courts—summer tournament winners in the early 1970s. *Courtesy of the Mountainside Recreation Department.*

people standing and waiting to get a court." Interest in the sport at that time reached nationwide and farther, she remembers.

Midget football, soccer, a variety of adult sports activities and trips—museum and theatre trips to New York City, baseball trips to Yankee and Shea Stadiums, senior citizen day trips—joined the roster. Population, both resident and school age, was up and so were the number and variety of things to do in the borough.

The late 1970s and early 1980s witnessed a change in demographics. The town was growing up, moms returned to the workforce and parent volunteerism declined. Such developments were catalysts for rethinking in the recreational field. For starters, nonresidents were accepted for membership in the Mountainside Community Pool in 1976. In the early '80s, rock 'n' roll dances for adults were held at the Elks Club. Then, in 1986, a preschool playground was built on the field near Deerfield School to prepare for a new wave of young homeowners and their children. In the '90s, the children's sports programs were expanded to include younger age groups.

A joint venture of the Borough of Mountainside, Children's Specialized Hospital and the County of Union, the Echo Lake Fitness Trail became a reality on June 22, 1985, less than two years following its inception. At nine-tenths of a mile in length (4,603 feet), it includes eighteen par course stations (individual exercises are spread out over eighteen stations along the track; the course is designed with warm-up and stretching exercises, followed by those that are more challenging and ending with cool-down varieties) and ten game-field wheel course stations with instructions on proper use and cardiovascular benefits. Adding to the tranquility of the surroundings, a sixty-foot, maintenance-free footbridge spans a stream and overlooks a wooded extension of Echo Lake Park immediately behind Children's Specialized Hospital. The walking, jogging and exercise facility is readily accessible to its patients via a path to the trail and to local residents with ingress and egress at each terminus.

For the next ten years or so, renovations and enhancements to recreation in Mountainside garnered the attention of those in charge. Changes at the pool started with a wooden deck opposite the entrance for shade and game players in 1989. Then, in 1995, a completely new zero-depth pool for the younger set replaced the baby pool, enabling toddlers to walk into the water as if they were at a beach on the ocean. That same year saw renovation of the bathhouse, which included expansion of the snack bar, the addition of a first-aid room and the replacement of the sun deck with a pitched roof. New lighting on playing fields and the rebuilding of tennis courts kept the borough up to speed with neighboring towns and technology.

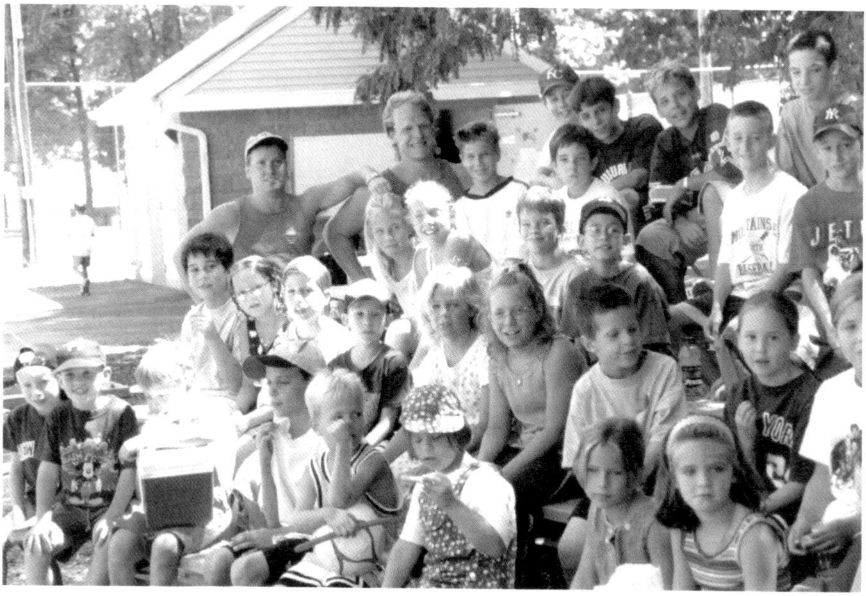

Attendees at summer recreation with counselors Ricky Brahm and Scott Laudati (rear left). *Courtesy of Maureen Giannone.*

In 1998, the recreation commission disbanded to make room for the Recreation Department, which would be under the auspices of the mayor and council. That same year saw the need for an expansion of the program's staff, and Frank Masella was hired as assistant recreation director. Three years later, Masella was named Young Professional of the Year by the New Jersey Recreation and Parks Association. When Sue Winans retired in 2005, he was named recreation director.

In the Swim

In 2002, Recreation Director and Pool Administrator Susan Winans concluded her annual report on the Mountainside Community Pool by saying, "The pool remains the single most popular recreation facility in Mountainside. Economic conditions, elementary school enrollment, and the weather appear to be the factors which influence membership and attendance the most."

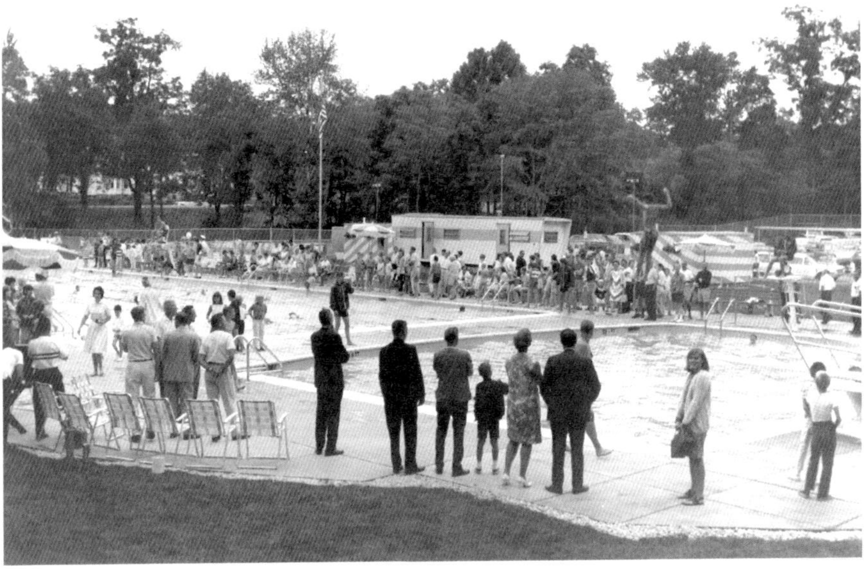

The crowd gathers for opening day ceremonies in 1966. The main building was not yet built; note the trailer and temporary buildings in the background. *Courtesy of the Mountainside Recreation Department.*

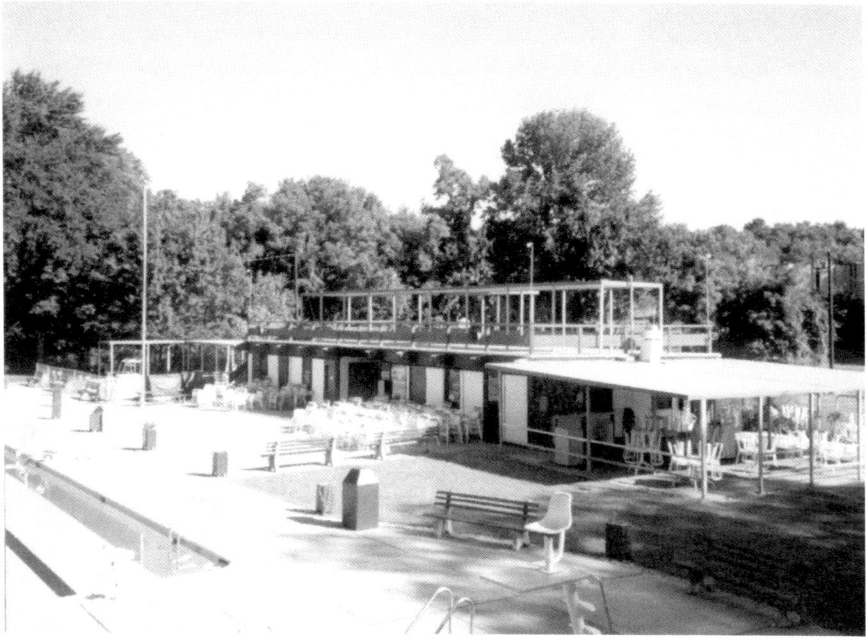

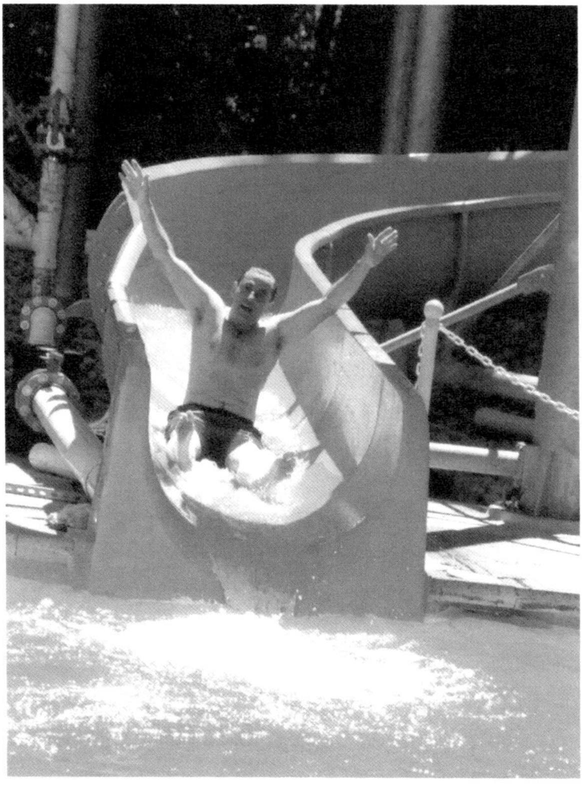

Above: The sun deck at the pool, 1995. *Courtesy of the Mountainside Recreation Department.*

Left: Tom McGowen, the first person to go down the new water slide in August 2006. *Courtesy of Maureen Giannone.*

Opening in 1966 with 727 families and portable trailers for bathhouses, membership increased to 800 by the later years of the decade. Permanent bathhouses opened in 1967. When the school population peaked in the early 1970s, so did pool membership. When a downward trend in the school-age population was forecast for the 1980s, the pool committee opened membership to nonresidents. In 1977, forty-one non-Mountainsiders joined the pool, and this trend increased sixfold over the next dozen summers.

True to expectations, resident pool membership ebbed to an average of 423 families per season in the 1980s, reflecting the decline in elementary school enrollment and changing demographics. In 1988, it was noted that resident memberships would not increase dramatically in the next five years. A summer of poor weather in 1989 also prompted a declining membership in subsequent years.

Nonetheless, Mountainsiders continue to be the backbone of the pool. In 2002, following an upward movement in school population, the pool had 492 resident families in attendance, the highest since 1994.

Improvement, as well as maintenance, has been a key element in the pool's success and manicured appearance since its early days. In 2006, for example, water slides replaced two of the diving boards at the diving tank, providing additional water activities for the young and young at heart.

CHILDREN'S SPECIALIZED HOSPITAL

From its simple beginnings as a country home for underprivileged city children, Children's Specialized Hospital has evolved into the nation's largest pediatric rehabilitation hospital. In 1891, twenty-four women from Westfield, of which Mountainside was then a part, raised $136 to bring eight children from New York City to the Levi Cory House on the corner of New Providence Road and Mountain Avenue. For the first half dozen years, the house was rented only during the four summer months to bring children to the "country" for a respite from city heat. Near the end of that period, a need was seen for medical care for urban youngsters. In 1895, the first sick child was taken in, and in 1898, the first crippled child was admitted.

In 1896, the home moved from Bird's Corner to its ten-acre location on New Providence Road. Known then as the Children's Country Home, it was purchased from the Thomas Drew farm for $6,225. His descendants were the renowned acting Barrymore family—John, Ethel, Lionel and Maurice—who may have used the home as a summer residence at one time.

In the ensuing decades, much of the facility's work was centered on children stricken with pneumonia and influenza. Then, in 1923, it became a year-round operation, also treating handicapped children. When the polio epidemic hit New Jersey in 1942, the hospital began to care for its victims; by 1945, the demands had forced the home to restrict admission only to those stricken with the disease.

In 1956, the Salk vaccine, proven effective, permitted Children's Country Home to open its doors to those with other physical disabilities. A half dozen years later, the name was changed to Children's Specialized Hospital to reflect the real nature of the work being done.

Construction projects over the next two decades allowed expansion of service areas, as well as providing a sixty-bed inpatient unit. In 1988, a long-term care unit began to provide aid for twenty-five children with complex medical problems. That same year saw the opening of an outpatient center in Fanwood, and in 1992, the hospital reached into the southern part of the state with the opening of a thirty-bed unit in Toms River.

By the start of the millennium, Children's had seven sites from which to serve its patients. Each location has its own specialty. In addition, the Fanwood campus provides primary education for children up to the age of ten. In 2007, staff in all locations treated over sixteen thousand patients from across the country and around the globe.

For over a century, Children's Specialized Hospital has been an integral part of the borough of Mountainside. Similar to other institutions in town, its caring and nurturing helps so many to realize their potential.

Rahway Valley Sewerage Authority

In 1928, when nine nearby municipalities joined to create a wastewater treatment plant and a trunk sewer system, known as the Rahway Valley Joint Meeting, Mountainside still relied on septic systems. Springfield, Kenilworth, Roselle Park, Cranford, Westfield, Garwood, Clark, Rahway and Woodbridge, participants in what became the Rahway Valley Sewerage Authority in 1951, paid according to usage.

As Mountainside grew, it became apparent that the introduction of a sanitary sewage system was imperative. Population expansion was causing problems with the existing septic system, and all indications were that a more sophisticated method of collecting and treating wastewater would have to be instituted. Therefore, in 1951 Mountainside entered into an agreement with Cranford for the purchase of space in its trunk system and, thereby, in the Rahway Valley Sewerage Authority treatment plant. According to the agreement, Mountainside paid its proportionate share of Cranford's assessment from RVSA.

This method worked satisfactorily for a number of years. It is important to remember, however, that the entire borough was not "sewered" at one time. Work on the system was done gradually, depending on population density in a given area of town and on funds available.

A second variable in the equation was the fact that Mountainside was not represented on the governing board of the authority, since technically it was not a member. Nevertheless, it was paying into the operations of the RVSA while not being afforded input as to how the monies were being spent.

In the mid-1980s, when Mountainside approached RVSA regarding membership, it was met with resistance and then with opposition. To protect residents' interests, Mountainside filed suit in 1987 seeking membership in RVSA. The suit continued into the '90s, and in April 1994 Mountainside's right to become a member was established. Certain conditions—dealing with the capacity and flow going into the trunk line that connected the borough with Cranford's trunk line—had to be met.

Finally, in the spring of 1999, after meeting the criteria set by the RVSA, Mountainside formally requested membership in the authority. Membership was granted on April 15, 1999, and Bart Barre became the first Mountainside representative to the Rahway Valley Sewerage Authority.

Chapter 9

NO MAN IS AN ISLAND

Organizations

English poet John Donne believed that while each of us functions as an individual, everyone is also part of something much larger. In "Meditation 17," he reflected, "No man is an island entire of itself; every man is a piece of the continent, a part of the main…I am involved in mankind." Similarly, while time alone and with one's family may be a top priority, life in Mountainside offers numerous organizations and activities from which to choose in order to be involved in the community. Whether a new resident or community elder, Mountainsiders don't shy away from an opportunity to bring good will together.

Welcome to Mountainside

One of the first greetings a new resident might receive is from the Mountainside Newcomers Club. Since 1954, this group has provided a chance for newcomers to meet others and to participate in their community. Newcomers also welcomes established residents who have had a lifestyle change, such as marriage or the birth of a child, and those who might benefit from a reintroduction to the town or support from others in a similar situation.

Newcomers board members plan a range of activities for parents and children to participate in and enjoy while extending their friendships.

Programs like Mommy and Me offer moms and toddlers the opportunity to mingle, as do holiday events like Easter egg hunts and Halloween pumpkin picking. Three social events are planned annually for adult members: the Winter Cocktail Party, the Summer Barbeque and the Fall Progressive Dinner. Moms exclusively are invited to attend the monthly Lunch Bunch and Ladies' Night Out. Late in the twentieth century, this hospitable group held an annual holiday luncheon to raise funds for community scholarships, as well as a summer pool party for adults.

At holiday time, Santa (aka one of the dads in town) visits individual homes and distributes gifts (those that he conveniently finds hidden outside the front door) to excited believers in participating Mountainside homes. For many years, the club ran a holiday luncheon and auction at which money was raised to benefit the borough volunteer organizations and for scholarships.

PLAY BALL!

Mountainside Youth Baseball

On the first Saturday of April each year, Mountainside experiences a spring awakening when baseball's opening day parade is held. Little League, founded by Carol Stotz in 1939 in Williamsport, Pennsylvania, found its way to Mountainside in 1954, becoming known as Mountainside Youth Baseball in the early 1990s. Girls were invited to join in the 1980s, encouraging all youth between the ages of six and fourteen to participate. By the turn of the twenty-first century, more than eight hundred players and coaches (for both baseball and softball) marched in the parade.

Over two dozen teams and clinics in five different age groups play on five different fields; the fields are maintained by volunteer parents. This level of commitment took on a new face in 1994, when several board members cosigned a loan to construct a snack bar and field house. Thanks to the generosity of families and the borough council, three of the fields have lights and scoreboards.

No volunteer better exemplifies the dedication of Mountainside to its baseball league than Chuck Fernicola. Since 1969, Fernicola has been the manager of the Mountainside Blue Stars. Now as a senior citizen he can still be seen weeding, raking or coaching around the baseball diamond. And he never had a son of his own in the program!

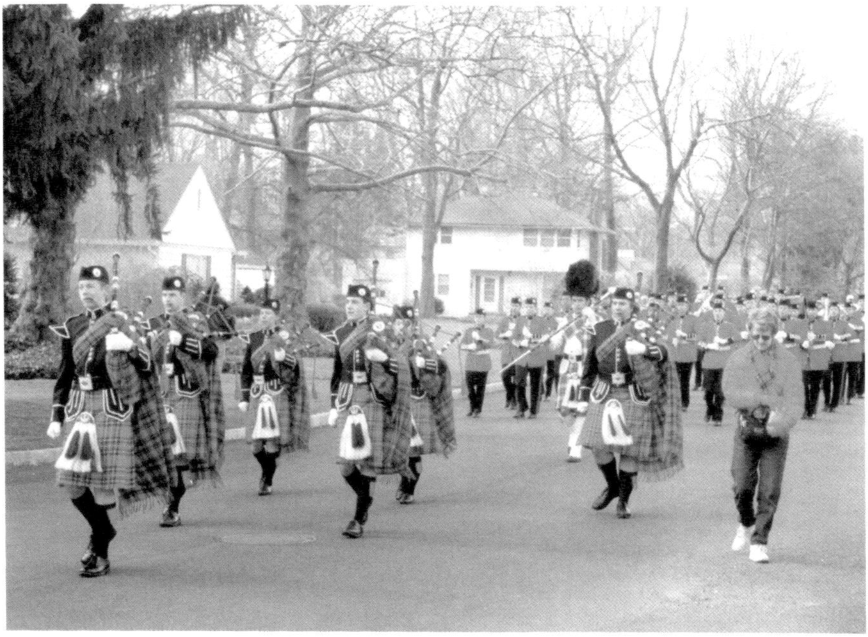

Opening day baseball parade, April 9. 2002. *Courtesy of Maureen Giannone.*

Since 2000, Mountainside Youth Baseball has seen fit to recognize sportsmanship on and off the fields. At each level, a player and coach are recognized not only for their ability but also for their commitment to good behavior. These awards are given in the names of two former MYB players: Scott Burdge, who died at the age of twelve in a bicycle accident in 1977, and Ryan Faella, who died suddenly in 2000 in his sleep of an unknown brain tumor when he was thirteen. At the foot of the flagpole at the major league field are plaques in memory of these boys.

Mountainside Softball Association

When the Recreation Department approached Peter Spadaccini in 2000 to coach a team in the Parkway Invitational Softball League, it had little idea of the implications that move would have on borough athletics. Pete's management led his girls to the league championship, and by 2005 there were two teams composed of twelve- and fourteen-year-olds.

Clearly seeing a void in the female sports arena, in 2005 nine residents formed the not-for-profit Mountainside Softball Association. The first board

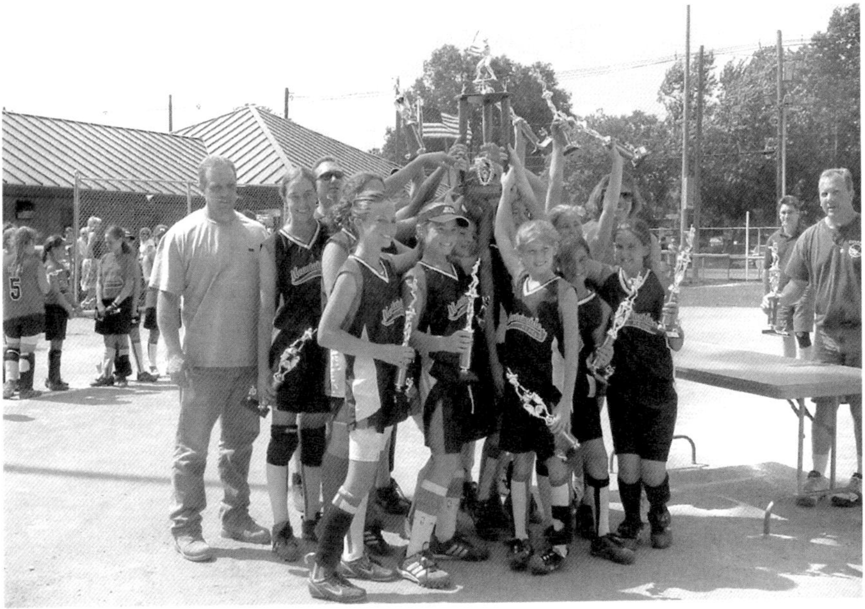

Girls' softball team, 2006. *Courtesy of the Borough of Mountainside.*

of directors was made up of the following residents: Spadaccini, president; Bill Buteau, vice-president; Margie Pires, treasurer; and Chris Palumbo, secretary. Other founding members were Tom and Heather Murphy, Bill Corrigan, Ed Kozowski and John Liss.

This independent program, with three teams during its first three seasons, runs over the summer for girls between the ages of nine and fifteen. Additional tryouts are held, and the most talented girls are chosen to play in a fast-paced traveling league. As a coach, Margie Pires states that the mission of the MSA is "to teach young women the skills that are needed to play softball safely and properly for the rest of their lives."

Giving Back to the Community

Mountainside Women's Club

In 1956, residents organized the Mountainside Women's Club, which was the local chapter of the New Jersey State Federation of Women's

Clubs (NJSFWC) and its national counterpart, the General Federation of Women's Clubs. Since 1894, the state organization has provided training and education, enabling women to make a difference in the lives of others. In 1918, the NJSFWC founded New Jersey College for Women, known today as Douglass College at Rutgers University, and continues to support the institution in the form of scholarships and other donations. The state group's intuition saw the need for the preservation of the Palisades. Its efforts led to the formation of the Palisades Interstate Park Commission, which still plays an integral part in the conservation of the more than 100,000-acre territory.

Locally over the years, the Mountainside Women's Club contributed to various state and national projects, raised funds for nearby organizations and presented combined physical fitness and academic awards at both Deerfield and Governor Livingston High Schools. In the early years of the new millennium, the Mountainside Women's Club disbanded as a result of a continued decrease in membership, although many participants have moved on to other community organizations.

The Foothill Club

As a result of the Newcomers bylaws, which established a two-year maximum involvement to preserve its title, a group of twenty-three women who were no longer eligible for membership formed a new club for both social projects and community service. Hanna Tritschler was one of the founders of this new organization. "The women enjoyed working and being together and wanted to continue these relationships," recalls her daughter, Evelyn Holcombe, who subsequently won the contest that named the group. In 1963, the Foothill Club, named to reflect Mountainside's location in the foothills of the Watchungs, elected Evelyn Lugannan as its first president.

That same year, Dr. David Samuelson, director of development at the Janet Memorial Home, a residential treatment center for adolescents in Elizabeth, was a speaker at one of the meetings. Other talks running the gamut from representatives of Habitat for Humanity and Summit-based Elder Care to the Seeing Eye trainers and puppies from Morristown have enriched the minds of the members, and social events of various types raised money for charitable causes. In 1964, for example, proceeds from a square dance were donated to the library, and in 1965, a check for $210 was presented to the Visiting Nurse Association of Westfield and Mountainside.

In 1972, a needy child was provided with a summer pool membership, and that same year money was given to Fern Hyde, welfare director, to aid the elderly on limited incomes. Sometime later, Foothill purchased a wheelchair for town use. In 1973, a spruce tree was planted at Deerfield School and dedicated to Marine Captain James Egan of Mountainside, listed as missing in action in Vietnam in 1966.

Foothill continues the women's club practice of yearly awards for physical fitness and academic achievement at Deerfield School, as well as conducting food collections at Thanksgiving, Christmas and Easter and giving donations to various civic groups.

Elks Club

From its modest beginnings in 1868, when it was formed to elude New York City drinking laws, the Benevolent and Protective Order of Elks began as a social club. It has since evolved into a major American fraternal and charitable service organization with more than a million members, both male and female. Part of its mission—to inculcate the principles of charity, justice, brotherly love and fidelity—is accomplished in serving people and communities through drug awareness programs, youth activities, scholarships and vets services.

The Mountainside-Westfield Elks received its charter in 1932 and held meetings in a speakeasy on Route 29 until it moved across the street (now Route 22) later that same year. In the 1950s, the Gramps family donated their homestead to the Elks Club for its exclusive use. At that time there was a picnic grove in the back—that wooded area became the site of the Mountainside Indoor Tennis Club.

Currently, Mountainside Lodge #1585 encompasses the surrounding towns of Westfield, Garwood, Clark, Fanwood and Scotch Plains. Like the national organization, these Elks are involved with their communities and with veterans, particularly those at the veterans' hospital in Lyons, New Jersey. One of the fundraising projects enables Lodge #1585 to pay the hospital directly for merchandise in its gift shop and present coupon books to the patients so that they may "purchase" items either without charge or at greatly reduced prices.

Nationally, the Elks provide more than $3 million in scholarships to high school seniors each year.

Rotary Club

Formed in 1905 by Illinois attorney Paul P. Harris, Rotary is an international organization of professional and business leaders. Its mission is to encourage high ethical standards in the workplace, to build good will and peace in the world and to provide humanitarian service. The Rotarian's motto, "Service Above Self," is exemplified in its commitment to society. The club strongly demonstrated its drive when it instituted the PolioPlus program, participation in the worldwide effort to immunize all children against polio and eradicate the disease. Since 1998, Rotary International has been a driving force in reducing the number of polio cases, which have decreased worldwide by 99 percent.

Chartered in September 1961, the Mountainside Rotary Club began with Elmer Hoffarth as its first president. The charter-night dinner was held at the Chi-Am Chateau. Although the site of the weekly meetings changed over the years, the club gravitated back to its original location, with lunchtime meetings first at Steak & Ale (on the original Chi-Am Chateau property) and more recently at Famous Dave's (currently on the same site).

Locally, Rotary raises money through the sale of ads that are placed within an annual community calendar. In addition to donating to local groups and causes, Rotary presents savings bonds to two Deerfield School graduates each year and scholarships to two Mountainside seniors at Governor Livingston. At holiday time, the members run a Salvation Army–sponsored breakfast for children in Union County on Christmas Eve morning.

Member efforts are also recognized and rewarded by the organization. In 1996, Joy Fickett, a Mountainside Rotarian, was one of 113 New Jersey residents selected to carry the Olympic torch when it came to the state. Fickett was responsible for raising money for Rotary International's Gift of Life Program, which arranges for children from foreign countries to undergo surgeries in the United States. By sponsoring Rotary dances, she raised $5,000 to cover the cost of operations for two children from Trinidad, and in the mid-1990s, she ran a marathon for a ten-year-old Syrian girl who needed open-heart surgery.

Lions Club

Another organization whose mandate limited members' participation based on keeping a younger constituency was the Junior Chamber of Commerce. In 1963, those retirees who were "over the hill" at the age of thirty-two decided to start a local Lions Club to maintain their camaraderie and commitment to volunteerism. Lions International, the world's largest and most active service organization, counts in its membership 1.3 million men and women in over two hundred countries and geographic areas.

Dedicated primarily to the prevention of blindness, this organization also promotes programs and offers aid to the blind. One of six recycling centers for eyeglasses in the United States is located in Trenton, New Jersey. Over one million pairs of glasses a year are refurbished and sent to third-world countries. Orders with specific age and corrective needs are filled for those otherwise unable to afford glasses.

Individual clubs, like the one in Mountainside, obtain discarded U.S. Postal Service receptacles, which are restored and set up in convenient locations throughout the community ready to accept donations. Members regularly collect and mend the eyeglasses and transport them to the recycling center. There, advanced equipment "reads" the prescriptions of each pair of glasses, which are then restored, sterilized and packaged for shipment to the needy.

In Mountainside, the Lions Club annually lights and maintains the town's Christmas tree on the southeast corner of Route 22 and New Providence Road. Founder and current president Frank Magnolia recalls how an old army surplus gasoline-powered generator was originally used to provide the electricity needed to light the holiday tree. During the fuel shortage in 1973, the familiar holiday tree was decorated, although in order to conserve energy it was not lit. Yet holiday spirit continued in glee of its town's prideful efforts. Each year, Lou Strohmeyer added additional bulbs and wiring to accommodate the average annual growth of one to two feet. For several years after the start of the new millennium, the tree began to deteriorate. Tree experts tried various methods of salvaging and reviving the Route 22 landmark, including deep-root feeding, but they all failed. Borough officials announced that the tree would be replaced. In 2007, after forty-four years of standing tall, the old tree was lit for the last time, and a smaller, neighboring tree took its place.

Mountainside PAL

In existence as a national organization since the 1930s, the Police Athletic League of New Jersey was founded in 1990. Mountainside's PAL was formed in 1999 and adheres to the same tenets as its parent group.

Simply stated, PAL is a crime-prevention program designed to promote positive interactions between the police and youth of a community. Its basic conviction is that if a youngster understands and respects the role of a law enforcement officer and has a relationship with a number of these people through his growing years, he will continue to have an awareness of and a favorable attitude toward the work of police officers as he matures.

Mountainside's PAL sponsors activities throughout the four seasons to encourage the spirit of benevolence, good will, friendship, tolerance and other values considered not only American but human as well. Fall soccer, high school recreation basketball, traveling basketball teams, flag football and an annual cop trot are only several of the dozen or more ways that the local PAL's goals are accomplished. The cop trot 5K race brings in between $16,000 and $20,000. Monies raised help defray the cost of the July 4 fireworks held in town each year.

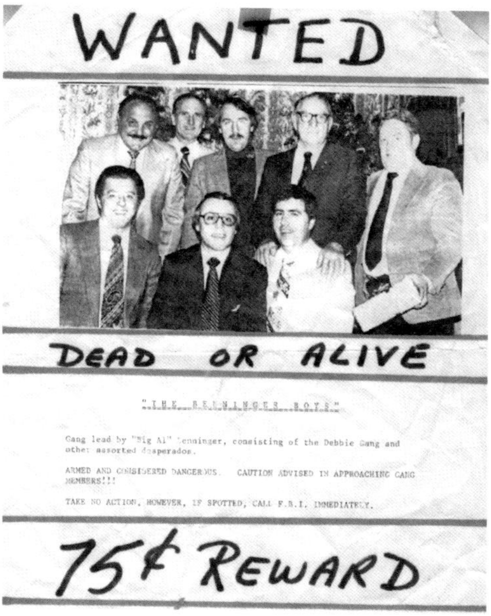

Members of the Bestowers assemble around the Christmas tree during twentieth annual party in 1980. *From left to right, top row*: Judge Robert Ruggerio, Steve Escoff, George Benninger, Albert Benninger and James Debbie Sr.; *bottom row*: Robert Viglianti, Richard Benninger and James Debbie Jr. *Courtesy of the* Mountainside Echo.

The Bestowers

Time and again the giving spirit of Mountainsiders has manifested itself in tangible ways. Calling themselves the Bestowers, a group of people began a holiday tradition in 1960 that lasted for twenty-five years.

Seeing the less-fortunate around them, the Bestowers decided to make Christmas morning a joyful and memorable time for them. James Debbie Sr., Gene Mitchell, Albert Benninger, George Coughlin and Werner Schon were several of those who organized a mid-December party, the prime purpose of which was to buy gifts and raise money for children and senior citizens who otherwise would not have had the means to enjoy this aspect of the holiday season.

During the first year of this tradition, $750 was raised by auctioning gifts donated by local merchants and businesses. The money was given to St. Joseph's Villa in Montvale for orphans and other children often forgotten at this time of year. At the initial party, a priest, sixteen nuns and fifty children entertained the guests with Christmas carols. "It was the most beautiful sound you ever heard," reminisced Benninger, twenty years later. Ten years after its formation, the group gave all its donations and toys to a town in Pennsylvania that had been devastated by a flood.

Originally, the gathering was a potluck buffet, with residents taking food to share with other attendees. Over the years, as additional guests attended and the proceeds grew, the organizations that benefited increased as well. The party became somewhat more formal and expensive: it was catered and competed with other holiday affairs. Sometime in the mid-1980s, the event met its demise.

Mountainside Historic Preservation Committee

Established in 1977 to preserve and maintain the town's history and historical sites, the Mountainside Historic Preservation Committee believes that history is a part of culture and it should be kept alive so that future generations can learn from it. With this in mind, the committee strives to identify and keep intact, when possible, buildings and artifacts pertinent to the development of Mountainside.

The Deacon Andrew Hetfield House is the headquarters of this group, and its major achievement was the rescue of the structure from demolition. In 1985, under the direction of the late Fern Carter Hyde, the committee was instrumental in moving the house from its location on Route 22 to Constitution Plaza near the library, where it continues to be restored and maintained. The Hetfield House is on the National and State Registers of Historic Places.

The Mountainside Historic Preservation Committee raises money from its various projects, one of which is the brick walkway leading to the Hetfield House. Residents and neighbors purchase inscribed bricks to honor families and organizations that have cared for the borough over the years. Monies raised from this walkway funded the writing of a second volume of Mountainside's history.

Scouting in Mountainside

Scouting evolved early in the 1900s simultaneously in Britain and America to provide an aspect of education that schools couldn't, or didn't, provide. Chicago publisher William D. Boyce incorporated the Boy Scouts of America in 1910 to develop young men with quality in character, citizenship and physical fitness.

Scouting for both boys and girls made a number of false starts in the late 1930s and early 1940s. Groups disbanded due to small numbers and joined with those in other towns. Scouting made its permanent appearance in Mountainside in 1955 with the formation of Cub Scout Pack 177. Four years later, Boy Scout Troop 177 began its activities. Troop 177 is run by a troop committee, consisting of four to six senior scouts and four adult leaders. While individual traits like resourcefulness, initiative and self-reliance are inculcated, understanding of and involvement in the world and the community are also fostered.

Typically, a boy joins the Cub Scouts in the spring of kindergarten and is eligible to become a Boy Scout when he is in the fifth grade, but as longtime scouting mom Jo Vargo points out, "You don't have to be a Cub Scout to be a Boy Scout. Boys can enter at any point in time." She describes the Cub Scout program as "family-oriented" and Boy Scouts as "scout-driven and much more independent."

Vargo, who describes herself as "a huge believer in the program," says that boys learn about "being good people with a sense of family and citizenship and a desire to give back to the community." For a nine-year period, due to a void of adult leadership, Mountainsiders went to Berkeley Heights for scouting; Troop 177 was reinstated in 1998 and has been thriving ever since. In fact, says Vargo, "leadership has grown." And, contrary to popular belief, there *are* female scout masters. When one local mom admitted, "I tried and tried to get my husband to be a leader," Vargo retorted, "Well, what about *you*!"

Troop 177's community service projects currently include assisting Cub Scout Pack 177 in collecting food for an annual Thanksgiving Food Drive at the Community Presbyterian Church, donating one Saturday each month preparing and serving meals for the homeless in Newark and maintaining the "Triangle" at the northeast corner of New Providence Road and Route 22 through the New Jersey State "Adopt A Spot" program. In the wake of the terrorist attack on the World Trade Center, Cub Scout Pack 177 raised $900 through the sale of popcorn and donated this money toward the purchase of a defibrillator for the fire department in memory of September 11, 2001.

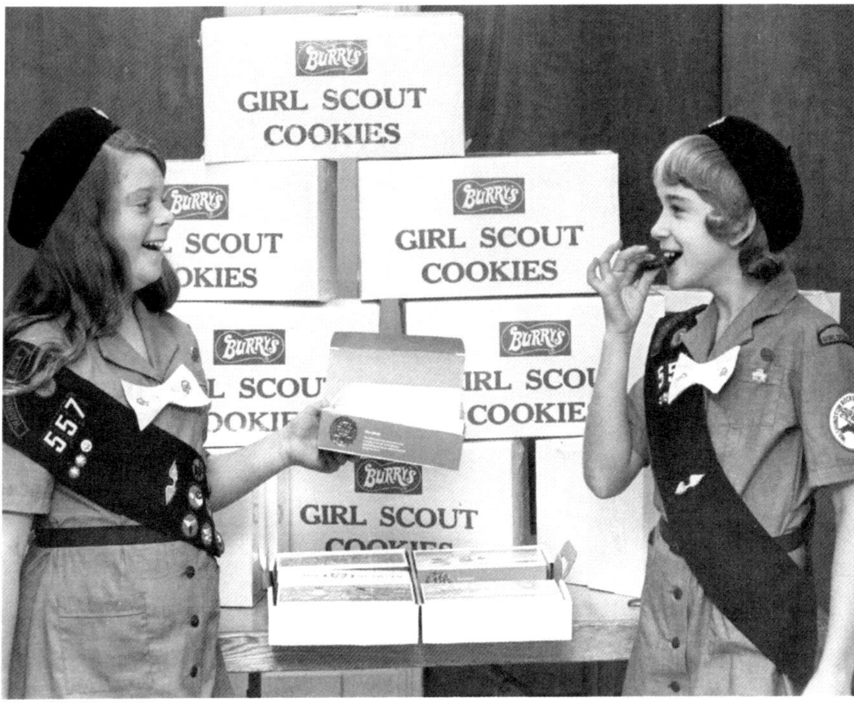

Girl Scout cookie tasters Christine Hartnett and Kathleen Kelly, early 1970s. *Courtesy of the Mountainside Recreation Department.*

Juliette Gordon Low gathered eighteen girls together as the first Girl Scout troop in Savannah, Georgia, on March 12, 1912. Nearly a century later, and with 3.6 million members, her vision of developing young women with the skills necessary to become leaders is still being realized across the United States.

The first Girl Scout troop started in town in 1941. As time has passed, the focus of scouting has broadened tremendously. Early on, according to local scout leader Mary Greeley, scouting was "geared to preparing girls to be housewives. Badges were based on domestic areas: cooking, sewing and first aid. While girls still work for badges, they are now aimed at careers: science, technology, nature, business and finance."

At the turn of the twenty-first century, roughly two hundred girls were participating in scouting, one of the largest ratios of participants to the number of girls available in this area of the state. Greeley concurs that the borough has "an active high school group," which is unusual since this is a time when teenagers' interests expand widely. In town, the girls must perform one service for the community and another for senior citizens every year in order to receive a community service badge. "It stands to reason," says Greeley, "that you have a better understanding of the town you live in if you participate in that town."

In 2008, the number of councils overseeing scouting activities in the state decreased from eleven to four in order to prevent duplication of services. Another sure advantage in this reduction is that girls will work more closely with peers in nearby cities and town, thereby learning about other socioeconomic groups and not just their own somewhat more homogeneous town troop.

The Maturing of Mountainside

In a report released by the U.S. Census Bureau in July 2007, 12.1 percent of Americans could accurately identify themselves as senior citizens. Fully 25 percent of Mountainside's residents proudly boast of being sixty-five years of age or older. Studies have not been undertaken to determine the possible reasons for this local statistic, but certainly the active and stimulating lifestyle offered by the two senior groups has contributed to the well-being of the mature members of the population and has encouraged them to remain in town.

In 1965, a group of folks founded the Senior Citizens' Club "to promote a friendly and positive atmosphere and to sponsor a feeling of camaraderie" among the town's elders. The group meets twice a month at the Community Presbyterian Church, often with a speaker engaged to enlighten the attendees. Bus trips to nearby attractions broaden the offerings of the club.

Seeing the need for additional activities, a group of eight began Mountainside Active Retirees in 1983. Meeting bimonthly at Borough Hall, MAR's objective is "to promote the cultural, educational, recreational and social activities of active senior citizens and to afford the members the opportunity to meet with their peers." Like its sister organization, MAR offers trips and speakers. Membership in the two groups tends to overlap, and participants view them as complementary rather than competing clubs.

Let There Be Music

With Bea Reich as its first president, the Mountainside Music Association raised its baton in 1959. Its goal was to encourage and foster an appreciation of and participation in music in the schools and in the community. One tiny community succeeded in bringing forth an amazing number of talented, enthusiastic people gifted in costuming, stagecraft, lighting and designing, as well as performing. For more than thirty years, they enriched the lives of those around them.

Music teacher Aden Lewis was recruited as musical director. The program for the thirtieth anniversary production recalls that "his presence and musical influence and guidance were magical, eliciting the best in everyone and turning the first production, as well as the others to come, into first-rate professional quality musicals that attracted wide attention."

With the profit of $900 from *Make Mine Manhattan*, the initial production, MMA purchased stage equipment for the schools. Over the years, additional purchases relating to music were made for the district schools, and funds were also used for professional artists to appear at school and community programs. Further, MMA brought residents with diverse backgrounds together harmoniously through decades of crises and turmoil in the real world.

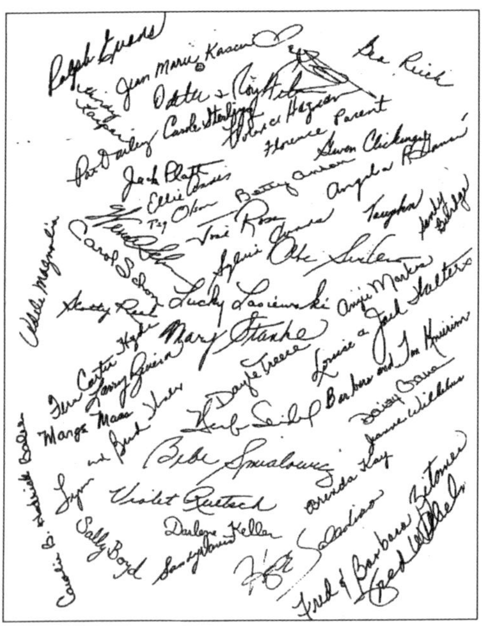

Participating "players" signed the program for the 1989 MMA production of *Everything Old Is New Again*. The revue was the thirtieth-anniversary celebration comprising parts of old shows and featuring many of the original performers in their same roles. According to the program, it was "a sentimental journey and reunion of old friends" and was conceived and produced by MMA's beloved impresario Jeanne Wilhelms.

Another Branch of Volunteerism

Sensing a need for volunteer representation from the community to a hospital within its boundaries, Jean Pascuiti and Elizabeth Bellezza started a branch of TWIG at Children's Specialized Hospital in 1984. TWIG is but one branch in the auxiliary of several groups assisting the staff and patients.

Forty women established an active presence of Mountainside residents by donating thousands of hours of time to patients through tutoring, hosting evening parties and arranging horseback riding for those usually seeing the world from a wheelchair. Bellezza recalls that during riding lessons there was a volunteer on either side of the horse, someone leading the horse and a physical therapist nearby. "You could see the child's muscles relax while he was riding," she says. This was such a unique opportunity for physically challenged youngsters that one patient during the early years came from eastern Long Island to participate.

Once a month, TWIG members lend a hand in other ways as well: reading to the children, working with arts and crafts, helping in recreation and music therapy and preparing the day carts for the housekeeping service. "It's definitely not a sad place," says 2007 corresponding secretary Laura Patterson. She remembers herself as a ten-year-old singing and talking with the kids and being introduced to the facility as part of a volunteer group from Westfield. "It's hands-on volunteering," says Patterson. "It's wonderful to stimulate the youngsters in various ways and get them to smile."

A Windfall in Mountainside: The Watts Foundation

Blanche and George Watts lived in Mountainside for about fifty years. Having no children and little family, in 1999 they were encouraged by their attorney Thomas Phelan to leave their assets to the place they loved. And they did.

Blanche Watts was a schoolteacher during her years of employment, and George Watts worked for Western Electric—seemingly modest means of making a livelihood. From most external evidence, they lived frugally. It was indeed a surprise when the Wattses' will was probated. After willing a sizeable bequest to a family member, Blanche and George Watts left the remainder of their estate to fund a free-standing foundation. The amount left for that purpose was $3.5 million.

Established in 2005, the purpose of the Watts Mountainside Community Foundation is to provide grants to nonprofit organizations that benefit the citizens of Mountainside. A board of nine members administers the foundation. Thus far, money has been given for the purchase of a community bus, construction of an ecology classroom at Trailside Museum, acquisition of video equipment for a variety of venues in town, assistance in refurbishing fields and stages at local schools and a number of other programs in Mountainside. In addition, an annual $10,000, four-year scholarship (total of $40,000) is awarded to a graduating high school senior, and a $5,000 one-time award is given to another college-bound senior.

Enhancement of the monetary value of the Watts Mountainside Community Foundation was realized when Mary P. Komich, daughter of former mayor Joseph Komich, added approximately $700,000 when she died as a way of honoring her family.

Chapter 10

MOTHER NATURE WITH SOME HELP FROM HER FRIENDS

Environs

One of Mountainside's visually appealing attractions is related to its geographic position between two county parks: Watchung Reservation on the north, forested and natural for the most part, and Echo Lake Park on the south, more manicured and planned. Both are part of the Union County Park System, designed by the Olmsted Brothers, descendants of Frederick Law Olmsted, nineteenth-century founder of American landscape architecture and the nation's foremost park maker.

Watchung Reservation

The Lenni-Lenape Indians, who in the sixteenth century built their winter villages in the protected valley between the first and second Watchung Mountain ridges, had a decidedly more pragmatic view of the nearly 2,000 wooded acres of what would much later become Watchung Reservation than do contemporary residents. So did English miners of the late 1660s who were searching for mineral deposits in the mountains of what is now the northern part of Mountainside. During the 1920s, a number of the borough's families donated or sold 830 acres of their land to the Union County Park Commission, which was formed in 1921 to provide a park system, a feat not able to be accomplished by individual communities. This land was added to that given by four other neighboring communities to form Watchung Reservation.

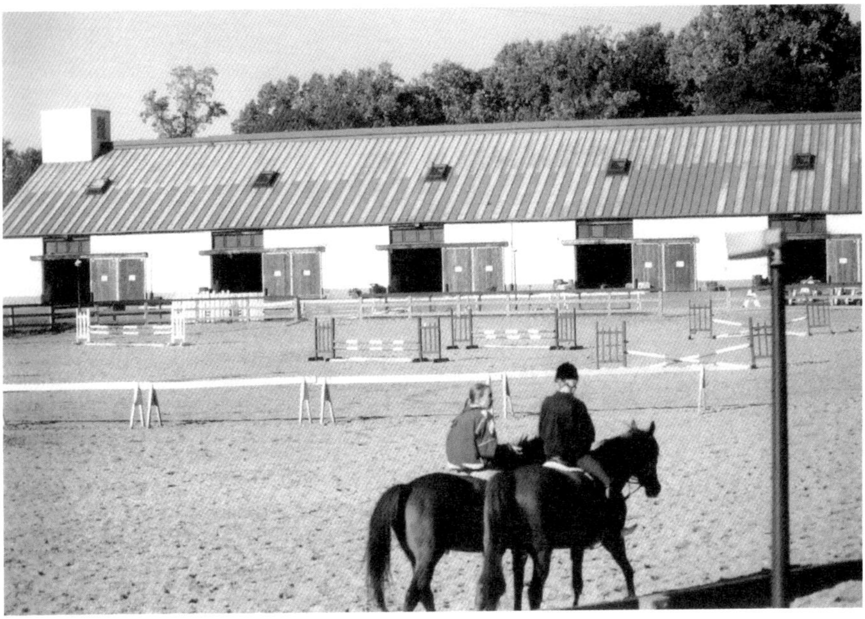

Back to the stables after a ride. *Courtesy of Westfield Historical Society.*

Today, much of the 1,945-acre parcel of land, almost half of which is within the boundaries of Mountainside, is forested and preserved for its natural offerings. Set aside as a reservation in 1924–25 by the Union County Park Commission, it is the largest park in the county system. Hiking and horseback riding are the primary pursuits of those who travel the more than thirteen miles of marked walking paths and the over twenty-five miles of bridle trails. Winter snows provide opportunities for cross-country skiing, while warmer weather invites fishing in three bodies of water. Picnicking and boating, affording less vigorous activity, round out the park's offerings.

Twice since the park's beginnings, higher levels of government have used its land for nonrecreational purposes. In 1955, the U.S. Department of Defense entered into an agreement with the Union County Park Commission to use 76.02 acres of land for a Nike missile base. The U.S. Army operated this base between 1957 and 1963. Then, in the early 1980s, after years of litigation and public protest, New Jersey's Department of Transportation received approval to build a 5.5-mile portion of Interstate 78 through the northern fringe of the reservation in order to complete the 144.0-mile highway that runs from Union Township, Pennsylvania, through the Holland Tunnel into New York City. The major concern of the populace in the building of this relatively short section of I-78 was its environmental impact. One of the adaptations to the east–west link that was completed in 1986 was the construction of land bridges for animal migration within the park.

Within the reservation's boundaries are three facilities that provide for special interests. At the eastern end of the park, on the site of the old Nike missile base in Mountainside, is the Watchung Stable complex. Owned and operated by Union County since 1933, the main barn houses nearly one hundred horses, both county and privately owned. Four riding rings, a show ring, an outside hunter course, storage and equipment areas and an administration building compose this facility built in 1988. Prior to this date, a stable was located at the northeastern edge of the park; that barn is gone, and today the former stable administration building houses the Union County K-9 unit.

Built in 1941 as the state's first nature center, Trailside Nature and Science Center exhibits flora and fauna of the area. Its planetarium seats fifty, and its grounds feature areas with herbs, wildflowers and butterflies. Princeton architect Michael Graves designed the 1974 visitor center. Renovations and additions to this building over a three-year period more than doubled its size when it reopened in 2006. Exhibits correlate with New Jersey core curriculum standards and with Boy and Girl Scout merit badge programs.

In the western part of Watchung Reservation is the Deserted Village, which over the course of three centuries has been a farming community, a mill town and a summer resort. Known as Feltville for a period of time, the property was named for David Felt, who ran a stationery business in New York City.

In 1844, Felt began buying property from the descendants of Peter Willcocks, who had farmed the land for a century or more. Felt wanted to establish a paper mill and provide a pleasant lifestyle for his employees, unlike that of urban mill sites of the times. He constructed an entire town, including dams to supply power for the mill, and provided housing, education and religious services for those who worked in his mill.

Feltville thrived for only fifteen years before David Felt sold his property. It is speculated that his decision was based either on the failing health of his brother, who had been managing the business in New York, or on ties to the secessionist South that strained the business as the Civil War approached. By 1872, Felt had sold most of his stationery business and filed for bankruptcy. As the years passed and houses in the former company town became unoccupied, Feltville became known as the Deserted Village.

In 1882, Feltville was purchased by Warren Ackerman, who converted it into a summer resort called Glenside Park. Dwellings were renovated and expanded. The resort offered numerous outdoor activities for guests and proximity to the train in Summit so that fathers and husbands could join their families on the weekends. It flourished until about 1916, when the popularity of the automobile allowed city people to travel farther away for leisure and vacation. The property was purchased by the Union County Park Commission when it formed in the 1920s, and the houses were rented out until the 1960s. An Outdoor Education Center used some of the houses as classrooms until it closed in 1985.

Echo Lake Park

Part of Mountainside's southern boundary is also parkland. Echo Lake Park's 147 acres are shared by the borough and neighboring Westfield. In the late 1700s, a working mill was located at the eastern edge of the park near Springfield Avenue. Owned originally by the Frazee family, it was passed down through the family until sometime in the 1890s, when it became the Parkhurst Mill. Aaron Parkhurst was one of the petitioners who proposed that Mountainside secede from Westfield. His son, William Parkhurst Sr., sold the mill and much of the surrounding property to the County of Union. It was developed by the Union County Park System in 1924 and given its name because of the echo that resounded from the fifty-foot slope on the southern side of the lake.

On both sides of the 1.1-mile east–west drive are facilities for all kinds of recreational activities, depending on the season: picnicking, boating, skating and snowboarding. Watching the variety of ducks on each of the three lakes has provided pleasure for children over many years. Free outdoor concerts on an eastern hillside attract music lovers from near and far on summer evenings. Known as "flagpole hill," this is the site where pasteboard from the Parkhurst Mill was laid out to dry during the late part of the nineteenth century. Once dry, Aaron Parkhurst would deliver the pasteboard in his horse-drawn wagon to factories in Newark, where it was made into cardboard boxes. In 2001, a dog park opened on another one of the hillsides. There, in a fenced-in, three-acre area, pets can run free and frolic with other canines, as well as with their human companions.

Echo Lake Park was closed to vehicular traffic for two years following a torrential rain storm on August 2, 1973. Three bridges and two dams were destroyed and had to be reconstructed at a cost of $973,000. Initially, the

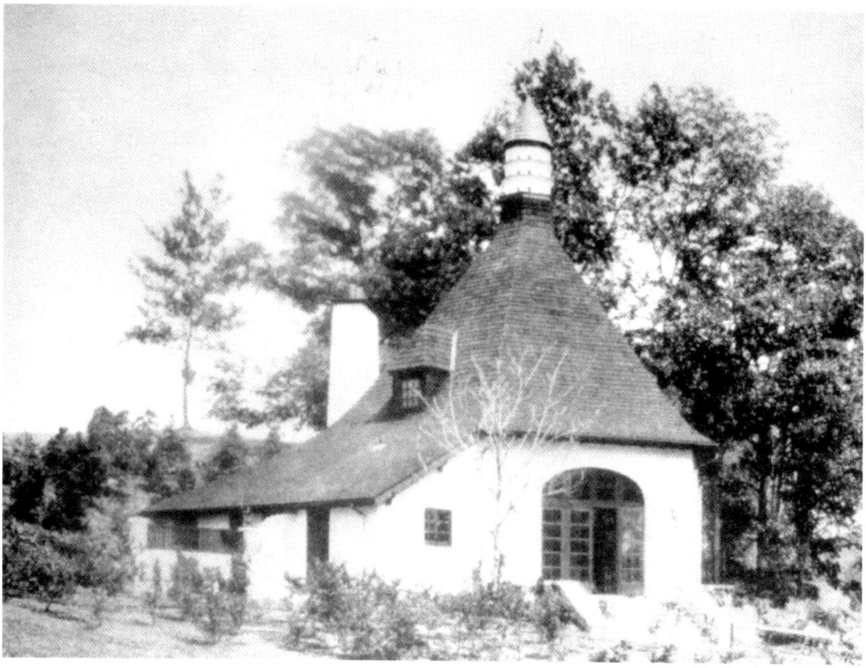

Refreshment pavilion, Echo Lake Park, completed February 1925. *Courtesy of the Westfield Historical Society.*

Union County Park Commission footed the bill. Later, the Federal Disaster Assistance Administration made full reimbursement to the commission.

In 1985, a fitness trail was installed in an extension of the park located west of Mountain Avenue. Following the terrorist attacks of September 11, 2001, a memorial plaza was added behind the flagpole hill to commemorate area victims of the tragedy.

Mountainside is indeed fortunate to be a part of and surrounded by these two county woodlands. In addition, Baltusrol Golf Club's world-renowned course constitutes a portion of the eastern boundary of the borough. Beauty, privacy and land stability combine to enhance the already attractive makeup of the town itself.

Chapter 11

MOMENTS TO REMEMBER

In this chapter, a baker's dozen of both former and longtime residents share their recollections of a time when Mountainside Borough was considerably more homogeneous and rural than it is today.

Arthur J. Brahm's Boyhood in Mountainside

My first memory in Mountainside was living on Central Avenue (1940). We were the last house on the paved road, which ended just below where Wood Valley Road meets Central Avenue. Across the street was the Weber farm. When I was older, we would help Mr. Weber load his flatbed truck with vegetables and then get a fun, bumpy ride back to the barn.

One of my fondest memories was hiking up the dirt road to the spring on Tracy Drive at the end of Central Avenue. There we would have a cold drink. We might then continue up Tracy Drive to the "lookout" tower, a wooden structure at the time, or on to the Trailside Museum or Surprise Lake for a day of exploring and fun.

When I was old enough to cross Route 22, Echo Lake Park offered us fishing, renting a row boat (twenty-five cents per hour) or meeting friends for a game of softball or marbles. Ice skating was another activity to fill our time in the winter.

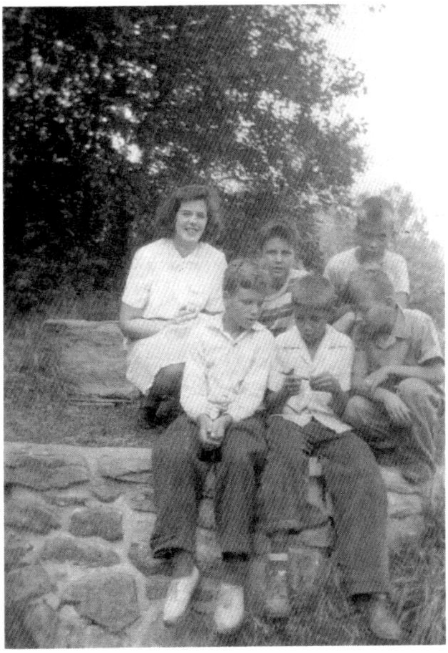

I recall when it would snow and I heard the rumble of the snow plow coming down the street. I would look out the window and see the name "Heckel" on the truck and hope there would be no school the next day.

We did not have television while we were growing up, so our imaginations were our entertainment, and we were never bored.

I entered high school in 1949 and the town by then was growing rapidly. The good planning by the mayors and councils helped to make this the beautiful town that it has become today.

Brahm married Peggy Chattin, a third-generation Mountainsider. They now live in Montague, New Jersey.

Above: Spring on Tracy Drive at the top of Central Avenue. Remnants of the wall and the large stone on top are still visible today, but the spring is no longer running, August 4, 1946. *From left to right, front row*: Arthur Brahm, Donald Pittenger and George Robbins; *second row*: Hope Cookes, John Sheehan and Richard Robbins. *Courtesy of Arthur Brahm.*

CHRONE'S TAVERN: A LANDMARK

"My grandfather took over in 1946," says Mike Chrone, the current proprietor of Chrone's Tavern on Mountain Avenue.

> *Before that it was Pop Whelan's and was on the corner where the gas station is* [Woodland and Mountain]. *Bliwise owned the property at the time; we paid him rent. It was Bliwise's decision to tear the building down and build the gas station and this place in 1951: two rentals instead of one. He owned the property until the late '60s when we bought it.*

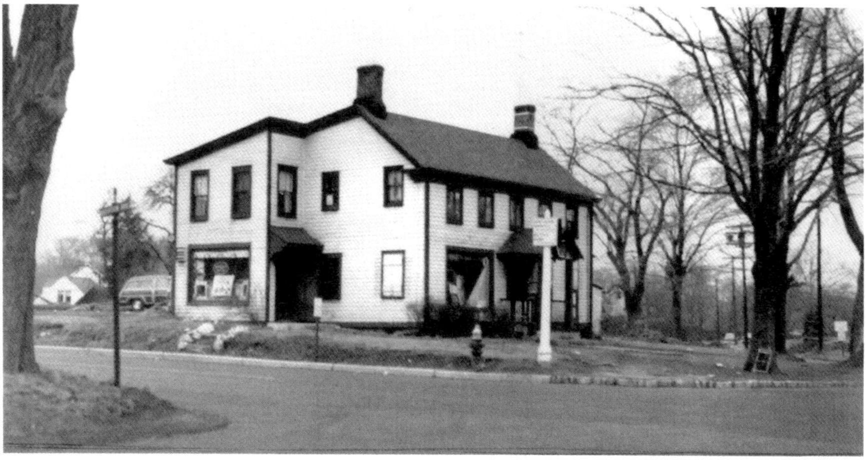

Pop Whelan's, later Chrone's. *Courtesy of the Mountainside Historic Preservation Committee.*

According to Chrone, the tavern is the same size it was in 1951, except for the solarium in the front, which was added later. "It was just a local bar, same as it is now." And then he says, rather matter-of-factly, "Actually, I was told that Al Capone used to stop in."

Connie Dorio Moves to the "Country"

When Connie and John Dorio bought property in the Pioneer Forest section (area west of Apple Tree Lane and south of Orchard Road) of Mountainside, they had to access it via a dirt road. That was in 1951, and John had found the lot while helping his brother build a house nearby. He was from Linden; Connie was from the Vailsburg section of Newark. They were city people.

The two Dorio brothers built the house on what was supposed to be called Pioneer Road but instead was named Force Drive in memory of Harold Force, a resident of Central Avenue who drowned during a training accident in the South soon after enlisting in the U.S. Army.

"We moved in during 1952. Before too long, houses started popping up all around," says Connie. Three children joined the Dorio family before long: John, Cynthia and Deborah. Cindy Dorio West is on record as the first child baptized in Our Lady of Lourdes parish when St. James in Springfield was still the site for all services, before the church was built on Central Avenue.

Elizabeth Hahn on Iceboating

Because of my husband's activity in iceboating, we came to buy a house in Mountainside in 1959. Knowing that we were house hunting, a fellow iceboater, living in Westfield, learned that a house on Coles Avenue was for sale. We were from Bloomfield, so we asked, "Where is Mountainside?" Short story: Saw it on Friday, bought it on Sunday.

It was a log cabin and had a big oak tree growing up and out the roof of the dining room. Months later, we had termites for breakfast, hundreds of them. That meant sawing the tree in slices and removing it. Outside though, we had so many dogwoods that it looked like fairyland in spring.

Years later, our Westfield friend built a house on the corner of Deer Path and Tanager Way. The outside cellar entrance was large enough to get Yankee iceboats in and out. One year we took advantage of this: we hid our children's Christmas present down there; it was a sailfish boat.

Growing Up in a Small Town

Ruthie Zimmermann Goense says that her parents met while learning to speak English: "Luisa was from Germany, Robert from Switzerland. My father hid the books on my mother; she was in the class after his. She had to ask him where her books were." That, apparently, was the beginning of a romance. The Zimmermanns came to Mountainside in 1937 from Union. Ruthie was born in the borough and has lived here all her life. Her three children were raised here, and two of the three are rearing their own kids in town.

The Zimmermann house was built in 1792. My parents rented for the first three years from George Knoll, who owned a lot of property in town; then they bought it. The Zimmermann farm had thirty-seven acres. My father still had a job milking cows at Ideal Dairy in Union. Then he got a job with the landscaper next door to us. Most of what was raised on the farm was for the family, not for public market. My maternal grandmother, who lived with us through the war years until she could go back to Germany, worked on the Weber farm across the road.

We got to play only with the kids who lived on Central Avenue because there wasn't an east–west connection to the other main streets. It was

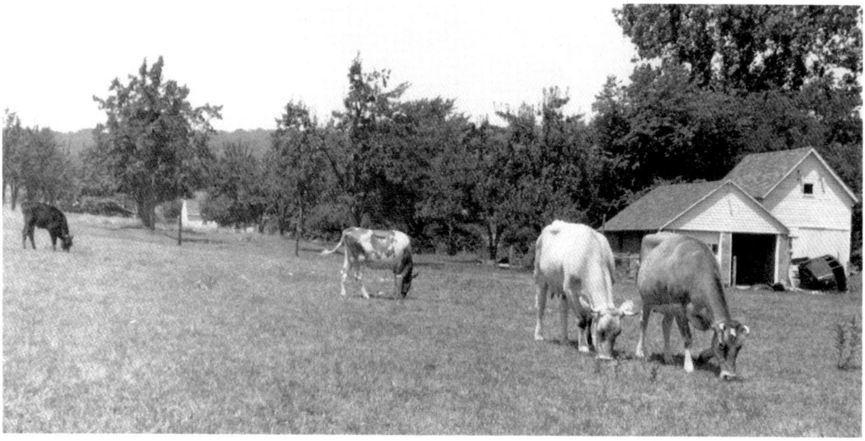

Cows on Zimmermann's farm, 1956. *Courtesy of Ruthie Goense.*

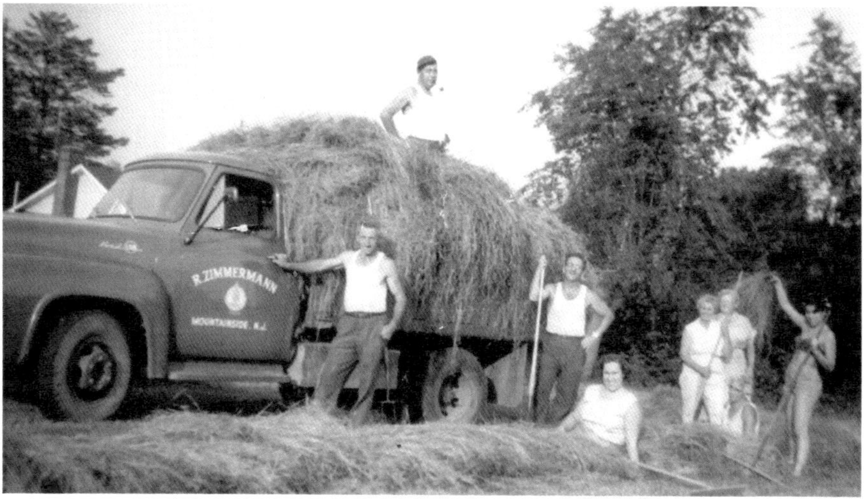

Haying time on Zimmermann's farm, 1956. *Courtesy of Ruthie Goense.*

all farmland, mostly vegetables and fruit. We played with kids in our immediate area, no matter what their age. We didn't see the other kids in town unless it was in school or Sunday school. Summit Road didn't connect with us [Central Avenue], *nor did New Providence Road. We walked to the Mountainside School from here. The cop would hold up the traffic on Route 22 so we could cross.*

Everybody knew everybody in Mountainside. If I did something I wasn't supposed to, my mother knew about it before I got home. Once,

I was on Route 22 with my bike, and somebody told my mother. When I got home, I was in real trouble because I wasn't supposed to be on the highway.

Ruthie and Jimmy Goense were the first couple to get married in Our Lady of Lourdes after it was incorporated. They were married in the rectory, the first house on the left on Wyoming Drive off Central Avenue, because the church wasn't ready for use. Ruthie remembers that it was a snowy January day. Husband-to-be Jimmy was concerned that he'd have to plow their way to the ceremony. He didn't have to!

Heckel's Farm, as Remembered by Carol Heckel Clark

When I was growing up in the late '40s, there were only eleven houses located on Summit Road. Charles Street did not exist; instead there was a dirt road leading back to the rest of the farm. The house above ours on Summit Road was the Darby House (now owned by the Jaffe family).

Our farm consisted of horse and cow barns, ducks, chickens, pigs and home-grown fruits and vegetables. These vegetables were planted in the area which is now Maple Court and continued on over to Weber's property. Also along Charles Street were a pasture and more space to grow vegetables.

If you were going down Charles Street you would see a picnic grove located on what is now Linda Drive. On Saturdays and Sundays, local organizations, such as the Summit Fire Department, would hold picnics. Just across from the grove was the greenhouse, where the plants were started as seedlings and later planted.

Near the greenhouse was the practice shooting range for the Mountainside Police Department. At that time there was a hill behind the practice range (so they were shooting into a sandbank), but when Charles Street was put through in the '50s this hill was cut down and the soil removed. No one who attended these picnics or practice shootings would recognize the area today. It definitely did not look like the present Linda Drive. Theoretically, Linda Drive should have been called Old Grove, as that is where Heckel's grove actually was.

From the back of our house to Linda Drive was an apple and peach orchard. At the end of Charles Street just before Rolling Rock Road, there

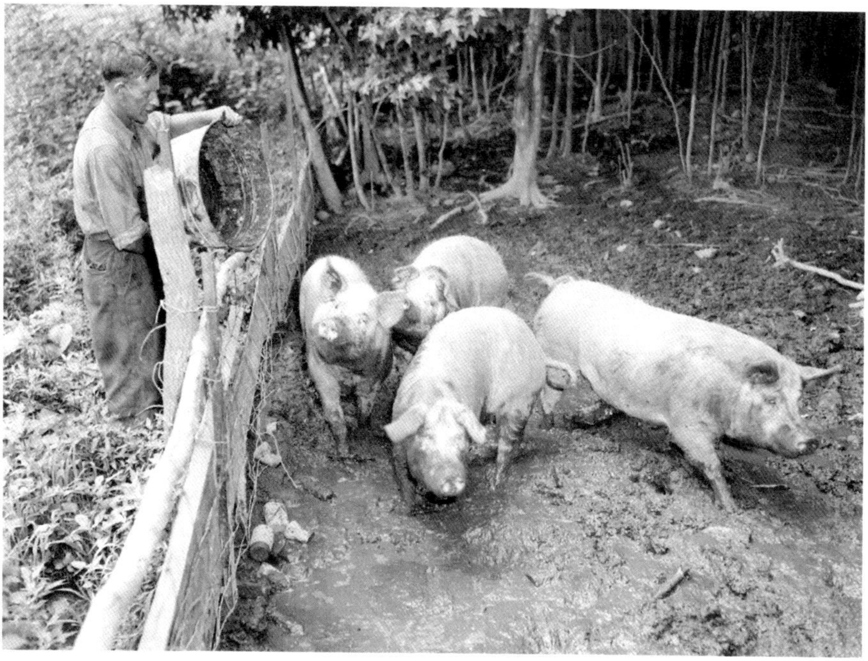

Al Heckel feeding his pigs, 1940s. *Courtesy of Carol Clark.*

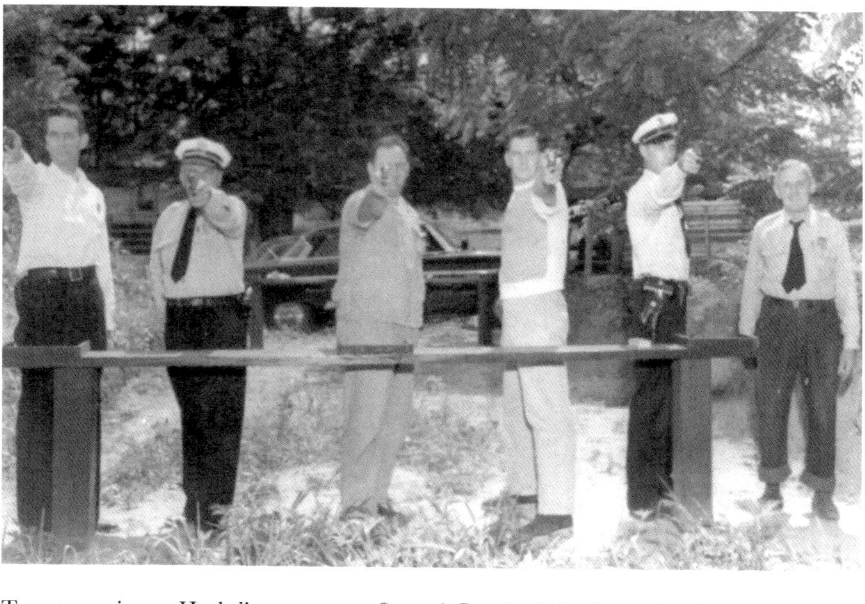

Target practice on Heckel's property on Summit Road, 1950s. *From left to right*: Lieutenant Christian Fritz, Chief Charles Honecker, Patrolman William Lenehan, Patrolman Edward Mullin, Patrolman Charles Doyle and an unidentified special patrolman. *Courtesy of the Mountainside Police Department.*

was a garbage dump where the local disposal service dumped all the trash. There was another dump at the end of Linda Drive, backing up to Elston Drive. The pig farm was located in this area.

Many changes have been made over the past fifty years to all the properties and land, but I am glad that I was around to watch the progress as Mountainside moved forward.

Mayor Bruce Geiger Remembers

My wife, Ronnie, and I lived in Mountainside for almost thirty years. We raised three children and were active in community life. In the spring of 1962, we moved to Saddlebrook Road, a new subdivision, with new houses that cost 30 to 40k. When we sold, our house had appreciated ten times.

We were active in Republican politics, and I was elected to council for three terms between 1974 and 1982 during the time Tom Ricciardi was mayor. I succeeded him as mayor in 1983 for one term. We moved to Dutchess County, New York, for a few years and then moved permanently to Florida in 1990.

The period 1974 through 1990 were formative years for the borough of Mountainside. The mayor and most members of council during this period fought to keep Mountainside a community of owner-occupied, single-family homes with good schools and low taxes. The new homes that were built during this period seemed to be larger and more expensive than the average existing homes. There seemed to be no end to the people that desired to live in Mountainside.

During this period, infrastructure projects were initiated that resulted in sanitary sewer service to every home. Storm water collection systems were designed and built. Some other projects included a new firehouse, improvements to Borough Hall, the swimming pool and the library. As a result of a study commissioned by Mountainside, Interstate 78 was built through the reservation on the west side of the ridge instead of on the east side of the ridge through the heart of our residential districts.

Many wonderful people served on the various boards and committees without salary or pensions. The planning board and board of adjustment spent many hours hearing development applications and made the hard decisions required to maintain the single-family character of Mountainside.

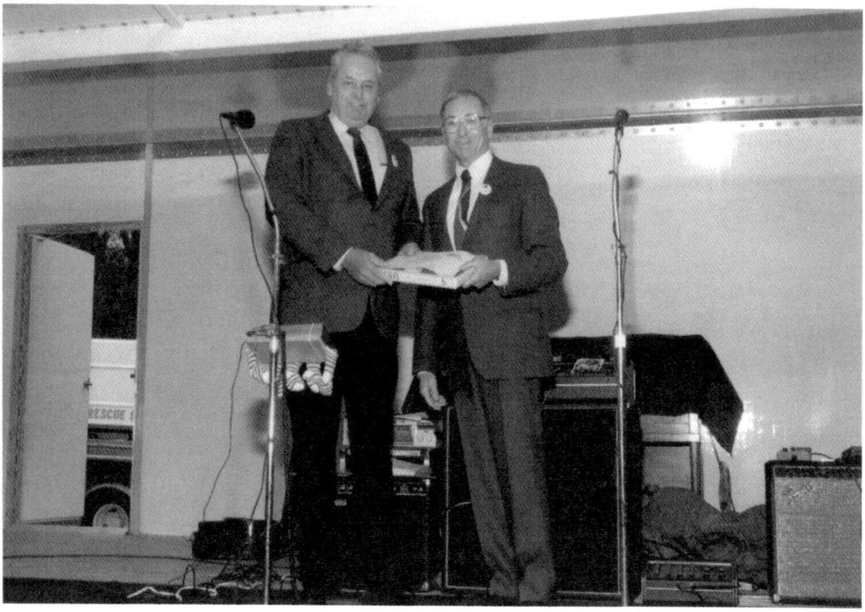

Retirement of Bruce Geiger from the mayorship. Representative Matthew Rinaldo presents flag, circa 1987. *Courtesy of Bruce and Ronnie Geiger.*

From my perspective, the reason Mountainside is such a special community is because Fred Wilhelms and Tom Ricciardi, the two mayors that preceded me, had a clear vision of what was required to control growth and nurture a community. The solid foundation created by these two men underpins the community of Mountainside today.

Mayor Robert F. Viglianti Reminisces

Hetfield House Newsletter, *September 1995*

I firmly believe that one, if not the main, reason for Mountainside success has been the tremendous willingness of men and women to volunteer and the quality of their time and effort over the years giving so much of themselves to their community. There is no dollar amount one could pay to a person who is serving out of love and dedication and not for a paycheck.

I have seen hundreds of residents who have served so willingly without pay. First to come to mind is John E. Keuler, a founding member of the rescue squad and a longtime member of the Mountainside Fire Department. In the sense of being dollar rich, John was a poor man simply because he was always willing to give to others for free. Even in his work as an electrician, many said John didn't charge if he felt his customer was having hard times. He also lost income because of the hours, days and weeks he volunteered as a rescue squad member or a firefighter, but in the end John was rich. He had "Mountainside Pride."

Several ladies must be mentioned, who were the "daytime squad" for many, many years: Mary Steiner, Helen Hay and, later, Sandy Levine. Ruth Keuler, John's wife, not only served as a loyal member but was an instructor, well known in the area. Today [1995] *we still have Kit Carson, a native Mountainside resident and teacher in Deerfield, and Bill Van Blarcom, the squad's longtime treasurer and past council member, plus many residents and nonresidents who give of their time and talents to provide us with emergency care.*

The Mountainside Fire Department will always be known by the statewide slogan started by Ron Huter, "Look for 2 ways out." Then there were Doc Porter, Bob Butler, Joe Hershey, Bob Wyckoff, Alan Hambacher, Ed Colline, Bruce Geiger and many others who served as chief. I must mention also Bob Farley and Jay Kelk, both of whom have served as chief and are still active today.

We are most fortunate to have families who have been a source of support and commitment for generations: Honeckers, Maxwells, Brahms, Bliwises, Pfeifers, McGuire/Harts, Roeders/Debbies, Heckels, Webers, etc. There exists a small group of residents whose pride for Mountainside will live on in our history. Jean Hershey's book on Mountainside; Harry Devlin's drawing of the Hetfield House; the Bass family's "Firefighter" monument; the rescue squad building, dedicated to John Keuler, and streets named for the Heckels, Blazos, Miarmis, Dunns, Ackermans, Mary Allen and Coles are all part of our heritage and pride of our community.

One could not forget Emily and Elmer Hoffarth. Emily, one of the nicest ladies I ever met, was a major driving force in the history of our library. Her portrait adorns its lobby today in recognition and appreciation of her efforts and love of our community. Elmer, on the other hand, sounded gruff and tough. Let me say that Elmer lived, ate and slept Mountainside. He was a long, long time borough clerk, and he ran a tight ship. But when it came to Emily and Mountainside, he had a heart of gold and enough love for several men.

Another borough employee, part time, was Fern Hyde. Boy, for such a quiet, sweet lady Fern could and did become a tiger when she wanted something for her town. Fern was the main thrust behind the saving, moving and renovating of the Hetfield House. I can still see her on Route 22 that famous day when the Hetfield House was being moved to its new location.

The support and work of Mabel Young was so appreciated by Mountainside residents that they created the Mabel Young Award to be given each year to a Mountainside resident who displays through his or her actions true love and dedication to our community. How much more of an honor could be bestowed on an individual than to have an award named after her?

To bestow…what a wonderful thought. Many years ago several residents got together to create what later became simply the Bestowers. This organization throughout the years has donated thousands of dollars and food to the needy. This is really "Mountainside Proud."

Another of the more obvious reflections of Mountainside's community pride is seen in our section of Route 22. When compared to neighboring communities you can see that governing bodies of the past had pride in our development; thus we have green grass and trees while others have asphalt, asphalt, asphalt. This was not only good planning but pride in one's community. Look at our industrial area. All are campus-like settings and not the norm generally seen throughout north and central New Jersey.

Mountainside pride may have started in 1895 with the founding of our community, but it has grown each and every year. It has grown through our rescue squad, fire and police departments, from our Historic Preservation Committee in their constant work on the Hetfield House to the upgrading of "Children's Country Home" to the renowned Children's Specialized Hospital. It has grown to become one of the finest residential communities in all of Union County and Central New Jersey.

Yes, Mountainside is one hundred years proud—one hundred years proud of her residents. I'm most honored to be the mayor during this celebration. I wish all future mayors, that they, too, be blessed with such a loyal, dedicated group of volunteers that I have had the fortune of working with.

MEETING HOUSE LANE MEMORIES

Bobbi Weeks, October 21, 2008

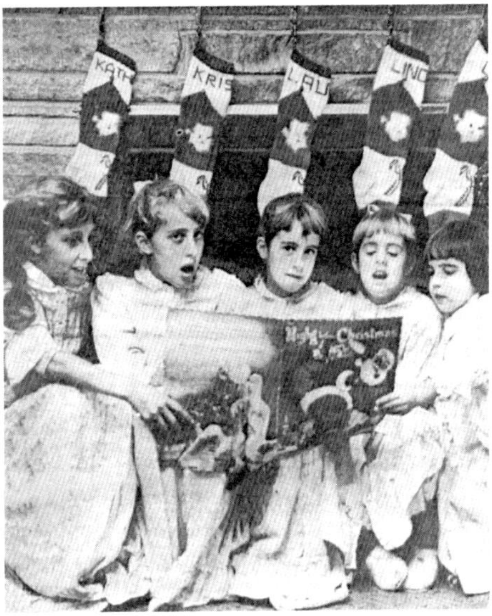

This 1965 local article captures the spirit of the season, presenting Ted and Bobbi Weeks's five daughters: Kathleen, eleven; Kristy, nine; Laurie, seven; Lindsay, five; and Leslie, three. *Courtesy of the* Mountainside Echo.

Back in 1956, I had to convince the street pavers to allow me and the moving truck following me to drive on the street to our new home, the only one on that dirt road in Mountainside. It was a move we've never regretted as this has been a lovely town in which to raise our five daughters.

Two of our daughters also decided to raise their families here. We remember most gratefully how supportive the town was when our twenty-two-year-old daughter died. There was standing room only at the memorial service.

Bobbi and Ted Weeks have lived on Meeting House Lane since 1956.

RECOLLECTIONS OF EIGHTY-TWO-YEAR-OLD EVELYNE WEBER WASHBURN

Conrad Weber, my grandfather, bought the farm in 1907. The Weber land ran from the brook down on Central Avenue before you get to Blazo Terrace to the beginning of the reservation property.

Conrad's son Henry, my father, married Emma Pfeiffer. Henry was a farmer, but he also helped to organize the fire department. [Henry was, in fact, one of the founders of the Mountainside Volunteer Fire Department.]

My father had three sisters. The farm was left to my father to farm, but the property belonged to all four of them. The first portion to be sold was

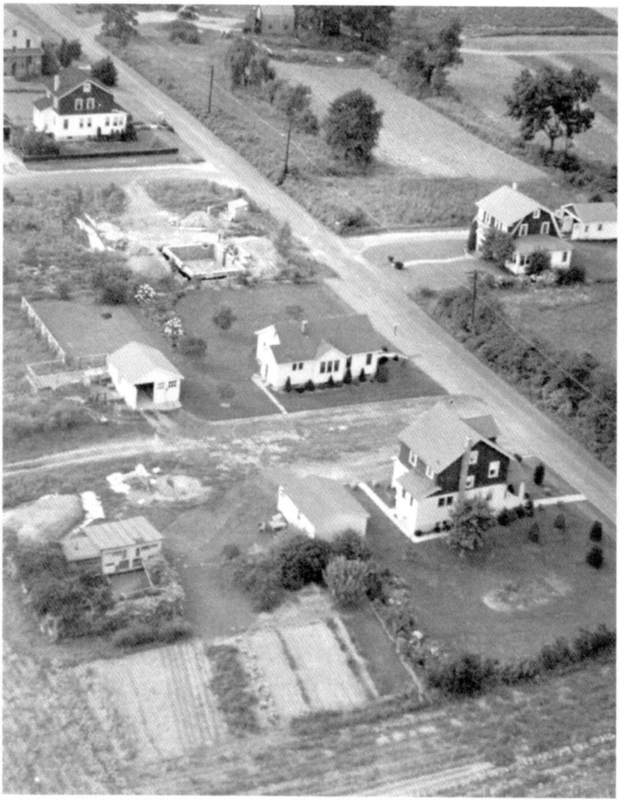

Left: View of Central Avenue looking north. The Weber house and farm are visible on the right. Our Lady of Lourdes is now north of the Weber house; Deerfield School is to the south. The second house on the left is the home of the Martin family. *Courtesy of Cathy Martin Adamek.*

Below: Weber House, circa 1920s. *Courtesy of Evelyn Weber Washburn.*

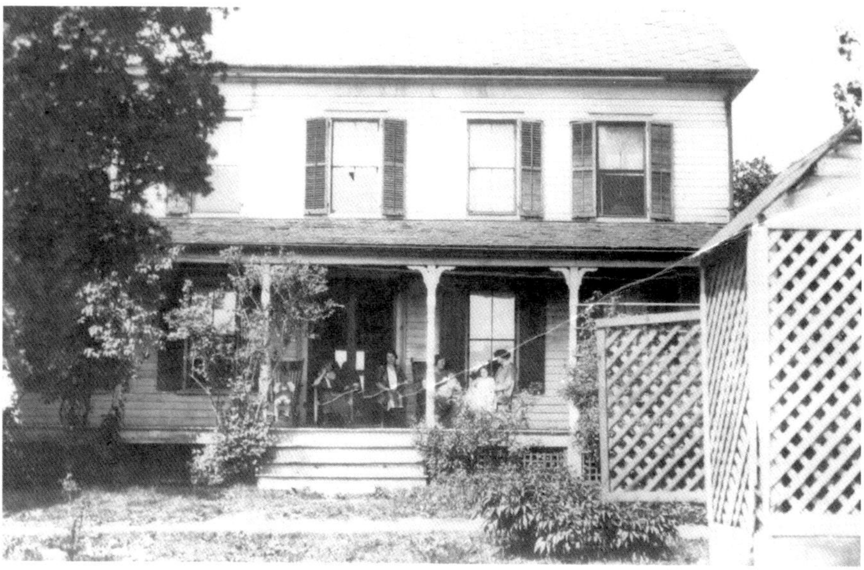

where Wyoming Drive is now. It was sold to a builder, and all those homes up to Short Drive were built. After that, [her father and his sisters] *sold land to the town of Mountainside for Deerfield School. The land north of that was purchased by the Diocese of Newark (ten acres on Central Avenue). Our house stood where Our Lady of Lourdes now is, back from the road a way, but it was on that property.*

Each of the three sisters and brother had a piece of property along Central Avenue that was deeded to them by my grandmother, who died in 1927. The dimension of each of those lots was 200 feet front by 375 feet deep. At that time, two of my aunts built homes; the third one never used her property.

My father, who married Emma Pfeiffer, built a house on their lot at 292 Central Avenue. He built the house on only a one-hundred-foot front, so there was another lot next door that was vacant; he farmed that just about until he died. Prior to his death, I sold the lot because he was in a nursing home. We had no use for it, and we could use the money to care for him. A house was built there next door to ours. [Both houses still stand.]

Emma Weber and the Library

My mother was a housewife, but she also worked out of the home. She worked cleaning houses, as well as working on the farm. Then when we—my brother and two sisters and I—were of high school age, she got her LPN degree and became a nurse. She specialized in baby care; she always adored children and babies. Just about every doctor we had in the area recommended her to take care of newborns. She would go to their homes and stay a period of two weeks to a month, and we took care of ourselves and our home and our dad.

She loved to read. She had a great deal of energy and wanted to learn. In the days when she was young she didn't get to have a formal education. She was still an avid reader. She loved the idea of people learning, and she thought there was something she could do about it. She had a lot of help from other women in the community. She was president of the Regional Board of Education. My mother was in the choir of the chapel. She was in just about everything. She worked on the Community Presbyterian Church as well.

My brother and two sisters and I had the first library cards issued at the time. The library was upstairs in the old Borough Hall. I know that my mother spent a lot of time working there at night. She'd stack books and search for books. She was extremely active. Then they needed the space for offices and for the police headquarters. The library moved to the old school [Echobrook] *to a classroom, then to the basement. She had the present library built, too. She was the one who instigated: "We need it." She wrote many letters to the state; she was very involved in it. She did a tremendous job in this town. I don't know how she did it all. She was in the Ladies' Aid Society. She rolled bandages for the war effort. She had four children. She died about twenty years ago at the age of eighty-eight.*

Woodacres Farm Provided Happy Childhood Memories for Ella Chattin Wright

From the Mountainside Echo *at the Time of the Centennial*

As a four-year-old, moving into Woodacres Farm in 1917 was very exciting. It didn't bother me that although the house was wired for electricity, the lines had not yet come up New Providence Road. The lamps and kerosene stove had to do for a year or so, although we did have a telephone and indoor plumbing.

When we first moved to Mountainside, New Providence Road was a one-lane dirt road, always full of ruts, and was either dusty, muddy or covered with snow, so transportation to town—even with a horse—was difficult.

There were many buildings to explore: a barn with a hay mow, a chicken and brooder house, a pump house, a carriage shed in which we had a buggy, a surrey with fringe on top and some farm equipment. Most unusual was a huge wooden water tower and tank that very often sprang leaks. My brothers could climb up to repair it, but I was never allowed up there, so it remained a place of mystery.

However, there was a lovely brook in back of the barn, which I could wade in and fall into, and alongside it in a small pasture was a log cabin playhouse to enjoy. Also there were many old fruit trees that were great for climbing, as well as for fruit.

There was a large pasture behind the buildings, which was perfect for sled riding in the winter and romping with my animal friends in the summer. My father loved pets, so we had an abundance of them, and they were my toys and my friends. Dad commuted to New York every day so he was a "gentleman farmer" on weekends with a horse to ride, fancy pigeons and collie dogs to raise, and a small vegetable garden to tend.

My impression of the farm is one of a homestead, as I don't recall living anywhere else. It was a happy place for me as I loved the outdoors, especially horseback riding, and I enjoyed being able to have pets, such as a pony, horses, puppies and kittens.

Chattin died in 2006 at the age of ninety-three.

JEANNE WILHELMS TALKS ABOUT WORKING AND PLAYING TOGETHER

When Fred was mayor, our marvelous swimming pool was built. It was in July 1966, and the hope was that by August 1 the pool would be open, but there was still so much to accomplish. Every evening during that month, many Mountainsiders turned out to speed the completion process. It reminded me of an old-fashioned barn-raising. There were two trailers on the site to be used as restrooms, and the ladies of the town painted them in bright colorful stripes. The young people didn't shirk either. Doug Ivory, a local teenager, handled a wheelbarrow loaded with small rocks and pushed them all round the pool. They are the very same rocks you see today in the trenches bordering the sidewalks. It is my belief that all those who labored to complete the pool took a proprietary interest in the facility, especially the teenagers. I heard one young man reprimand an adult for lighting a cigarette and tossing the match on the ground.

The Mountainside Music Association was a wonderful organization, which raised money for the music program in the schools. We presented variety shows. I wrote and co-directed about twelve of them with Aden Lewis, the music teacher in the schools. This was a labor of love, and our performers were residents who were extremely talented. We had cast members who were shy, as well as confident ones, and we liked to tell them that could make them a "star." We showcased many of our teachers, leading citizens and ordinary folks who just wanted to be in the chorus. Isn't it funny how everybody loves to warm himself in the spotlight!

Jeanne and Fred Wilhelms came to town in 1952. Fred was mayor from 1964 through 1969. He passed away in 1994.

You Can Go Home Again

It has been a real cultural shock to me going back to Mountainside after forty-plus years. So many things have changed, but many of the people have remained the same. I can't get over how good you and your sister look. I can still see the teenage Carol Heckel in your face. I spent a great deal of my youth on Summit Road being good friends with the Halls and being in the class with Ed Hall. We were constantly riding our bikes up and down Summit Road. It was great sport to ride to the top of Summit Road and then come zooming down.

My grandfather and my grand uncle both came to Mountainside around 1885–90, and my grandfather first farmed the property that your family later farmed. When my grandfather farmed the property, it was known as the Ideal Farm.

My father lived on the corner of Central Avenue and Route 29, now Route 22. He had a large St. Bernard dog; the dog would pull my father on roller skates down to what my father referred to as his grandmother's house. [She lived in the Smith Williams house on Route 22.] *Not many cars on the road then.*

My great-grandmother slept on a rope bed without springs and with a horsehair mattress. Later, my brother George spent the first ten years of his life on the same bed and mattress. He hated the horsehair mattress because it was prickly.

The above is from a letter written by Richard Robbins on May 2, 2004, to Carol Heckel Clark of 308 Summit Road. Robbins, now a Florida resident, lived on Central Avenue.

BIBLIOGRAPHY

Hershey, Jean Hesketh. *History of Mountainside: 1895–1945.* N.p., 1976.

Kellogg, William O. *American History: The Easy Way*. Hauppauge, NY: Barron's, 2001.

McDuffie, Jerome, Gary Wayne Piggram, Steven E. Woodworth and Paul R. Babbitt. *United States History, Super Review*. Piscataway, NJ: Research and Education Association, 2005.

Pearson Education. "This Year in History." Infoplease. http://www.infoplease.com/yearbyyear.html.

Union County Survey of Historic Sites. N.p.: Central Piedmont Regional Planning Commission, 1971.

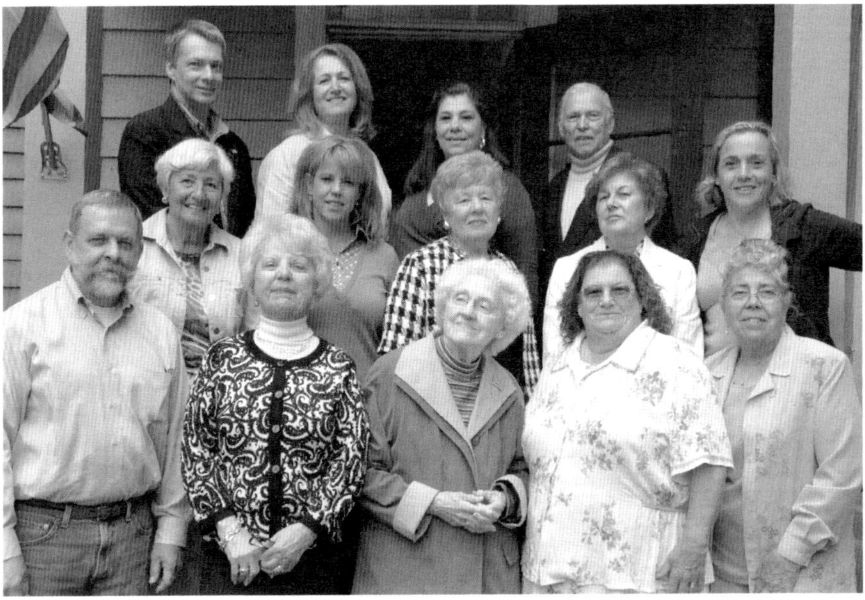

The Mountainside Historic Preservation Committee. *From left to right, first row, bottom*: Scott Daniels, president; Diane Ruggiero; Eleanor Pfeifer; Sharon Green; and Ruth Goense; *second row, middle*: Carol Clark, Maureen Giannone, Alice Cowell, Lenore Toner and Nancy Spadaccini; *top row*: Glen Mortimer, Carol Goggi, Cynthia West and Donald Jeka. *Not pictured*: Thomas McGee. *Photo taken by Chris Petraccoro.*

ABOUT THE AUTHOR

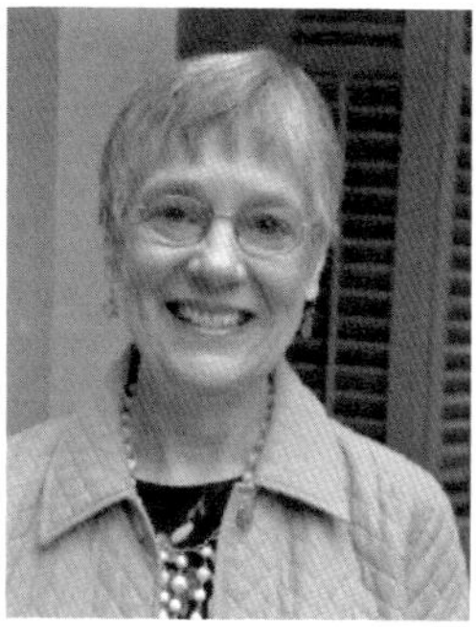

A lifelong resident of Union County, Connie McNamara has lived in Mountainside since 1974. She graduated from Douglass College and earned an MA from Seton Hall University. She taught high school English for more than thirty years, during which time she served as advisor of the school paper, which won numerous awards from the Columbia Scholastic Press Association of Columbia University. A stint at *Newsweek* magazine as a researcher and reporter interrupted her career in the educational arena for a time. Later, as assistant editor at *New Jersey Savvy Living*, she renewed her calling to the communications field. Since then, she has been a freelance writer.